TERRITORIES
OF THE VOICE

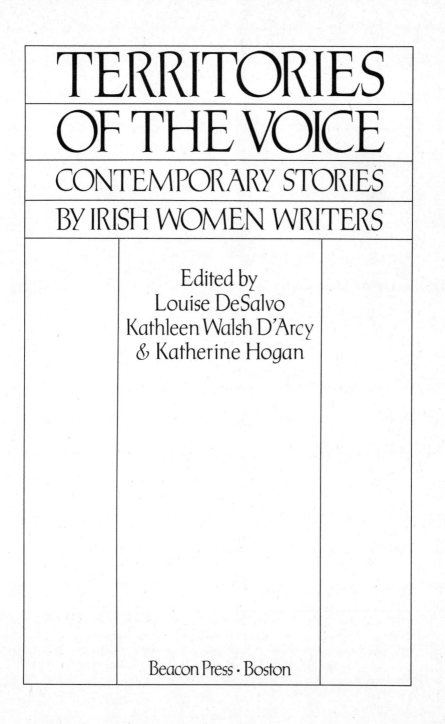

TERRITORIES OF THE VOICE

CONTEMPORARY STORIES

BY IRISH WOMEN WRITERS

Edited by
Louise DeSalvo
Kathleen Walsh D'Arcy
& Katherine Hogan

Beacon Press · Boston

Beacon Press
25 Beacon Street
Boston, Massachusetts 02108-2800

Beacon Press books
are published under the auspices of
the Unitarian Universalist Association of Congregations.

Copyright page continues on pages 267–69.

96 95 94 93 92 91   8 7 6 5 4 3

Text design by Christine Leonard Raquepaw

Library of Congress Cataloging-in-Publication Data
Territories of the voice : contemporary stories by Irish women writers
/ edited by Louise DeSalvo, Kathleen Walsh D'Arcy & Katherine Hogan.
    p.   cm.
  ISBN 0-8070-8320-8 (cloth)
  ISBN 0-8070-8325-9 (paper)
  1. Short stories, English—Irish authors.   2. Short stories,
English—Women authors.   3. Women—Northern Ireland—Fiction.
4. Women—Ireland—Fiction.   5. English fiction—20th century.
I. DeSalvo, Louise A.   II. D'Arcy, Kathleen Walsh.   III. Hogan,
Katherine.
PR8876.2.W65T4   1989
823' .01089287—dc20   89-42597

Taom

The unexpected tide,
the great wave,
uncontained,
breasts the rock,
overwhelms the heart,
in spring
or winter.

Surfacing from a fading language,
the word comes when needed.
A dark sound surges and ebbs,
its accuracy steadying the heart.

Certain kernels of sound
reverberate like seasoned timber,
    unmuted truths of a people's winters,
    stirrings of a thousand different springs.

    There are small unassailable words
    that diminish caesars,
    territories of the voice
    that intimate across death and generation
    how a secret was imparted,
        that first articulation,
        when the vowel was caught
        between a strong and a tender consonant,
        when someone, in anguish,
        made a green and mortal sound
        that lived until now,
        a testimony
        to waves succumbed to
        and survived.

—Moya Cannon

For

Margaret Coughlin Hogan
Mildred Calabrese Sciacchetano
Kathleen Kearney Walsh

We think back through our mothers if we are women. . . .
—Virginia Woolf

Contents

Acknowledgments

The editors would like to thank the following for their help and co-operation: Nuala Archer, Therese Caherty, Siobhán Campbell, Rosette Capotorto, Angela Carter, Roisin Conroy, Pauline Cummins, Philip D'Arcy, Ernest DeSalvo, Noreen Donoghue, Charlotte Francis, Suzanne Gluck, Eileen Godlis, Michael Greaves, James M. Haule, Robert Hogan, Ruth Hooley, Maureen Hossbacher, Mary Paul Keane, Noreen Kelly, Carolyn Larson, Sarah Leddy, John Liddy, Philip MacDermott, David Marcus, Elizabeth Oldman, Hilary Parker, Lester Probst, Ursula Pattison, Mavis E. Pindard, Charlotte Ramsay, Gregory Rodowsky, Deborah Rogers, Catherine Rose, Ann Sandhorst, William Schwalbe, Claudia Shaffer, Elizabeth Stevens, Julia Simpson, Clare Summerfield, Barbara Vagg, John A. Ware.

We would like to thank Joanne Wyckoff, our editor at Beacon Press, for enthusiastically taking on this project. Finally, we thank the writers who agreed to have their work represented in this collection. A special thanks to Rita Kelly for translating the Irish in her story.

Introduction

This is the first collection of contemporary short stories by Irish women writers to appear in the United States. Our aim has been to provide a sampler of short stories for readers not familiar with the breadth and range of short fiction written by contemporary Irish women.

We have taken the title of our collection, *Territories of the Voice*, from Moya Cannon's remarkable poem "Taom," which, in Irish, means "a great wave" and is used to describe an overwhelming wave of emotion. We have included the poem as epigraph because it signifies not only the tremendous outpouring, "the great wave" of contemporary Irish women's writing, but also the powerful impact of these works upon readers. Cannon's poem points to the importance of claiming a language that has been used by others to define who one is, to use that language now to make "a testimony" to what has been "succumbed to and survived." Cannon's vision compels us to listen to the "stirrings of a thousand different springs," the newly articulated testimonies of many, many women writers whose "unmuted truths" about their experiences are depicted with an "accuracy steadying the heart." Reading such testimonies involves one in a communal act that begins with the creation of the work of art by the writer. Although a genuine encounter with a work of art may be disturbing, it is also, paradoxically, a profoundly centering experience, even though the truths described may be of terrible ordeals lived through, the "truths of a people's winters." For Cannon, both the suffering and the survival are necessary to the artistic agenda set forth here. Saturated with woman-identified images, the poem conveys writing's awesome power to fight against oppression: its power to "diminish caesars."

Moya Cannon's poem is a paean to the hope implicit in the creative act as well as the hope that the work of art will come to the reader, to the world, at the right time, that the word will come, as she puts it, when it is needed.

Territories of the Voice represents the explosion of contemporary Irish women's writing. Almost all of the stories were written after 1960, the date that Janet Madden-Simpson marks as the beginning of contemporary Irish women's literature, a time when "currents of feminine revolt" increasingly came to the surface. They represent the period during which Irish women "began to look at themselves differently" and to express themselves differently and during which a far wider social range of Irish women have been writing and publishing for the first time.[1]

Early in the selection process, we prepared a "wish list" of some thirty writers of fiction whom we had encountered, either in our reading here or during our stays in Ireland; attendance at international conferences, such as the one in Dublin in 1987, brought us into contact with the work of others. Through the years we added other names to our list. We decided early that we would choose stories that met two criteria: the story should be representative of the entire oeuvre of the writer, and the story should tell the reader something about the nature of the lives of women in Ireland. As our anthology progressed, we tried to ensure that the stories we selected provided portraits of, for example, urban women and rural women, women from the Republic of Ireland and women from the North, Catholic women and Protestant women, portraits of women who loved men and women who loved women, visions of elder women thinking back through their lives and portraits of young girls, adolescent women, mothers, widows, and women living alone. Most importantly, we had to love the stories, to be excited by them as works of art, as well as by what they demonstrated about the diversity of experience of the lives of women in Ireland. We wanted this to be a woman-centered collection and so virtually all the stories included here are about women, often narrated by first-person women narrators. ("Trio," by Jennifer Johnston, however, presents a kaleidoscope of viewpoints toward women through male narrators.)

In addition, we wanted the collection to reflect certain of the major concerns that women are treating in their art in Ireland today: the fact that abortion is illegal, in the North and in the South; the impact of the prohibition against divorce in the South; the issue of the silence surrounding incest, sexual abuse, and sexual repression; the daily reality of life as it is lived in a war zone. And we wanted to provide something of the range of literary styles being employed by Irish women today: the sharp, hilarious satire of a writer like Clare Boylan; the lyrical, elegiac prose of a writer like Mary Lavin; the oral folk-tale quality of the work of Anne Le Marquand Hartigan; the use of the Irish language by Rita Kelly;[2] the experimental prose represented by Bernadette Matthews; the realism of an Anne Devlin.

Although our volume is comprehensive, we have not aimed at a definitive edition, including a selection from all of the writers whose work we have read, in part because of limitations of space, in part because certain authors' previous publication agreements made it impossible for us to secure the rights to stories we would have liked to include.

The most invigorating and surely the most pleasurable aspect of preparing this volume was that it gave us the opportunity to read extensively in the work of contemporary Irish women writers of fiction and to correspond with them, meet them, and hear them speak about their work and their future plans. During the bleakest of days, our mailboxes would bring us a new story, fresh from the pages of the *Irish Times,* or a letter including an open invitation to visit any time we were in Ireland. We have made a good many friends in the process of preparing this volume and we thank these writers for their trust in committing their work to our scheme. We believe that if this volume impels a reader unfamiliar or newly familiar with the work of Irish women writers to read beyond it, it will have served its purpose well. We hope that it will introduce readers to writers whose work they will want to pursue. (The Notes on the Contributors contain the names of major works by our authors.) Certain writers included here—Elizabeth Bowen, Julia O'Faolain, and Edna O'Brien, for example—will be familiar to many, but some will be new to most readers outside of Ireland.

When the idea for this anthology first arose, some seven or eight years ago, very few works by Irish women writers were available outside of Ireland. Interested readers had to buy books in Ireland, rely on Irish friends to send books over, or get in touch with Angela Carter at Keshcarrigan Bookshop (renamed Irish Books and Graphics) in New York City, whose newsletters kept interested readers informed of newly available titles in stock, such as *The Head of Family* by Eilis Dillon, the historical novelist from Galway, or *No Mate for the Magpie* by Frances Molloy.

Recently, however, because of increasing interest in works of fiction written by women throughout the world, and because of increased contact among writers and publishers brought about by international conferences of women, the works of Irish women writers are becoming more easily available. There has even been a made-for-television adaptation of Anne Devlin's story, "Naming the Names," which has surely stirred interest in her work and that of other Irish women writers. In the United States, for example, Mary Beckett's collection, *A Belfast Woman*, whose title story is one of the finest evocations of a woman's life in Belfast that we have read, has recently been published, as has her novel, *Give Them Stones*. Other recent publications, including a number of overtly political novels, are Julia O'Faolain's *No Country for Young Men*; Linda Anderson's portrait of modern Belfast, *We Can't All Be Heroes, You Know*; Deirdre Madden's tale set in Belfast in the sixties, *Hidden Symptoms*; Mary Leland's novel set in Ireland during the politically turbulent time of the 1930s, *The Killeen*; as well as Clare Boylan's, *Last Resorts* and *Holy Pictures*, in Penguin paperbacks, and Maeve Binchy's work in mass-market editions.

A special feature issue of contemporary Irish women's writing (which quickly became a collector's item) was put together through the prodigious efforts of Nuala Archer of the *Midland Review* at Oklahoma State University. This issue published for the first time in the United States the work of forty-one poets, fiction writers, and essayists, such as Moya Cannon and Medbh McGuckian. Given the quality of the poetry in that volume, one can only hope that other editions of poetry by Irish women will soon appear.

In her introduction to that volume, Archer observed that there is "a prejudice against the emergence of women's writings in the Republic of Ireland" and she quoted Ruth Hooley's statement that "in Northern Ireland there is little evidence" of interest in the work of women writers.[3] Ruth Hooley, like Archer, is the editor of a ground-breaking volume, *The Female Line*, a collection of writings by Northern Irish women, published in 1985 by the Northern Ireland Women's Rights Movement.

But the publication of Irish women's writing has been urged on by the work of many like Nuala Archer and Ruth Hooley, who have devoted enormous energy to the project of redressing the imbalances they have identified. Poolbeg Press, for example, has published many of the collections from which stories in this volume have been taken. David Marcus, the editor of a series of anthologies, such as *Tears of the Shamrock: An Anthology of Contemporary Short Stories on the Theme of Ireland's Struggle towards Nationhood* and *Best Irish Short Stories*, has brought the work of many women writers such as Ann McKay into view. There is the work of community writing groups, and the publication of volumes of their work such as *Write Up Your Street: An Anthology of Community Writing*, by Women's Community Press, which, in the words of the introduction to that volume, presents a "serious challenge to the accepted notion of 'literature' being the preserve of a privileged elite."[4]

And there is the work of Catherine Rose at the now defunct Arlen House Publishers, the noted feminist publishing imprint in Ireland, and that of Mary Paul Keane and Roisin Conroy at Attic Press (whose logo, the letter A, is formed by a woman and a pencil, the woman in the process of pressing the enormous pencil into place). The publishing program at Attic Press includes books on women's history such as Rosemary Cullen Owens's *Smashing Times: A History of the Irish Women's Suffrage Movement*, guides to health care, such as that compiled by Ursula Barry, *Lifting the Lid: A Handbook of Facts and Information on Ireland*, short story collections and novels, such as Leland Bardwell's *Different Kinds of Love*, Evelyn Conlon's *My Head Is Opening*, and Melissa Murray's *Changelings*, and the nonfiction works of Nell McCafferty and Liz Steiner-Scott.[5]

In the stories included in this volume, the reader will meet women who form, as one of our writers put it, "the backbone of the country," in portraits that do not idealize but rather describe "the fat, the veins, the sighs" as well as the happiness "seeping" into the body on a sunny day. The reader will meet elder women, sisters who have "wild and secret" games, a young Catholic mother in the North, a community of women who live against the backdrop of the relentless "thunder of the ocean," a fisherwoman responsible for her brother, a woman pregnant with her married lover's child, who must go to England for an abortion, and an IRA woman whose grandfather was an Ulster Volunteer.

In these pages are portraits of all the stages of a woman's life, including school life and adolescence. There is a young woman thinking of the "heroes" of her "wet dreams" despite the "rigourously inbred

protestant morality" that has nurtured her; an adolescent's love for her
uncle at a time when "every sensation was acute"; the coming into
sexual awareness of a young woman at a time when it was thought
immodest to swim in front of a male bus driver; the love and passion
of a young woman for the nun who teaches her; girls bracing themselves
against "the assault of man, the enemy"; and a girl's desperate cheerless
unhealthy life in a convent to which she has been consigned.

And there are portraits of mothers and of pregnancy, a condition
which one woman likens to "a bird trapped in an oil spill." One mother
is only fourteen years old, pregnant with a baby that resulted from her
being raped by her father's drunken crony; and there is her mother,
who tries to make peace with what has happened, but whose rage
surfaces only in the ferocious images of her dreams. Abortion is not
legal in Ireland and this girl-mother doesn't have the means to go to
England to terminate her pregnancy. One mother calls her lover from
a glassed-in telephone booth to escape her problems. There are portraits
of women who choose a strong and able solitude, women who choose
to live with women, women who believe themselves duty-bound to
live with relatives, and women who live in communities of women.
There are portraits of teachers, one who enables but another who uses
the behavior of the father of one of her students as a "textbook" example
about the evils of drink. And there are portraits of the work that women
do—working in a lending library, as a nurse's aide, running a tea house,
selling potatoes, tilling the soil, fishing, raising children, teaching,
working in a hotel.

Taken together, these portraits demonstrate the enormous variety of
the experiences of Ireland's women, and we hope they will contribute
to the effort being made to break down the prejudice that the lives of
any group of women are monotypic.

Accounts of Irish literary history, to date, have been male-dominated
and male-centered, even though the first writer of fiction in Ireland
was a woman, Maria Edgeworth. A history of women's writing in
Ireland and the place of women's writing in the literary history of Ireland
is just beginning to be established through the work of writers such as
Janet Madden-Simpson and Nuala Archer. But much work remains,
particularly around the question of whether contemporary writing has
been influenced by Irish women writers of the nineteenth century.

Maria Edgeworth's *Castle Rackrent*, published in 1800, details the
behavior of an "incompetent, wasteful" and "downright cruel" privi-

leged family from the viewpoint of Thady Quirk, a family retainer. It was Ireland's first published novel and the first regional novel in the English language. It employs literary techniques (such as monologue) that, according to the literary critic Anthony Cronin, anticipate the work of Irish writers such as Samuel Beckett, especially in *Malone Dies*, James Joyce in *Ulysses*,[6] and the contemporary writer, Dorothy Nelson, whose novel *Tar and Feathers* is a depiction through monologue of a working-class family in crisis. Maria Edgeworth's critique of the life of privilege in Ireland also anticipates the highly acclaimed oeuvre of Jennifer Johnston, whose work is represented here by the story "Trio," and that of Molly Keane, especially her novel *Time after Time*.[7] Johnston, like Edgeworth, writes novels of social criticism, such as *The Gates* (1973), which are often set in the "big houses" of Ireland and detail the decline of the Anglo-Irish.

Any history of women's writing in Ireland must of course pay attention to the work of Edith Somerville and Violet Martin, writing as Somerville and Ross, who collaborated to produce the finest nineteenth-century Irish novel, *The Real Charlotte*.[8] Anthony Cronin has written that one of the significant contributions of their collaboration was their creation of "a strong-minded woman" character who attempted to "reverse or control circumstance; to acquire or defend property; to improve or enhance her own or her family's social position." Theirs is a "sharp-witted and perceptive social drama" of people who wish to advance themselves but who nonetheless are bound by society's convention, with tragic results for some of the players.[9] A recent analysis of their work by Hilary Robinson has demonstrated their significant contribution to Irish letters.[10]

Janet Madden-Simpson has written of a "lost" Irish feminist foremother, Sarah Grand. Grand's novel, *The Beth Book* (1897), subtitled *A Study of the Life of a Woman of Genius*, sold 20,000 copies in the week following its publication, and is now available in the Virago Modern Classics series. It contains "sustained critiques of such issues as marriage, the education of girls, the physical and social degradation of women, the rights of women to work and the possibility of restructuring society," and its use of stream-of-consciousness as a literary technique predates that of James Joyce by several years.[11] Yet, until recently, Grand's contribution to Irish fiction had not been acknowledged.

Madden-Simpson's anthology, *Woman's Part*, representing the works of women writers from 1890 through 1960, has done its part in redressing the imbalance of male-dominated anthologies, and includes stories by women writers such as George Egerton, M. E. Francis, Jane Barlow, and Katherine Tynan. Tynan, whose work continuously addressed the issue of women's rights, produced a massive body of work over the years that included over a hundred novels and twelve collections of short stories, in addition to plays, poetry collections, memoirs, essays, criticism, and biographies.[12]

Evelyn Conlon, a writer whose work is represented in this volume, has said that when she started writing, for her, there were no models in Ireland for the work that she wanted to do; there was no body of literature available to her written by women with whom she identified, for she had not grown up in a "great house." Instead, Conlon looked to writers outside of Ireland for inspiration, to writers like Toni Cade Bambara and Grace Paley, who explore in their fiction what it feels like to be a working-class woman, who examine the experiences of a community of women rather than the life of a single protagonist, writers who are interested in expressing the strengths of the women who live within a society fundamentally hostile to their well-being rather than examining the social failings of women of privilege. Conlon has remarked that for her, the recent outpouring of writing by women can be attributed to several factors: the widening of educational opportunities for women; the availability of birth control; the impact of the women's movement, which has helped Irish women think about themselves in new and empowering ways; and the impact of the electrification program on the lives of women in the countryside, which has made the work of rural women less arduous and enabled them to read and write at night.

Nuala Archer has argued that many of the "outpourings of recent writings" by women "from every part of Ireland," often living in "isolated and harassed economic circumstances," are by intention "unsettling" works of art. She has suggested that these socially conscious writers manifest a "full array of feminisms."[13] Many of these artists critique Irish society from new vantage points—in classrooms, in kitchens, playgrounds, and supermarkets. Their "unsettling" voices embrace infants and elders, every generation and social category of Ireland's people. Their tales uncover lost histories, finally filling in the blanks and breaking a long silence. Certain contemporary Irish women writers have appropriated the function of the *seanchai* (pronounced "shankwee"), the Irish storyteller, whose tales preserve the history, culture, and language of an entire people.

Readers will come to this volume with varying levels of knowledge about the history of Ireland. But any reader will probably want to remember that abortion is illegal both in the Republic of Ireland and in the North under the 1861 Offences Against the Person Act, a British law enacted by a Protestant Parliament. In the Republic there is an information ban on abortion and referral to clinics in Britain (it is against the law to offer abortion counseling of any kind, including disseminating the names, locations, or telephone numbers of foreign abortion clinics), where abortion has been legal for over twenty years; abortion counseling is, however, permitted in the North. (It has been estimated that each year well over 3,000 Irish women go to Britain for abortions.)

The reader will probably want to bear in mind that it was not until the Family Planning Act of 1979 that married Irish women in the Republic were legally entitled to fertility control, that birth control is still not readily available for all in the Republic, and that divorce is illegal. In 1986 an attempt was made to remove the existing constitutional prohibition on divorce, but it was defeated. Moreover, married women do not have personal entitlement to social insurance protection and health or dental care in their own right.[14]

Readers interested in the relationship between Irish women's fiction and the changing shape of the lives of women in Ireland will want to read books such as Jenny Beale's *Women in Ireland: Voices of Change*; Margaret MacCurtain and Donncha O'Corrain's *Women in Irish Society*; Ailbhe Smyth's *Women's Rights in Ireland*; Eileen Evason's and Clara Clark's *Women and Social Policy—North and South*; and Andrew Rynne's *Abortion: The Irish Question*.[15] These books provide important information about a number of issues: the recent controversies over the voting on two constitutional amendments, one on divorce (which was voted down), the other on abortion (which was upheld); the impact of feminists on social welfare legislation; the differences in social welfare legislation in the North and South; the establishment of rape crisis centers and associations of single mothers; the effect of the widening of educational and employment opportunities for women; and the profound changes in women's lives that have come with Ireland's joining the Common Market.

An undercurrent in much Irish fiction is the scarring effect of poverty. The Republic now has a 20 percent unemployment rate, and between the years 1982 and 1987, over 150,000 people emigrated to the United States. In the North, the unemployment rate for males in Catholic communities is two and a half times higher than the rate for Protestant men, and in Catholic areas like Andersontown, Ballymurphy, and the Falls Road, unemployment among men may reach 60 or 70 percent, or perhaps higher, which has presented extraordinary problems for family life. In the North, many live in what can only be called a war zone, where soldiers on patrol (there are over 10,000 British soldiers, 8,000 locally recruited soldiers, and 12,000 armed paramilitaries enforcing British policy in the North), checkpoints, snipers, riots, assassinations, diplock courts (i.e., courts that hold trial without jury), strip-searching of women, internment without trial, and midnight searches without warrants are daily facts of life. A generation of children have grown up who know nothing but a life filled with violence. These realities are described in works such as Rona M. Fields's *Northern Ireland: Society under Siege*; Eileen Fairweather, Roisin McDonough, and Melanie McFadyean's *Only the Rivers Run Free: Northern Ireland—The Women's War*; and Elizabeth Shannon's most recent *I Am of Ireland: Women of the North Speak Out.*[16]

In stories such as Anne Devlin's "Naming the Names," Fiona Barr's "The Wall Reader," and Brenda Murphy's "A Curse," these realities are in the forefront of the narrative; in others, such as Mary Beckett's "Failing Years," they are present in a more subtle way—in the train that does not run straight through from Dublin to Belfast because the tracks have been bombed out; in an elder woman's nostalgic longing for the Belfast of her childhood.

Readers familiar with current events in Ireland might see correspondences too between events narrated in Leland Bardwell's "Dove of Peace" and the tragedy of Ann Lovett, who, at the age of fifteen, gave birth alone to a full-term baby in the Grotto of Our Lady in her home town of Granard, County Longford; both were found dead. Ann was a convent school girl and no one claims to have known that she was pregnant. But her death made headlines and precipitated much discussion about its implications. Éilís Ní Dhuibhne's "Midwife to the Fairies" resonates with implications when read against the history of the "Kerry Babies" case. Joanne Hayes, a single mother living on the family farm, gave birth to a child on April 13, 1984, in a field on that farm; the baby died and was buried there, but its death was not reported to local authorities. On April 14 a baby's body washed up on White Strand beach in Cahirciveen, County Kerry; the baby's neck had been broken and he had been stabbed twenty-eight times. Rumor linked it to Joanne Hayes and she was charged with the Cahirciveen baby's murder. Readers interested in this complex case (Hayes and her family confessed to charges under investigation but were subsequently cleared), which was accompanied by an outpouring of support for Joanne Hayes by feminists and eventually by local townspeople as well, should read the renowned journalist Nell McCafferty's account, A Woman to Blame.[17] Whatever else the Kerry Babies case reveals, it demonstrates the stigma attached to single parenthood in Ireland; whatever else Ann Lovett's story exemplifies, it suggests that the shame, terror, and confusion that must accompany an adolescent pregnancy—when accurate information about sexuality is virtually unobtainable—can be deadly.

The issues that Irish women writers of fiction often address are those that any reader would do well to confront. The position of Irish women in Irish society is similar to that of other women throughout the world. In the United States, as more rightist political groups are calling for a return to control over women's reproduction, several of the stories in this volume—Ní Dhuibhne's, O'Carroll's "The Day of the Christening," Julia O'Faolain's "Melancholy Baby"—are well worth pondering. The problems explored by many Irish women writers such as Bardwell and O'Carroll—living within a tightly enmeshed family from which it is difficult or impossible to extricate oneself because of a legal system that predicates a male-headed household as the social norm— are problems that, to a greater or lesser extent, women throughout the world confront. They explore the consequences of living in a culture that does not meet the pressing economic and social needs of women, a culture, like that of the United States, in which women and children make up the vast majority of the poor.

Women writers in Ireland bravely and eloquently explore what it means to define oneself with dignity. Their "great wave" of writing breaks through what Evelyn Conlon calls the "haze of enforced isolation," uncovering "a mass of past and future women."

Notes

1. See *Woman's Part: An Anthology of Short Fiction by and about Irish Women 1890–1960* (Dublin: Arlen House; London and New York: Marion Boyars, 1984).

2. Unfamiliar terms, including many Irish words and phrases, are listed in the Glossary, p. 264.

3. Nuala Archer, introduction, *Midland Review* 3 (Winter 1986):xii.

4. Introduction, *Write Up Your Street: An Anthology of Community Writing* (Dublin: Women's Community Press, 19XX), 6.

5. Readers wanting to keep abreast of Attic Press's outstanding publishing schedule, including a forthcoming novel by Nell McCafferty, can write the press at 44 Essex Street, Dublin 2, Ireland.

6. Anthony Cronin, *Heritage Now: Irish Literature in the English Language* (New York: St. Martin's Press, 1982), 25.

7. Molly Keane, *Time after Time* (New York: Alfred A. Knopf, 1984).

8. See Janet Madden-Simpson, "Womanwriting: The Arts of Textual Politics," *Midland Review* 3 (Winter 1986).

9. Cronin, *Heritage Now*, 85.

10. Hilary Robinson, *Somerville and Ross: A Critical Appreciation* (Dublin: Gill and Macmillan, 1980).

11. Madden-Simpson, "Womanwriting," 126.

12. See the biographical note on Tynan in, e.g., Frank L. Kersnowski et al., *A Bibliography of Modern Irish and Anglo-Irish Literature* (San Antonio, Tex.: Trinity University Press, 1976).

13. Archer, introduction, *Midland Review* 3 (Winter 1986):xi.

14. See Ailbhe Smyth, *Women's Rights in Ireland* (Dublin: Irish Council for Civil Liberties/Ward River Press, 1982); for a full account of the divorce referendum, see Jenny Beale, *Women in Ireland: Voices of Change* (Bloomington and Indianapolis: Indiana University Press, 1987).

15. MacCurtain and O'Corrain, *Women in Irish Society: The Historical Dimension* (Dublin: Arlen House, 1978); Smyth, *Women's Rights in Ireland*: see n. 14 above; Evason and Clark, *Women and Social Policy*: submission to the New Ireland Forum, 1983; Rynne, *Abortion*: Ward River Press, 1982.

16. Elizabeth Shannon, *I Am of Ireland: Women of the North Speak Out* (New York: Little, Brown, 1989).

17. Nell McCafferty, *A Woman to Blame* (Dublin: Attic Press, 1985).

In the Middle of the Fields

Mary Lavin

Like a rock in the sea, she was islanded by fields, the heavy grass washing about the house, and the cattle wading in it as in water. Even their gentle stirrings were a loss when they moved away at evening to the shelter of the woods. A rainy day might strike a wet flash from a hay barn on the far side of the river—not even a habitation! And yet she was less lonely for him here in Meath than elsewhere. Anxieties by day, and cares, and at night vague, nameless fears—these were the stones across the mouth of the tomb. But who understood that? They thought she hugged tight every memory she had of him. What did they know about memory? What was it but another name for dry love and barren longing? They even tried to unload upon her their own small purposeless memories. "I imagine I see him every time I look out there," they would say as they glanced nervously over the darkening fields when they were leaving. "I think I ought to see him coming through the trees." Oh, for God's sake! she'd think. I'd forgotten him for a minute!

It wasn't him *she* saw when she looked out at the fields. It was the ugly tufts of tow and scutch that whitened the tops of the grass and gave it the look of a sea in storm, spattered with broken foam. That grass would have to be topped. And how much would it cost?

At least Ned, the old herd, knew the man to do it for her. "Bartley Crossen is your man, Ma'am. Your husband knew him well."

She couldn't place him at first. Then she remembered. "Oh, yes—that's his hay barn we see, isn't it? Why, of course! I know him well—by sight, I mean." And so she did—splashing past on the road in a big

1

muddy car, the wheels always caked with clay, and the wife in the front seat beside him.

"I'll get him to call around and have a word with you, Ma'am," said the herd.

"Before dark!" she cautioned.

But there was no need to tell him. The old man knew how she always tried to be upstairs before it got dark, locking herself into her room, which opened off the room where the children slept, praying devoutly that she wouldn't have to come down again for anything—above all, not to answer the door. That was what in particular she dreaded: a knock after dark.

"Ah, sure, who'd come near you, Ma'am, knowing you're a woman alone with small children that might be wakened and set crying? And, for that matter, where could you be safer than in the middle of the fields, with the innocent beasts asleep around you?"

If he himself had to come to the house late at night for any reason—to get hot water to stoup the foot of a beast, or to call the vet—he took care to shout out long before he got to the gable. "It's me, Ma'am!" he'd shout. "Coming! Coming!" she'd cry, gratefully, as quick on his words as their echo. Unlocking her door, she'd run down and throw open the hall door. No matter what the hour! No matter how black the night! "Go back to your bed now, you, Ma'am," he'd say from the darkness, where she could see the swinging yard lamp coming nearer and nearer like the light of a little boat drawing near to a jetty. "I'll put out the lights and let myself out." Relaxed by the thought that there was someone in the house, she would indeed scuttle back into bed, and, what was more, she'd be nearly asleep before she'd hear the door slam. It used to sound like the slam of a door a million miles away.

There was no need to worry. He'd see that Crossen came early.

It was well before dark when Crossen did drive up to the door. The wife was with him, as usual, sitting up in the front seat the way people sat up in the well of little tub traps long ago, their knees pressed together, allowing no slump. The herd had come with them, but only he and Crossen got out.

"Won't your wife come inside and wait, Mr. Crossen?" she asked.

"Oh, not at all, Ma'am. She likes sitting in the car. Now, where's this grass that's to be cut? Are there any stones lying about that would blunt the blade?" Going around the gable of the house, he looked out over the land.

"There's not a stone or a stump in it," Ned said. "You'd run your blade over the whole of it while you'd be whetting it twenty times in another place!"

"I can see that," said Bartley Crossen, but absently, she thought.

He had walked across the lawn to the rickety wooden gate that led into the pasture, and leaned on it. He didn't seem to be looking at the fields at all, though, but at the small string of stunted thorns that grew along the riverbank, their branches leaning so heavily out over the water that their roots were almost dragged clear of the clay.

Suddenly he turned around and gave a sigh. "Ah, sure, I didn't need to look! I know it well!" As she showed surprise, he gave a little laugh, like a young man. "I courted a girl down there when I was a lad," he said. "That's a queer length of time ago now, I can tell you!" He turned to the old man. "You might remember it." Then he looked back at her. "I don't suppose you were thought of at all in those days, Ma'am," he said, and there was something kindly in his look and in his words. "You'd like the mowing done soon, I suppose? How about first thing in the morning?"

Her face lit up. But there was the price to settle. "It won't be as dear as cutting meadow, will it?"

"Ah, I won't be too hard on you, Ma'am," he said. "I can promise you that!"

"That's very kind of you," she said, but a little doubtfully.

Behind Crossen's back, Ned nodded his head in approval. "Let it go at that, Ma'am," he whispered as they walked back towards the car. "He's a man you can trust."

And when Crossen and the wife had driven away, he reassured her again. "A decent man," he said. Then he gave a laugh—it, too, was a young kind of laugh for a man of his age; it was like a nudge. "Did you hear what he said, though—about the girl he courted down there? Do you know who that was? It was his first wife! You know he was twice married? Ah, well, it's so long ago I wouldn't wonder if you never heard it. Look at the way he spoke about her himself, as if she was some girl he'd all but forgotten! The thorn trees brought her to his mind! That's where they used to meet, being only youngsters, when they first took up with each other.

"Poor Bridie Logan—she was as wild as a hare. And she was mad

3

with love, young as she was! They were company-keeping while they were still going to school. Only nobody took it seriously—him least of all, maybe—till the winter he went away to the agricultural college in Clonakilty. She started writing to him then. I used to see her running up to the postbox at the crossroads every other evening. And sure, the whole village knew where the letter was going. His people were fit to be tied when he came home in the summer and said he wasn't going back, but was going to marry Bridie. All the same, his father set them up in a cottage on his own land. It's the cottage that's used now for stall-feds—it's back of the new house. Oh, but you can't judge it now for what it was then! Giddy and all as she was—as light-headed as a thistle—you should have seen the way she kept that cottage. She'd have had it scrubbed away if she didn't start having a baby. He wouldn't let her take the scrubbing brush into her hands after that!"

"But she wasn't delicate, was she?"

"Bridie? She was as strong as a kid goat, that one! But I told you she was mad about him, didn't I? Well, after she was married to him she was no better—worse, you'd say. She couldn't do enough for him! It was like as if she was driven on by some kind of a fever. You'd only to look in her eyes to see it. Do you know! From that day to this, I don't believe I ever saw a woman so full of going as that one! Did you ever happen to see little birds flying about in the air like they were flying for the divilment of it and nothing else? And did you ever see the way they give a sort of a little leap in the air, like they were forcing themselves to go a bit higher still—higher than they ought? Well, it struck me that was the way Bridie was acting, as she rushed about that cottage doing this and doing that to make him prouder and prouder of her. As if he could be any prouder than he was already and the child getting noticeable!"

"She didn't die in childbed?"

"No. Not in a manner of speaking, anyway. She had the child, nice and easy, and in their own cottage, too, only costing him a few shillings for one of those women that went in for that kind of job long ago. And all went well. It was no time till she was let up on her feet again. I was there the first morning she had the place to herself! She was up and dressed when I got there, just as he was going out to milk.

" 'Oh, it's great to be able to go out again,' she said, taking a great breath of the morning air as she stood at the door looking after him. 'Wait! Why don't I come with you to milk!' she called out suddenly after him. Then she threw a glance back at the baby asleep in its crib by the window.

" 'Oh, it's too far for you, Bridie!' he cried. The cows were down in the little field by the river—you know the field, alongside the road at the foot of the hill on this side of the village. And knowing she'd start coaxing him, he made out of the gate with the cans.

" 'Good man!' I said to myself. But the next thing I knew, she'd darted across the yard.

" 'I can go on the bike if it's too far to walk!' she said. And up she got on her old bike, and out she pedalled through the gate.

" 'Bridie, are you out of your mind?' he shouted as she whizzed past him.

" 'Arrah, what harm can it do me?' she shouted back.

"I went stiff with fright looking after her. And I thought it was the same with him, when he threw down the cans and started down the hill after her. But looking back on it, I think it was the same fever as always was raging in her that started raging in him, too. Mad with love, that's what they were, both of them—she only wanting to draw him on, and he only too willing!

" 'Wait for me!' he shouted, but before she'd even got to the bottom she started to brake the bike, putting down her foot like you'd see a youngster do, and raising up such a cloud of dust we could hardly see her."

"She braked too hard!"

"Not her! In the twinkle of an eye she'd stopped the bike, jumped off, turned it round, and was pedalling madly up the hill again, her head down on the handle-bars like a racing cyclist. But that was the finish of her!"

"Oh, no! What happened?"

"She stopped pedalling all of a sudden, and the bike half stopped, and then it started to go back down the hill a bit, as if it skidded on the loose gravel at the side of the road. That's what I thought happened, and him, too, I suppose, because we both began to run down the hill. She didn't get time to fall before we got to her. But what use was that? It was some kind of internal bleeding that took her. We got her into the bed, and the neighbours came running, but she was gone before the night."

"Oh, such a thing to happen! And the baby?"

"Well, it was a strong child! And it grew into a fine lump of a lad.

5

That's the fellow that drives the tractor for him now—the oldest son, Bartley."

"Well, I suppose his second marriage had more to it, when all was said and done."

"That's it. And she's a good woman—the second one. The way she brought up that child of Bridie's! And filled the cradle, year after year, with sons of her own. Ah sure, things always work out for the best in the end, no matter what!" he said, and he started to walk away.

"Wait a minute, Ned," she said urgently. "Do you really think he forgot about her—for years, I mean?"

"I'd swear it," said the old man. And then he looked hard at her. "It will be the same with you, too," he added kindly. "Take my word for it. Everything passes in time and is forgotten."

As she shook her head doubtfully, he shook his emphatically. "When the tree falls, how can the shadow stand?" he said. And he walked away.

I wonder! she thought as she walked back to the house, and she envied the practical country way that made good the defaults of nature as readily as the broken sod knits back into the sward.

Again that night, when she went up to her room, she looked down towards the river and she thought of Crossen. Had he really forgotten? It was hard for her to believe, and with a sigh she picked up her hairbrush and pulled it through her hair. Like everything else about her lately, her hair was sluggish and hung heavily down, but after a few minutes under the quickening strokes of the brush, it lightened and lifted, and soon it flew about her face like the spray above a weir. It had always been the same, even when she was a child. She had only to suffer the first painful drag of the bristles when her mother would cry out, "Look! Look! That's electricity!" and a blue spark would shine for an instant like a star in the grey depths of the mirror.

That was all they knew of electricity in those dim-lit days when valleys of shadow lay deep between one piece of furniture and another. Was it because rooms were so badly lit then that they saw it so often, that little blue star? Suddenly she was overcome by longing to see it again, and, standing up impetuously, she switched off the light.

It was just then that, down below, the iron fist of the knocker was lifted and, with a loud, confident hand, brought down on the door.

It wasn't a furtive knock. She admitted that even as she sat stark with fright in the darkness. And then a voice that was vaguely familiar called out—and confidently—from below.

"It's me, Ma'am! I hope I'm not disturbing you!"

"Oh, Mr. Crossen!" she cried out with relief, and, unlocking her door, she ran across the landing and threw up the window on that side of the house. "I'll be right down!" she called.

"Oh, don't come down, Ma'am!" he shouted. "I only want one word with you."

"But of course I'll come down!" She went back to get her dressing-gown and pin up her hair, but as she did she heard him stomping his feet on the gravel. It had been a mild day, but with night a chill had come in the air, and, for all that it was late spring, there was a cutting east wind coming across the river. "I'll run down and let you in from the cold," she called, and, twisting up her hair, she held it against her head with her hand without waiting to pin it, and she ran down the stairs in her bare feet to unbolt the door.

"You were going to bed, Ma'am!" he said accusingly the minute she opened the door. And where he had been so impatient a minute beforehand, he stood stock-still in the open doorway. "I saw the lights were out downstairs when I was coming up the drive," he said contritely. "But I didn't think you'd gone up for the night!"

"Neither had I!" she said lyingly, to put him at his ease. "I was just upstairs brushing my hair. You must excuse me," she added, because a breeze from the door was blowing her dressing-gown from her knees, and to pull it across she had to take her hand from her hair, so that the hair fell down about her shoulders. "Would you mind closing the door for me?" she said, with some embarrassment, and she began to back up the stairs. "Please go inside to the sitting-room, won't you?" she said, nodding towards the door of the small room off the hall. "Put on the light. I'll be down in a minute."

But although he had obediently stepped inside the door, and closed it, he stood stoutly in the middle of the hall. "I shouldn't have come in at all," he said. "I know you were going to bed! Look at you!" he cried again in the same accusing voice, as if he dared her this time to deny it. He was looking at her hair. "Excuse my saying so, Ma'am, but I never saw such a fine head of hair. God bless it!" he said quickly, as if afraid he had been rude. "Doesn't a small thing make a big differ," he said impulsively. "You look like a young girl!"

In spite of herself, she smiled with pleasure. She wanted no more of it, all the same. "Well, I don't feel like one!" she said sharply.

What was meant for a quite opposite effect, however, seemed to delight him and put him wonderfully at ease. "Ah sure, you're a sensible woman! I can see that," he said, and, coming to the foot of the stairs, he leaned comfortably across the newel post. "Let you stay the way you are, Ma'am," he said. "I've only a word to say to you, and it's not worth your while going up them stairs. Let me have my say here and now and be off about my business! The wife will be waiting up for me, and I don't want that!"

She hesitated. Was the reference to his wife meant to put her at *her* ease? "I think I ought to get my slippers," she said cautiously. Her feet were cold.

"Oh, yes, put something on your feet!" he cried, only then seeing that she was in her bare feet. "But as to the rest, I'm long gone beyond taking any account of what a woman has on her. I'm gone beyond taking notice of women at all."

She had seen something to put on her feet. Under the table in the hall was a pair of old boots belonging to Richard, with fleece lining in them. She hadn't been able to make up her mind to give them away with the rest of his clothes, and although they were big and clumsy on her, she often stuck her feet into them when she came in from the fields with mud on her shoes. "Well, come in where it's warm, so," she said. She came back down the few steps and stuck her feet into the boots, and then she opened the door of the sitting-room.

She was glad she'd come down. He'd never have been able to put on the light. "There's something wrong with the centre light," she said as she groped along the wainscot to find the plug of the reading lamp. It was in an awkward place, behind the desk. She had to go down on her knees.

"What's wrong with it?" he asked, as, with a countryman's interest in practicalities, he clicked the switch up and down to no effect.

"Oh, nothing much, I'm sure," she said absently. "There!" She had found the plug, and the room was lit up with a bright white glow.

"Why don't you leave the plug in the socket, anyway?" he asked critically.

"I don't know," she said. "I think someone told me it's safer, with reading lamps, to pull them out at night. There might be a short circuit, or mice might nibble at the cord, or something—I forget what I was told. I got into the habit of doing it, and now I keep on." She felt a bit silly.

But he was concerned about it. "I don't think any harm could be done," he said gravely. Then he turned away from the problem. "About tomorrow, Ma'am!" he said, somewhat offhandedly, she thought. "I was determined I'd see you tonight, because I'm not a man to break my word—above all, to a woman."

What was he getting at?

"Let me put it this way," he said quickly. "You'll understand, Ma'am, that as far as I am concerned, topping land is the same as cutting hay. The same time. The same labour cost. And the same wear and tear on the blade. You understand that?"

On her guard, she nodded.

"Well now, Ma'am, I'd be the first to admit that it's not quite the same for you. For you, topping doesn't give the immediate return you'd get from hay—"

"There's no return from it!" she exclaimed crossly.

"Oh, come now, Ma'am, come! Good grassland pays as well as anything—you know you won't get nice sweet pickings for your beasts from neglected land, but only dirty old tow grass knotting under their feet. It's just that it's not a quick return, and so—as you know—I made a special price for you."

"I do know!" she said impatiently. "But I thought that part of it was settled and done."

"Oh, I'm not going back on it, if that's what you think," he said affably. "I'm glad to do what I can for you, Ma'am, the more so seeing you have no man to attend to these things for you, but only yourself alone."

"Oh, I'm well able to look after myself!" she said, raising her voice.

Once again her words had an opposite effect to what she intended. He laughed good-humouredly. "That's what all women like to think!" he said. "Well, now," he said in a different tone of voice, and it annoyed her to see he seemed to think something had been settled between them, "it would suit me—and I'm sure it's all the same with you—if we could leave your little job till later in the week, say till nearer to the time of the haymaking generally. Because by then I'd have the cutting bar in good order, sharpened and ready for use. Whereas now, while there's still a bit of ploughing to be done here and there, I'll have to be chopping and changing, between the plough and the mower, putting one on one minute and the other the next!"

"As if anyone is still ploughing this time of year!" Her eyes hardened. "Who are you putting before me?" she demanded.

"Now, take it easy, Ma'am. No one. Leastways, not without getting leave first from you."

"Without telling me you're not coming, you mean!"

"Oh, now, Ma'am, don't get cross. I'm only trying to make matters easy for everyone."

But she was very angry now. "It's always the same story. I thought you'd treat me differently! I'm to wait till after this one, and after that one, and in the end my fields will go wild!"

He looked a bit shamefaced. "Ah now, Ma'am, that's not going to be the case at all. Although, mind you, some people don't hold with topping, you know!"

"I hold with it!"

"Oh, I suppose there's something in it," he said reluctantly. "But the way I look at it, cutting the weeds in July is a kind of a topping."

"Grass cut before it goes to seed gets so thick at the roots no weeds can come up!" she cried, so angry she didn't realize how authoritative she sounded.

"Faith, I never knew you were so well up, Ma'am!" he said, looking at her admiringly, but she saw he wasn't going to be put down by her. "All the same now, Ma'am, you can't say a few days here or there could make any difference?"

"A few days could make all the difference! This farm has a gravelly bottom to it, for all it's so lush. A few days of drought could burn it to the butt. And how could I mow it then? What cover would there be for the 'nice sweet pickings' you were talking about a minute ago?" Angrily, she mimicked his own accent without thinking.

He threw up his hands. "Ah well, I suppose a man may as well admit when he's bested," he said. "Even by a woman. And you can't say I broke my promise."

"I can't say but you tried hard enough," she said grudgingly, although she was mollified that she was getting her way. "Can I offer you anything?" she said then, anxious to convey an air of finality to their discussion.

"Oh, not at all, Ma'am! Nothing, thank you! I'll have to be getting home." He stood up.

She stood up, too.

"I hope you won't think I was trying to take advantage of you," he said as they went towards the door. "It's just that we must all make out as best we can for ourselves—isn't that so? Not but you're well able to look after yourself, I must say. No one ever thought you'd stay on here after your husband died. I suppose it's for the children you did it?" He looked up the well of the stairs. "Are they asleep?"

"Oh, long ago," she said indifferently. She opened the hall door.

The night air swept in immediately, as it had earlier. But this time, from far away, it bore along on it the faint scent of new-mown hay. "There's hay cut somewhere already!" she exclaimed in surprise. And she lifted her face to the sweetness of it.

For a minute, Crossen looked past her out into the darkness, then he looked back. "Aren't you ever lonely here at night?" he asked suddenly.

"You mean frightened?" she corrected quickly and coldly.

"Yes! Yes, that's what I meant," he said, taken aback. "Ah, but why would you be frightened! What safer place could you be under the sky than right here with your own fields all about you!"

What he said was so true, and he himself as he stood there, with his hat in his hand, so normal and natural it was indeed absurd to think that he would no sooner have gone out the door than she would be scurrying up the stairs like a child! "You may not believe it," she said, "but I am scared to death sometimes! I nearly died when I heard your knock on the door tonight. It's because I was scared that I was upstairs," she said, in a further burst of confidence. "I always go up the minute it gets dark. I don't feel so frightened up in my room."

"Isn't that strange now?" he said, and she could see he found it an incomprehensibly womanly thing to do. He was sympathetic all the same. "You shouldn't be alone! That's the truth of the matter," he said. "It's a shame!"

"Oh, it can't be helped," she said. There was something she wanted to shrug off in his sympathy, while at the same time there was something in it she wanted to take. "Would you like to do something for me?" she asked impulsively. "Would you wait and put out the lights down here and let me get back upstairs before you go?"

After she had spoken, for a minute she felt foolish, but she saw at once that, if anything, he thought it only too little to do for her. He was genuinely troubled about her. And it wasn't only the present mo-

11

ment that concerned him; he seemed to be considering the whole problem of her isolation and loneliness. "Is there nobody could stay here with you—at night even? It would have to be another woman, of course," he added quickly, and her heart was warmed by the way—without a word from her—he rejected that solution out of hand. "You don't want a woman about the place," he said flatly.

"Oh, I'm all right, really. I'll get used to it," she said.

"It's a shame, all the same," he said. He said it helplessly, though, and he motioned her towards the stairs. "You'll be all right for tonight, anyway," he said. "Go on up the stairs now, and I'll put out the lights." He had already turned around to go back into the sitting-room.

Yet it wasn't quite as she intended for some reason, and it was somewhat reluctantly that she started up the stairs.

"Wait a minute! How do I put out this one?" he called out before she was halfway up.

"Oh, I'd better put out that one myself," she said, thinking of the awkward position of the plug. She ran down again, and, going past him into the little room, she knelt and pulled at the cord. Instantly the room was deluged in darkness. And instantly she felt that she had done something stupid. It was not like turning out a light by a switch at the door and being able to step back at once into the lighted hall. She got to her feet as quickly as she could, but as she did, she saw that Crossen had come to the doorway. His bulk was blocked out against the light beyond. "I'll leave the rest to you," she said, in order to break the peculiar silence that had come down on the house.

But he didn't move. He stood there, the full of the doorway.

"The other switches are over there by the hall door," she said, unwilling to brush past him. Why didn't he move? "Over there," she repeated, stretching out her arm and pointing, but instead of moving he caught at her outstretched arm, and, putting out his other hand, he pressed his palm against the door-jamb, barring the way.

"Tell me," he whispered, his words falling over each other, "are you never lonely—at all?"

"What did you say?" she said in a clear voice, because the thickness of his voice sickened her. She had hardly heard what he said. Her one thought was to get past him.

He leaned forward. "What about a little kiss?" he whispered, and to get a better hold on her he let go the hand he had pressed against the wall, but before he caught at her with both hands she had wrenched her arm free of him, and, ignominiously ducking under his armpit, she was out next minute in the lighted hall.

Out there—because light was all the protection she needed from him, the old fool—she began to laugh. She had only to wait for him to come sheepishly out.

But there was something she hadn't counted on; she hadn't counted on there being anything pathetic in his sheepishness. There was something actually pitiful in the way he shambled into the light, not raising his eyes. And she was so surprisingly touched by him that before he had time to utter a word she put out her hand. "Don't feel too bad," she said. "I didn't mind."

Even then, he didn't look at her. He just took her hand and pressed it gratefully, his face still turned away. And to her dismay she saw that his nose was running water. Like a small boy, he wiped it with the back of his fist, streaking his face. "I don't know what came over me," he said slowly. "I'm getting on to be an old man now. I thought I was beyond all that." He wiped his face again. "Beyond letting myself go, anyway," he amended miserably.

"Oh, it was nothing," she said.

He shook his head. "It wasn't as if I had cause for what I did."

"But you did nothing," she protested.

"It wasn't nothing to me," he said dejectedly.

For a minute, they stood there silent. The hall door was still ajar, but she didn't dare to close it. What am I going to do with him now, she thought. I'll have him here all night if I'm not careful. What time was it, anyway? All scale and proportion seemed to have gone from the night. "Well, I'll see you in the morning, Mr. Crossen!" she said, as matter-of-factly as possible.

He nodded, but made no move. "You know I meant no disrespect to you, Ma'am, don't you?" he said then, looking imploringly at her. "I always had a great regard for you. And for your husband, too. I was thinking of him this very night when I was coming up to the house. And I thought of him again when you came to the door looking like a young girl. I thought what a pity it was him to be taken from you, and you both so young! Oh, what came over me at all? And what would Mona say if she knew?"

"But you wouldn't tell her, I hope!" she cried. What sort of a figure would she cut if he told about her coming down in her bare feet with her hair down her back! "Take care would you tell her!" she warned.

"I don't suppose I ought," he said, but he said it uncertainly and morosely, and he leaned back against the wall. "She's been a good woman, Mona. I wouldn't want anyone to think different. Even the boys could tell you. She's been a good mother to them all these years. She never made a bit of difference between them. Some say she was better to Bartley than to any of them! She reared him from a week old. She was living next door to us, you see, at the time—" He hesitated. "At the time I was left with him," he finished in a flat voice. "She came in that first night and took him home to her own bed—and, mind you, that wasn't a small thing for a woman who knew nothing about children, not being what you'd call a young girl at the time, in spite of the big family she gave me afterwards. She took him home that night, and she looked after him. It isn't every woman would care to be responsible for a newborn baby. That's a thing a man doesn't forget easy! There's many I know would say that if she hadn't taken him someone else would have, but no one only her would have done it the way she did.

"She used to have him all day in her own cottage, feeding him and the rest of it. But at night, when I'd be back from the fields, she'd bring him home and leave him down in his little crib by the fire alongside of me. She used to let on she had things to do in her own place, and she'd slip away and leave us alone, but that wasn't her real reason for leaving him. She knew the way I'd be sitting looking into the fire, wondering how I'd face the long years ahead, and she left the child there with me to break my thoughts. And she was right. I never got long to brood. The child would give a cry, or a whinge, and I'd have to run out and fetch her to him. Or else she'd hear him herself maybe, and run in without me having to call her at all. I used often think she must have kept every window and door in her place open, for fear she'd lose a sound from either of us. And so, bit by bit, I was knit back into a living man. I often wondered what would have become of me if it wasn't for her. There are men and when the bright way closes to them there's no knowing but they'll take a dark way. And I was that class of man.

"I told you she used to take the little fellow away in the day and bring him back at night? Well, of course, she used to take him away again coming on to the real dark of night. She'd take him away to her own bed. But as the months went on and he got bigger, I could see she hated taking him away from me at all. He was beginning to smile

14

and play with his fists and be real company. 'I wonder ought I leave him with you tonight,' she'd say then, night after night. And sometimes she'd run in and dump him down in the middle of the big double bed in the room off the kitchen, but the next minute she'd snatch him up again. 'I'd be afraid you'd overlie him! You might only smother him, God between us and all harm!' 'You'd better take him,' I'd say, I used to hate to see him go myself by this time. All the same, I was afraid he'd start crying in the night, and what would I do then? If I had to go out for her in the middle of the night, it could cause a lot of talk. There was talk enough as things were, I can tell you, although there was no grounds for it. I had no more notion of her than if she wasn't a woman at all—would you believe that? But one night when she took him up and put him down, and put him down and took him up, and went on and went on about leaving him or taking him, I had to laugh. 'It's a pity you can't stay along with him, and that would settle all,' I said. I was only joking her, but she got as red as fire, and next thing she burst out crying! But not before she'd caught up the child and wrapped her coat around him. Then, after giving me a terrible look, she ran out of the door with him.

"Well, that was the beginning of it. I'd no idea she had any feelings for me. I thought it was only for the child. But men are fools, as women well know, and she knew before me what was right and proper for us both. And for the child, too. Some women have great insight into these things! And God opened my own eyes then to the woman I had in her, and I saw it was better I took her than wasted away after the one that was gone. And wasn't I right?"

"Of course you were right," she said quickly.

But he slumped back against the wall, and the abject look came back into his eyes.

I'll never get rid of him, she thought desperately. "Ah, what ails you!" she cried impatiently. "Forget it, can't you?"

"I can't," he said simply. "And it's not only me—it's the wife I'm thinking about. I've shamed her!"

"Ah, for heaven's sake. It's nothing got to do with her at all."

Surprised, he looked up at her. "You're not blaming yourself, surely?" he asked.

She'd have laughed at that if she hadn't seen she was making headway—another stroke and she'd be rid of him. "Arrah, what are you blaming any of us for!" she cried. "It's got nothing to do with any of us—with you, or me, or the woman at home waiting for you. It was the other one! That girl—your first wife—Bridie! It was her! Blame her! She's the one did it!" The words had broken from her. For a moment, she thought she was hysterical and that she could not stop. "You thought you could forget her," she said, "but see what she did to you when she got the chance!" She stopped and looked at him.

He was standing at the open door. He didn't look back. "God rest her soul," he said, and he stepped into the night.

Housekeeper's Cut

Clare Boylan

Edward kept looking into the refrigerator. It gave him a sense of faith. This peculiar sensation billowed inside his chest in the manner competently wrought by carol singers and card senders at Christmas. It was not the same as religious faith. Edward was too modest for that. He was experiencing another sensation never before aspired to in his life, a faith in ordinary things.

There was butter and bacon, eggs, milk, ice-cream; a clutter of untidy vegetables—carrots, cabbage, onions, mushrooms. He had purchased them recklessly from a stall in a food market, cramming his string bag with scabby-looking roots with the air of a man who knows exactly what he is doing. He had no notion of any practical application for such primitive nutrients. They might have been employed by men who lived in caves to club their enemies. He was familiar with food that came in plastic bags and could be persuaded, with boiling water, to imitate a meal.

He knew, all the same, in the way a blind man knows that the world over his head is blue and grey and the world under his feet is green and grey and the top part is safer, that these items belonged at the very heart of things and that this was where he was going.

The thing that pleased him most was his roast. It held the centre of the refrigerator, lightly covered in butcher's paper. He had watched it in the meaty window for several minutes before striding in and claiming it. He did this by pointing because he had no idea what it was. He was appalled at the price. It cost over four pounds. He was neither poor nor mean, merely accustomed to buying a slice or two of roast beef from the delicatessen or a couple of spiced sausages, and there was always plenty of change left over from a pound. Now that it was his he could see that it was worth the money, swirling fat and flesh tied with a string in the middle; already he could hear the clash of knives being sharpened, the rattle and scrape of plates, like sounds of battle imagined by a child in a history class.

He used to meet Susan between meals. She was worn out from making excuses and he had to give her glasses of wine to make her look the way he imagined her when she was not there. She grumbled about the needs of her children, the demands of her husband, his capacity for chops and potatoes and apple tarts. It appeared that her whole life was dragged down by the weight of her husband's appetite; she was up at dawn wringing the vitamins from oranges, out hampered by enormous sacks of groceries during the day. Afternoons were taken up with peeling and grating, marinating, sieving. After a time her abused features would soften and she would say: "It would be different if it was for you. I always think of that when I'm cooking. I always pretend it's for you." She would come to him then, dipping her face to his lips. She sat across his legs as if he was a see-saw. "If you were with me," he would say, "I would give you six months of tremendous spoiling. Then I'd put you to work."

Sometimes he did, just to watch her, just for fun. He put her beside the cooker with mushrooms and cream, small morsels of fish, tasty things.

She was too tired. The food got burnt, the mushrooms went rubbery. Or they became distracted. He would come up behind her and put his arms around her and she would swivel round and burrow to him. When they were in bed smells of burning food and sounds of music drifted up from rooms below.

Inside her, he found a love that wanted to be taken advantage of and although he did not wish to hurt her, he found himself complaining about the comfortlessness of his life; the meals taken in restaurants with people who meant nothing, just to fill an evening. He dined out most evenings because he was lonely in the house without her. She never asked about his companions, but about the interior features of the restaurants, the designs on menus and then in detail, the meal. "It's a waste," he said, "to be anywhere without you."

When he went back to the city he forgot about her. There were moments when he felt a hollowness which he recognized as the place in him where she had been, but he had always known it would come to an end. He looked on love as a seasonal pleasure, like sunshine. Only a savage expected the sun to shine all year round.

She telephoned from public call boxes. Her voice was the ocean in a seashell. He remembered that they had made together a splash of happiness on a pale canvas but he knew that she did not carry this glow alone, without him. When they said goodbye for the last time, he had watched her running away, a drooping figure, disarrayed, a spirit fleeing an exorcism. He listened to the cascade of coins following the operator's instructions and then after a pause, her weary voice. "I miss you." He saw her in a headscarf with a bag of groceries at her side and small children clawing on the outside of the glass, trying to get at her.

He was at home now, busy, surrounded by people who were skilled in the pleasures of living—conversation and lovemaking—as people in the country had never been.

Even she, to whom he had leapt as determinedly as a salmon, held within her a soft hopelessness which begged, come in to me, fill me up, I have nothing else.

One day on the phone her voice sounded different: "I'm coming up," she said. He frowned into the machine receiving the bubbles of her tone. This possibility had not occurred to him. She was too firmly anchored with groceries. "Two whole days," she was telling him through her laughter, gasping about excuses and arrangements so complicated that he knew she would tunnel under the earth with her hands to reach him if necessary. "That will be very nice," he said inadequately. "I'll look forward to that." It was when he had replaced the receiver and was still washed by echoes of her foolish joy that he understood properly what she was saying. She had disposed, for a time, of all the open mouths that gaped at her for sustenance. She had put them aside. She was coming to do her proper task. He was tenderly agitated by the thought of her frail figure scurrying from one area of usefulness to another. This was blotted out by the shouts of his own areas of deprivation, crying out to be seen to. He wanted her to look after him.

When he met her at the station she was tremulously dressed up, a country woman on an outing. She threw him a reckless smile from under a hat. Alarming blue carnations sprang up around her skull. She dropped her cases and raced into his arms. Her feet flailed heedlessly and the flowers on her hat dipped like the neck of a heron. She thudded into him and he felt the needy probing of her tongue. He

19

held her patiently, employing his training as a man to grind down the stone in his chest, of disappointment, that she had not kept a part of herself solid and available to his needs.

"Look at that!" She kept stabbing at the window of the car with her gloved finger, demonstrating pigeons and churches and department stores. "Look!" "You sound like a tourist," he said. She kept quiet after that. She hadn't ever been to the city before.

Inside his flat she walked around all the rooms, inspecting his clothes on their hangers, patting the bed, trying out chairs. He was surprised when she sat down without giving a glance to the refrigerator. "What shall we do?" she said.

She was slouched in a red leather armchair, her white skirt bunched under her thighs. He imagined that she ought to be in the kitchen doing something with the roast. He could picture it bulging in a tin, strung about with peeled potatoes and onions. He wanted to watch her bending at the oven, her frowning face pink, her straight hair shrivelling into tiny curls around her face. He had bought an apron for her. It was white with a black and red frill at the bottom. It hung on a nail by the sink. He had no clear idea of what they would do with all the time they now had to spend together. She was the one who was married, who was skilled in the sectioning of time. He had vaguely imagined that women liked to be busy in a house, arranging flowers, punching pastry, stirring at saucepans on the stove, and that it was a man's role to encircle this ritual with refinement, music and drinks and occasional kisses, creating a territory for their contentment, a privacy for their love.

He had not set his heart on this course of events. He did not mind if she preferred to take a nap or read a book or sit on his knee. The thing that was foremost in his mind was that their pursuits of the afternoon would be overlaid by ovenly aromas, snaps and splutterings and the delicious sting on their senses of roasting meat.

He asked if she was hungry and she said that she was, standing up instantly, brushing down her skirt. She took a mirror from her bag and gazed at her face, pressing her lips together, peering into her eyes for flaws. He took her hand and led her through to the kitchen. He pulled open the door of the refrigerator as if he was drawing back a stage curtain and she peered, awed, at the overcrowding of nourishment. "What are you going to do with all this?" she said, and he laughed. "There's cold meat and cheese," he said. "We could have that for lunch." She stood gazing into the fridge with a melancholy expression while he removed the slices of ham and the tubs of potato salad and the oozing triangle of Brie.

When he had set the table and opened a bottle of wine he came back to find her still transfixed in front of the open cabinet with that expression housewives have, and he thought she was sizing up the contents, planning menus. "That," he said, pointing in at his slab of meat on the shelf as if it was a lovely trinket in a jeweller's window, "is for dinner." She sat down at the table without a word. He sensed, as she ate her ham and potatoes and swirled her wine around in the glass, that she was disappointed. This feeling communicated to himself and he poured wine into his leaden chest, blaming himself. He had probably pre-empted her plans for lunch. She might have been planning to surprise him with a homemade soup. She raised bleak eyes to him over her glass. She was not her normal self, full of cheerful complaint and breathless love. She was ill at ease and sad. "Aren't we going out?" she said. The thought to him was preposterous. Now that they finally had a stretch of privacy, she wanted to race out into the cold where they would be divided by elements and the curious looks of strangers.

He drove her to a park and they huddled under some trees against the cold, watching cricket players and a family of deer in the distance like an arrangement of dead branches. He had brought a box of sweets that she had sent him. It had seemed a sentimental gesture, saving them to share with her. Now that he was pulling off the wrapper he could see it was tactless, taking them out so much later. She would think he had not wanted them. He laid the open box in the grass. After a moment or two, the arrangement of confectionery was swarming with ants.

He was tired when he got home and beginning to get hungry. Susan wanted a bath. He took the meat from the fridge and laid it on a plate on the counter. He hazarded the skinning of several potatoes. He carried a clutch of jaundiced-looking parsnips and placed them in a bowl, close to the liquidizer. This tableau was completed with a blue tin of curry powder. Once, in a restaurant, he had been given a curried parsnip soup and it was delicious.

When she joined him in the kitchen she was wearing a black dress down to her feet. Her mouth was obscured in magenta. He put his arms around her and kissed her laundered neck but she struggled from

21

his grasp and pointed to the ranked ingredients. "What are you doing?" she said. "Just hamming." He smiled guiltily.

She looked from him to the food, back again. Her hands, he noticed, wrestled with the string of a tiny evening bag. "I thought," she said, "that we'd be going out." "Going where?" he said, exasperated. "I don't know." Her shoulders drooped. "The theatre, a restaurant." He could not keep her still, draw her back to the things that mattered. "Do you really want to go out?" She nodded her head. He sighed and went to telephone a theatre. When he came back the counter had been cleared of his work and offered instead a meagre plate of toast and a pot of tea.

In the city she was happy. She sipped cocktails and laughed, showing all her teeth, raising her eyebrows larkily. Although her clothes were not suited to the theatre, not suited to anything really, she carried her happiness with dignity. Men looked at her, old ones, young ones, brown, grey. She was aware of this but her eyes were for him. He thought he understood now. She was sure of herself on this neutral territory. She did not wish to be plucked by him from their complicated past. Here, she was a woman alone. She wanted him to court her. He took her hand and kissed her cheek, catching scents of gin and perfume. He felt desire. This seizure of lust was new. It had not touched him when they were in the park or shut up in his living quarters. He had felt love and compassion but no selfish stirrings.

During the play he watched her, writing his own theme, making her free and carefree as his needs required, as her loud laughter would lead anyone to believe.

Afterwards he turned the car quickly homeward. She kept looking out the window, like a child. When they were home she said fretfully: "We haven't had anything to eat, not really." He was no longer concerned about food. There was plenty, in any case, in the fridge. She cooked some eggs and a packet of little onions, frozen in sauce. It was a strange combination but he drove the food into his mouth and pronounced it delicious.

They went to bed. Their sex was full of need and passion. They came with angry shouts. They could not find their love. "I love you," she said. "Yes," he said. "Yes." And then they were silent, each saying to themselves: "Tomorrow will be different."

In the morning she was up early to make his breakfast, her toes crackling with joy as she reached up to shelves for coffee and marmalade. She felt wrapped around him as a cardigan. As she waited for the coffee to boil she sensed a warm splash on her feet and it was his seed, languorously detaching itself from her. She felt a minute sense of loss, wanting to let nothing go, wanting to be pregnant.

Edward had to work after breakfast. He did not mind leaving her on her own. She seemed happy as she punished pillows and washed out the breakfast things. He found himself whistling as he bent over his set square. After a time she came and sat beside him. She had been washing her hair. She combed it over her face in long strokes that emanated a faint creak. Inky streamers swam through the air and clung to his clothing. He could not work. He gave her an irritated glance and she went away. She came back dressed in high shoes and a blue suit—a costume, rather, he thought—her face matt and piqued with make-up. She was carrying cups of coffee. When she put his coffee down she quickly sought his hand with hers, and although their grasp was warm and steady there was some central part of them that was trembling and they could feel it through their palms. "Now," he thought, "we could go to bed. We could love each other." It made sense. They had always done their loving in the day. Her bright armour kept him distant.

"I'd like," she said, "to see the sights."

He took his hand away and wrapped it around the cup of coffee, needing warmth. He did not look at her. "There's nothing to see out there," he said. "Believe me. We could have a quiet lunch and listen to some music. We could read to each other." "But it's London!" she protested.

He said, thinking to stop her: "You go if you want. I must work for a little while. I couldn't bear to see the sights." He did look up then and saw her soft round face boxing up a huge hurt in an even larger resolve. She kissed the side of his face and he wanted the salt of her mouth but she was so different, so devoid of humour and generosity, that he believed even her taste might have changed. She clopped off on her high heels and he heard the sorrowful bang of the door.

He could not work. He was exasperated to distraction. There crept in on him thoughts, malice-filled whispers. He shook them off as if they were wasps at his ears.

He had established in his mind, long months before, that she was the one in his life who truly loved him, wanting nothing, knowing that nothing was possible. When they parted he had savoured the sorrow of it, knowing that this was real. They had been severed by fate, an outsider, a true professional. There would be no festering, only a clean grief gleaming like stainless steel around the core of a perfect happiness, safely invested in his centre. He had been content to leave it at that. He would have loved her, at the back of his head, until his death.

It was she who had come back like a vengeful spirit to incorporate him in her discontent, to mock his faith, to demonstrate to him, in her ghostly unreachableness, the great stretch of his own isolation.

He went to look for some lunch. There was nothing in the refrigerator that he could understand. He was exploring parcels of foil, hoping for some forgotten cheese, when he heard a commotion coming from the garden.

Susan was in a restaurant. She had a chocolate éclair that she was breaking with the side of her fork. She had taken a taxi to Madame Tussaud's and the Planetarium. Outside each was a long queue of foreigners and a man selling balloons on a stick for fifty pence. There was no glamour, no sense of discovery. They were like people queueing for food in the war. She had wanted him to take her to a gallery of famous paintings and show her the pictures he liked. No point in going on her own; she could never understand pictures, always wanted to see the scene as it really was.

She left the stoic queue and went back to the taxi rank. She could not think where to go. "Bond Street," she said to the driver, liking its sound. She did not know where it was but it seemed to her, as the streets unravelled like red and grey bandages, she was being taken further and further away from Edward. When they got to Bond Street, she was ordered out of the dark enclosure. She tried to thrust a fan of notes at the back of the driver's neck, through the sliding glass door, but he was suspicious and made her go out on the street and put them through a side window.

She stumbled along in front of the smart shops. She ached to be with Edward, to feel his hand or even the cloth of his jacket; and then, perversely, she felt lonely for home, wanting to butter toast for the children or to fluff the top of a shepherd's pie for her husband. She understood their needs. She knew how to respond. When she had exhausted several streets she found a café and she went in and ordered herself a cake. A tear dropped into it and she did not want to eat it. She would go back, she promised herself. She would talk to him.

He was standing at the window, shoulders bent, head at a quizzical angle and sunlight teasing his hair into infantile transparency. She had let herself in with the key he had given her and he did not notice her. Watching his back, she felt as if all the ordinary things had been vacuumed out of her body and replaced by love, lead-heavy, a burden. "I want to talk to you," she said. "Shhh," he said, not turning around. "Edward?" she begged. He turned to her. His face was white, filled with horror. "It's a bird," he said.

"What are you talking about?" She went to the window and looked out. She could see a ragged tomcat standing at a tree, his back arched. She ran to the back door and out into the garden, down the length of the path.

The tree was root deep in rattling leaves and when she got to it she could see that the leaves were in permanent motion as if agitated by a slow motor under the earth. She saw then that it was a dowdy grey bird, lopsided, helplessly urging an injured wing to flight. The cat held its victim with a gooseberry gaze. She picked up the cat and put it on the wall, slapping its behind to make it jump into the next garden. "Bring me a box," she shouted out to Edward's white face at the window. He advanced with a shoe box. She snatched it from him, piling it with leaves, roughly cramming in the damaged bird. She slammed the lid on the bird's head and carried it indoors. She looked, Edward thought, like a housewife who has just come upon some unpleasant item of refuse and means to deal with it; but when she got indoors she sat in a chair and emptied bird and leaves into her blue linen lap. She held the bird in cupped hands and crooned gently into its dank feathers.

He brought her tea and fed it to her, holding the cup to her mouth. She minded the bird like a baby, making noises with her lips, rocking back and forth as once she had minded him. He was unnerved by a pang of jealousy. "Did you have a nice morning?" he said. "Oh, yes," she said, distantly, rocking. He could see that she was in her element. He was excluded. He crumbled bread into a bowl of milk and pushed little spoons of it at the dry nib of the bird's beak. The bird seemed to be asleep. She pushed his hand aside and swept the bird, leaves and all, back into the box. "Open the bedroom window," she said. She followed him upstairs and put the box on the ledge without its lid. "If his wing isn't broken he'll fly away," she said. "But if it is broken?" he said helplessly. "He'll die," she said.

In the course of the morning he had taken the meat and vegetables from the fridge once more. There had been nothing readily edible and he was hungry. When they came downstairs again she saw them and said: "I have to phone my husband," as if they had reminded her of him, which they had.

He heard her on the phone. She sounded as if she was defending herself. She said then: "I miss you." It was an echo from his distant past. He went in and found her sitting on the sofa, her fist to her mouth, crying. He touched her hair lightly with his fingers, afraid to do more. "I'll just put the meat in the oven," he said hopefully. "What?" She glared at him. Her tearful face was full of scorn. "Have you still got your heart set on that?" "I bought it for you," he said. "You bought it for me? I have tasted prawns and sole in my life, you know. I have had fried steak." She was attacking him. He didn't know what was the matter. He assumed her husband had said something to upset her. "It's all right," he soothed. He tiptoed out as if she were sleeping.

The potatoes, peeled from yesterday, had blackened. He flung them hopefully into the tin. He peeled four onions and tucked them into the corners; in the centre, as he had imagined it, the round of juicy meat.

It looked perfectly fine. He put a pat of butter on the top and a sprinkling of salt and pepper. He cut up a clove of garlic and scattered it over the food. He thought he had seen other women doing something like this. He turned the oven up to a rousing temperature and pushed the tin inside. It was done. There was nothing to it.

He blamed himself for Susan's outburst. He should not have left her to wander around the city on her own. She was used to a more protected way of life. He must make it up to her.

He took champagne from a cool cupboard and dug it into a bowl with ice. He found music on the radio. He brought the wine with glasses to the bedroom. Music drifted up from downstairs. He drew the curtains and switched on a little lamp. "Susan," he called.

He heard her dragging steps on the stairs. A face loomed round the door, self-piteous. Her sharp eyes flashed about suspiciously, took in the details—and were radiant. She was a child; all troubles erased in a momentary delight. She ran to him and was caught in his arms. They stroked hair, pulled buttons, tasted flesh. She laughed greedily. At last they had met.

They made love boastfully, tenderly, certain of their territory. He held her feet in his hands. She took his fingers in her mouth. They embroidered one another's limbs with their attentions. He felt with his lips for the edges of her smile and could find no end. They were separated only by the selfishness of their happiness. Afterwards, she gave a deep unlikely chortle from her satisfied depths and he laughed at her.

They drank the champagne crouching at opposite ends of the bed in the intimate gloom, striking up flinty tales of childhood for sympathy.

When they crawled towards each other, he with bottle and she with empty glass, only their mouths met and he took the breakable things and put them on the floor because they had to make love again.

They emptied the bottle of champagne. They lay beside each other, gazing. "I must look awful," she said. He surveyed her snarled black hair and the matching dark scribble under a carelessly disposed arm; the smear of make-up under her eyes, her sated face scrubbed pink. "You look fine to me," he said. He felt exuberant, relieved, re-born, at ease. "You look," he teased, but truthfully, "like my mistress."

She swung away from him, rolled over and clung to her pillow, a mollusc on a rock. He could not tell what was in her head. He patted her back but she shook him off and murmured sadly through the pillow: "I smell something." She looked up at him, one moist eye rising above its ruined decor. He had offended her. But when the rest of her face rose above the sheets he could see that her eyes were watering with laughter.

"What is it?" he smiled tenderly. "It's perfect," she said. "It's exactly as it used to be—us, together, the music and the smell of burning food." She laughed.

He jumped out of bed and ran to the kitchen. Smoke gusted out around the oven door. The air was cruel with the taint of burning beast. He pulled open the oven door and his naked body was assaulted by the heat of hell. He dragged the roasting tin clear of the smoke with a cloth. The cloves of garlic rattled like blackened nails on the tarry ruin.

He was worn out. He felt betrayed. He could not believe that it had happened so quickly, so catastrophically. He felt his faith sliding away. "Edward?" Susan called out from the bedroom. "It's all right!" he shouted; and after he had said it he felt that it had to be. He opened the window to let out the smoke and went to the bathroom for a dressing-gown.

Bolstered by champagne and the satisfactoriness of the afternoon's loving he made himself believe that the meat could be repaired. He whistled loudly as if it was the dark and he was afraid. He forked the meat on to a scallopped plate and began to hack away with a sharp knife at the charred edges of the tormented flesh.

He was agreeably surprised to find that the meat was still quite rare on the inside—almost raw, in fact. He found it hard to make an impression with the knife but he put this down to lack of practice and the fact that the carving implements were not much in use. He sawed, glad of the little box of cress in the fridge which would decorate its wounds and the rest of the vegetables which Susan would cook and toss in butter while he put on his clothes.

Susan came up behind him. She had been standing in the doorway in a night-dress like a flourbag, frilled on cuff and sleeve. She tiptoed on bare feet, so that he sensed her at the last moment, tangled wraith blanched and billowing.

"It's no use," she whispered. "It's fine," he said. "It's not bad at all." "It's no use," she cried brokenly. "There's no Bisto, no stock cubes. There's nothing in your cupboards, nothing ordinary—no flour or custard, there isn't a packet of salt. It's all a pretence."

She put out a hand, and he reached for it, needing something to hold. Her hand shot past him. She struck at the meat. It sailed off the plate and landed on the floor, blood gathering at its edges. "That's all you think of me," she said violently, through trembling jaws. "You think that's good enough for me! Housekeeper's Cut! I wouldn't have that on my own table at home. I wouldn't give that to my children if they were hungry. That's all I'm worth."

They ate in an Italian restaurant close to where he lived. It was not a place he had been before. The tables were bright red and the menu leaned heavily to starch but there was no time to book a proper restaurant. He had to have something to eat.

"Have some veal," he said. "That should be good." He poured wine from a carafe into their glasses. She ordered a pizza. Her hair fell over her face. He could see her knuckles sawing over the fizzing red disc but none of it seemed to go to her mouth. The waiter said that the lady should have an ice-cream. She shook her head. "Cassata!" he proclaimed. "It means," he wheedled, "*married.*"

Edward laughed encouragement but she did not see. Her head was turned to the waiter, nodding, he could not tell whether in request or resignation.

In the morning she was gone. The sheets still burned with the heat of her body. She had been up at six, packing, making coffee, telephoning for a taxi. Her feet, on the floor made a rousing slap like the sound of clapping hands. At one point he heard her whistling. He knew that he should drive her to the station but he would not hasten her back to the disposal of her lawful dependants. He would not.

"Edward!" Her hands clung to the end of his bed and she cried out in distress, her face and her night-dress trailing white in the grey morning light. "Yes, love," he said inside, but he only opened a cautious eye and uttered a sleepy "Mmm?" "I bought nothing for the children," she said. "They'll be expecting presents. I always buy them something."

She stood at the window, dressed in hat and coat, in the last moments, waiting for her taxi. "Edward!" she cried. He sat up this time, ready to take her in his arms. "The bird!" she said. "He flew away."

When she was gone he traced with his fingers her body in the warm sheets, bones and hair and pillows of maternal flesh. He kept his eyes closed, kept her clenched in his heart. The day bore in on him, sunshine and telephone bells and the cold knowledge that she did not love him. All the time she pretended to care for him, she had been jealous of his wealth, greedy for glamour. She was a pilgrim, stealing relics of the saints.

It was not him she desired. She wanted to snatch for herself some part of a glittering life she imagined he was hoarding. He tried to bring her face to mind but all he could see was a glass box, clawed by children, and inside, a housewife in a headscarf, bags of groceries at her side.

Susan did not cry until she was on the train. The tears fell, then, big as melted ice cubes. There was a man sitting opposite with a little boy. The child had been given a magic drawing pad to occupy his hands and he made sketches of her melting face, squinting for perspective.

As the tears dashed from her eyes she felt that she was flying to pieces. Soon there would be nothing left of her; at any rate, nothing solid enough to contain the knowledge that he did not love her.

She had expected so little. She only wanted to fill up the gaps in their past. Often, when they were together, he had spoken of the hurt of being anywhere without her; the wasted nights with strangers; the meals in restaurants, not tasted. It was terrible to her that she had only given him her leftover time. She had to make it up to him. She wanted him to know that she would risk anything for him. She would shine beside him in the harsh glare of public envy. For a very little time she would be his for all the world to see, whatever the world might say.

Now she did not know what she would do except, in time, face up to her foolishness. He had not been proud of her. He wanted to hide her away. Established in his own smart and secret life, he had been ashamed of her.

The man on the seat opposite was embarrassed. It was her huge tears, her lack of discretion, the critical attention of his little boy. He felt threatened by their indifference to proper codes of behaviour. He snatched the magic pad and threw it roughly to the far end of the seat. The boy gazed idly out the window.

Accustomed to inspecting the creative efforts of the children, Susan reached for the sketch pad. The boy was not as clever as her own. His portrait was a clown's mask, upside down. She rubbed out his imprint and sat with the pad on her knee, acquainting herself with the raw, hurting feeling of her mind and her skin, settling into the pain. She had to stop crying. The children would notice. Tomorrow she would buy them presents. Tonight, they would have to content themselves with ice-cream. "Ice-cream" she scratched absently on the magic pad. Her tired mind grizzled over the necessities of tea and she wrote, without thinking, "eggs, bacon, cheese"; and then, since days did not exist on their own but merely as transport to other days, and since she on this vehicle of time was a stoker, she continued writing: "carrots, cabbage, onions, mushrooms."

Midwife to the Fairies

Éilís Ní Dhuibhne

We were looking at the "Late Late." It wasn't much good this night, there was a fellow from Russia, a film star or an actor or something—I'd never heard tell of him—and some young one from America who was after setting up a prostitute's hotel or call-in service or something. God, what Gay wants with that kind I don't know. All done up really snazzy, mind you, like a model or a television announcer or something. And she made a mint out of it, writing a book about her experiences if you don't mind. I do have to laugh!

I don't enjoy it as much of a Friday. It was much better of a Saturday. After the day's work and getting the bit of dinner ready for myself and Joe, sure I'm barely ready to sit down when it's on. It's not as relaxing like. I don't know, I do be all het up somehow on Fridays on account of it being such a busy day at the hospital and all, with all the cuts you really have to earn your keep there nowadays! Saturday is busy too of course—we have to go into Bray and do the bit of shopping like, and do the bit of hoovering and washing. But it's not the same, I feel that bit more relaxed, I suppose it's on account of not being at work really. Not that I'd want to change that or anything. No way. Sixteen years of being at home was more than enough for me. That's not to say, of course, that I minded it at the time. I didn't go half-cracked the way some of them do, or let on to do. Mind you, I've no belief in that pre-menstrual tension and post-natal depression and what have you. I come across it often enough, I needn't tell you, or I used to, I should say, in the course of my duty. Now with the maternity unit gone of course all that's changed. It's an ill wind, as they say. I'll say one thing for male patients, there's none of this depression carry-on

31

with them. Of course they all think they're dying, oh dying, of sore toes and colds in the head and anything at all, but it's easier to put up with than the post-natals. I'm telling no lie.

Well, anyway, we were watching Gaybo and I was out in the kitchen wetting a cup of tea, which we like to have around ten or so of a Friday. Most nights we wait till it's nearer bedtime, but on Fridays I usually do have some little treat I get on the way home from work in The Hot Bread Shop there on the corner of Corbawn Lane, in the new shopping centre. Some little extra, a few Danish pastries or doughnuts, some little treat like that. For a change more than anything. This night I'd a few Napoleons—you know, them cream slices with icing on top.

I was only after taking out the plug when the bell went. Joe answered it of course and I could hear him talking to whoever it was and I wondered who it could be at that hour. All the stories you hear about burglars and people being murdered in their own homes . . . there was a woman over in Dalkey not six months ago, hacked to pieces at ten o'clock in the morning. God help her! . . . I do be worried. Naturally. Though I keep the chain on all the time and I think that's the most important thing. As long as you keep the chain across you're all right. Well, anyway, I could hear them talking and I didn't go out. And after a few minutes I could hear him taking the chain off and letting whoever it was in. And then Joe came in to me and he says:

"There's a fellow here looking for you, Mary. He says it's urgent."

"What is it he wants? Sure I'm off duty now anyway, amn't I?"

I felt annoyed, I really did. The way people make use of you! You'd think there was no doctors or something. I'm supposed to be a nurse's aide, to work nine to five, Monday to Friday, except when I'm on nights. But do you think the crowd around here can get that into their heads? No way.

"I think you'd better have a word with him yourself, Mary. He says it's urgent like. He's in the hall."

I knew of course. I knew before I seen him or heard what he had to say. And I took off my apron and ran my comb through my hair to be ready. I made up my own mind that I'd have to go out with him in the cold and the dark and miss the rest of the "Late Late." But I didn't let on of course.

There was a handywoman in this part of the country and she used to

be called out at all times of the day and night. But one night a knock
came to her door. The woman got up at once and got ready to go out.
There was a man standing at the door with a mare.

He was a young fellow with black hair, hardly more than eighteen or
nineteen.

"Well," says I, "what's your trouble?"

"It's my wife," he said, embarrassed like. He'd already told Joe, I
don't know what he had to be embarrassed about. Usually you'd get
used to a thing like that. But anyway he was, or let on to be.

"She's expecting. She says it's on the way."

"And who might you be?"

"I'm her husband."

"I see," says I. And I did. I didn't come down in the last shower.
And with all the carry-on that goes on around here you'd want to be
thick or something not to get this particular message straight away. But
I didn't want to be too sure of myself. Just in case. Because, after all,
you can never be too sure of anything in this life. "And why?" says I
to him then. "Why isn't she in hospital, where she should be?"

"There isn't time," he said, as bold as brass. See what I mean about
getting used to it?

"Well," says I then, "closing maternity wards won't stop them having
babies." I laughed, trying to be a bit friendly like. But he didn't see
the joke. So, says I, "And where do you and your wife live?"

"We live on this side of Annamoe," he said, "and if you're coming
we'd better be going. It's on the way, she said."

"I'll come," I said. What else could I say? A call like that has to be
answered. My mother did it before me and her mother before her, and
they never let anyone down. And my mother said that her mother had
never lost a child. Not one. Her corporate works of mercy, she called
it. You get indulgence. And anyway I pitied him, he was only a young
fellow and he was nice-looking, too, he had a country look to him.
But of course I was under no obligation, none whatever, so I said,
"Not that I should come really. I'm off duty, you know, and anyway
what you need is the doctor."

"We'd rather have you," he said.

"Well, just this time."

"Let's go then!"

"Hold on a minute, I'll get the keys of the car from Joe."

"Oh, sure I'll run you down and back, don't bother about your own car."

"Thank you very much," I said. "But I'd rather take my own, if it's all the same to you. I'll follow on behind you." You can't be too careful.

So I went out to start the car. But lo and behold, it wouldn't go! Don't ask me why, that car is nearly new. We got it last winter from Mike Byrne, my cousin that has the garage outside Greystones. There's less than thirty thousand miles on her and she was serviced only there a month before Christmas. But it must have been the cold or something. I tried, and he tried, and Joe, of course, tried, and none of us could get a budge out of her. So in the heel of the hunt I'd to go with him. Joe didn't want me to, and then he wanted to come himself, and your man . . . Sean O'Toole, he said his name was . . . said OK, OK, but come on quick. So I told Joe to get back inside to the fire and I went with him. He'd an old Cortina, a real old banger, a real farmer's car.

"Do not be afraid!" said the rider to her. "I will bring you home to your own doorstep tomorrow morning!"

She got up behind him on the mare.

Neither of us said a word the whole way down. The engine made an awful racket, you couldn't hear a thing, and anyway he was a quiet fellow with not a lot to say for himself. All I could see were headlights, and now and then a signpost: Enniskerry, Sallygap, Glendalough. And after we turned off the main road into the mountains, there were no headlights either, and no house-lights, nothing except the black night. Annamoe is at the back of beyonds, you'd never know you were only ten miles from Bray there, it's really very remote altogether. And their house was down a lane where there was absolutely nothing to be seen at all, not a house, not even a sheep. The house you could hardly see either, actually. It was kind of buried like at the side of the road, in a kind of a hollow. You wouldn't know it was there at all until it was on top of you. Trees all around it too. He pulled up in front of a big five-bar gate and just gave an almighty honk on the horn, and I got a shock when the gate opened, just like that, the minute he honked. I never saw who did it. But looking back now I suppose it was one of the brothers. I suppose they were waiting for him like.

It was a big place, comfortable enough, really, and he took me into the kitchen and introduced me to whoever was there. Polite enough. A big room it was, with an old black range and a huge big dresser, painted red and filled with all kinds of delph and crockery and stuff. Oh you name it! And about half a dozen people were sitting around the room, or maybe more than that. All watching the telly. The "Late Late" was still on and your one, the call-girl one, was still on. She was talking to a priest about unemployment. And they were glued to it, the whole lot of them, what looked like the mother and father and a whole family of big grown men and women. His family or hers I didn't bother my head asking. And they weren't giving out information for nothing either. It was a funny set up, I could see that as clear as daylight, such a big crowd of them, all living together. For all the world like in "Dallas."

Well, there wasn't a lot of time to be lost. The mother offered me a cup of tea, I'll say that for her, and I said yes, I'd love one, and I was actually dying for a cup. I hadn't had a drop of tea since six o'clock and by this time it was after twelve. But I said I'd have a look at the patient first. So one of them, a sister I suppose it was, the youngest of them, she took me upstairs to the room where she was. The girl. Sarah. She was lying on the bed, on her own. No heat in the room, nothing.

After a while they came to a steep hill. A door opened in the side of the hill and they went in. They rode until they came to a big house and inside there were lots of people, eating and drinking. In a corner of the house there lay a woman in labour.

I didn't say a word, just put on the gloves and gave her the examination. She was the five fingers, nearly into the second stage, and she must have been feeling a good bit of pain but she didn't let on, not at all. Just lay there with her teeth gritted. She was a brave young one, I'll say that for her. The waters were gone and of course nobody had cleaned up the mess so I asked the other young one to do it, and to get a heater and a kettle of boiling water. I stayed with Sarah and the baby came just before one. A little girl. There was no trouble at all with the delivery and she seemed all right but small. I'd no way of weighing her, needless to say, but I'd be surprised if she was much more than five pounds.

"By rights she should be in an incubator," I said to Sarah, who was sitting up smoking a cigarette, if you don't mind. She said nothing.

What can you do? I washed the child . . . she was a nice little thing, God help her . . . I wrapped her in a blanket and put her in beside the mother. There was nowhere else for her. Not a cot, not even an old box. That's the way in these cases as often as not. Nobody wants to know.

I delivered the afterbirth and then I left. I couldn't wait to get back to my own bed. They'd brought me the cup of tea and all, but I didn't get time to drink it, being so busy and all. And afterwards the Missus, if that's what she was, wanted me to have a cup in the kitchen. But all I wanted then was to get out of the place. They were all so quiet and unfriendly like. Bar the mother. And even she wasn't going over-board, mind you. But the rest of them. All sitting like zombies looking at the late-night film. They gave me the creeps. I told them the child was too small, they'd have to do something about it, but they didn't let on they heard. The father, the ould fellow, that is to say, put a note in my hand . . . it was worth it from that point of view, I'll admit . . . and said, "Thank you." Not a word from the rest of them. Glued to the telly, as if nothing was after happening. I wanted to scream at them, really. But what could I do? Anyway the young fellow, Sean, the father as he said himself, drove me home. And that was that.

Well and good. I didn't say a word about what was after happening to anyone, excepting of course to Joe. I don't talk, it's not right. People have a right to their privacy, I always say, and with my calling you've to be very careful. But to tell the truth they were on my mind. The little girl, the little baby. I knew in my heart and soul I shouldn't have left her out there, down there in the back of beyonds, near Annamoe. She was much too tiny, she needed care. And the mother. Sarah, was on my mind as well. Mind you, she seemed to be well able to look after herself, but still and all, they weren't the friendliest crowd of people I'd ever come across. They were not.

But that was that.

Until about a week later, didn't I get the shock of my life when I opened the evening paper and saw your one, Sarah, staring out at me. Her round baby face, big head of red hair. And there was a big story about the baby. Someone was after finding it dead in a shoebox, in a kind of rubbish dump they had at the back of the house. And she was arrested, in for questioning, her and maybe Sean O'Toole as well. I'm not sure. In for questioning. I could have dropped down dead there and then.

I told Joe.

"Keep your mouth shut, woman," he said. "You did your job and were paid for it. This is none of your business."

And that was sound advice. But we can't always take sound advice. If we could the world would be a different place.

The thing dragged on. It was in the papers. It was on the telly. There was questioning, and more questioning, and trials and appeals and I don't know what. The whole country was in on it.

And it was on my conscience. It kept niggling at me all the time. I couldn't sleep, I got so I couldn't eat. I was all het up about it, in a terrible state really. Depressed, that's what I was, me who was never depressed before in my life. And I'm telling no lie when I say I was on my way to the doctor for a prescription for Valium when I realised there was only one thing to do. So instead of going down to the surgery, didn't I turn on my heel and walk over to the Garda barracks instead. I went in and I got talking to the sergeant straight away. Once I told them what it was about there was no delaying. And he was very interested in all I had to say, of course, and asked me if I'd be prepared to testify and I said of course I would. Which was the truth. I wouldn't want to but I would if I had to. Once I'd gone this far, of course I would.

Well, I walked out of that Garda station a new woman. It was a great load off my chest. It was like being to confession and getting absolution for a mortal sin. Not that I've ever committed a mortler, of course. But you know what I mean. I felt relieved.

Well and good.

Well. You'll never believe what happened to me next. I was just getting back to my car when a young fellow . . . I'd seen him somewhere before, I know that, but I couldn't place him. He might have been the fellow that came for me on the night, Sean, but he didn't look quite like him. I just couldn't place him at all . . . anyway, he was standing there, right in front of the car. And I said hello, just in case I really did know him, just in case it really was him. But he said nothing. He just looked behind him to see if anyone was coming, and when he saw that the coast was clear he just pulled out a big huge knife out of his breast pocket and pointed it at my stomach. He put the heart crossways in me. And then he says, in a real low voice, like a gangster in "Hill Street Blues" or something:

"Keep your mouth shut. Or else!"

And then he pushed a hundred pounds into my hand and he went off.

I was in bits. I could hardly drive myself home with the shock. I told Joe of course. But he didn't have a lot of sympathy for me.

"God Almighty, woman," he said, "what possessed you to go to the guards? You must be off your rocker. They'll be arresting you next!"

Well, I'd had my lesson. The guards called for me the next week but I said nothing. I said I knew nothing and I'd never heard tell of them all before, the family I mean. And there was nothing they could do, nothing. The sergeant hadn't taken a statement from me, and that was his mistake and my good luck I suppose, because I don't know what would have happened to me if I'd testified. I told a priest about the lie to the guards, in confession, to a Carmelite in White Friar Street, not to any priest I know. And he said God would understand. "You did your best, and that's all God will ask of you. He does not ask of us that we put our own lives in danger."

There was a fair one day at Baile an Droichid. And this woman used to make market socks and used to wash them and scour them and take them to the fair and get them sold. She used to make them up in dozen bunches and sell them at so much the dozen.

And as she walked over the bridge there was a great blast of wind. And who should it be but the people of the hill, the wee folk! And she looked among them and saw among them the same man who had taken her on the mare's back to see his wife.

"How are ye all? And how is the wife?" she said.

He stood and looked at her.

"Which eye do you see me with?" he asked.

"With the right eye," she said.

Before he said another word he raised his stick and stuck it in her eye and knocked her eye out on the road.

"You'll never see me again as long as you live," he said.

Sometimes I do think of the baby. She was a dawny little thing, there's no two ways about it. She might have had a chance, in intensive care. But who am I to judge?

Granny

Bernadette Matthews

The trees in my granny's garden were hung with apples. There were also there   bluebells nettles and frogs. One frog I remember well because my brother prodded it savagely before he put it back into the pond. My brother was a hunter and gave bacon and ham (all the best game) to my granny who cooked foul temper and my own peculiar hatred of pig meat from it. She did this to feed the swine who attended her doorstep in frocks of light   with whiskers twitching in the air   and grunting. She was everyway contented in those days   holding the world in her apron strings.

She also had attendant lords and ladies with whom she danced a jig of fierce hilarity   tapping on the floor with her two feet. The messages she spelt out were fire and brimstone ones and love of god   though sometimes she lifted her skirts too high   so elastic stockings and pygmalion repartees that farted in the air like explosive holy ghosts were also experienced. The days have shattered since my granny danced   before the fire   controlling witches and hobgoblins with the blazing line of her heritage. She gobbled the fat on my lines of grace like an animal and fed me molten wax images instead. The lingering smells of her I have are of hot heavy stocking feet   a comfortable dry sweat   and make-up ravaged by some savage alliance. She had hair that was white and clipped into her shapely habit of ease and once I remember she caught me in her orchard eating one of her apples   all ablaze and munching. Her eyes were colder than ice then and her mind a haunting song holding me there. Her tickets for fire and brimstone she sold to itinerants and travellers.

I remember her best in the rapidly diminishing ball of my future picking up the pieces   settling untidy strands of my hair   and wiping bubbles of foam from my mouth. Living like that I had to be constantly tidied up and fitted with pins for new dresses. I grew up under her feet   like a spell casting dominion on mother and father; pronouncing parents   brother and sister   electing kin—

but always remembering her stare when she caught me ablaze when they couldn't or wouldn't give enough for my election promise. I have two pictures of her still I can't reconcile   One of her in her dancing shoes. And one of her in her apron throwing out swill. Where did she get her fowl face from   her feathery perfumed body and the tickling grin of my future? From her I was cast in luck and beauty and some uncertain haberdashery I'm not unaware of.

Backways she was often steaming face packs   and making mud pies for umbrellas   she rented the air for thunder for my electric face   she harnessed the rain for tears when the ground beneath me had dried up.

She took my howling face sometimes and gave me rhapsodies in harmony.

My grandfather   meanwhile was retired out on the steps with his old dog and his pipe making his nets for her to cast her vision. Making his old man body supple and inclined for her make-up. Drinking whiskey out of a bottle when she wasn't looking   and clacking his teeth.

All and all they were as normal as could be.

When I grew up cast from her election spell   she had a fund of blessings for me   and a light shower for when I couldn't rain enough.

She blew out my candles when I was five with a wish from her eyes and I never knew I had looked on her with such certain knowledge and called her mother and mary and creation. She had handles for doors   and keys into bedrooms   and eyes that could see the furthest reaches of me   and when she blew (on your birthday make a wish) I wished for the rest of her rising and billowing like thunder in myself.

She gave me good notes on fowl appetites   and a reason for living I keep forgetting. She promised no century would be without me witnessing her   I found her when I was looking in books   I read her last look   a story about an apple and something I can't see clearly yet   her undying realm of stitching.

The Bride of Christ

Eithne Strong

About three weeks gone now, the term. The students did not all have their uniforms yet. It took the tailor close on six weeks from the first measurement to get them all covered. Not that the measuring made very much difference to the final turn-out. Square long-sleeved garment to the waist. Navy serge. "Blouse" it was called in the college prospectus. A shapeless overdress of the same material hung to the calves. In over twenty years the outline had not changed.

"Ugly," assessed Sister Benignus in the silence of her cold detachment. "But what does it matter what they wear? Marking time."

She walked along by the wall where the September figs were ripening. Away on the far side beyond the trellised clematis they were at recreation. Games were compulsory. Sauntering groups were forbidden during recreation. The girls from Dingle were good at camogie; their rapid Irish urgent with the game came to her, their fluency of throaty aspiration, liquid diphthong and beautiful attenuation giving the tongue its living grace. Listening to them, richly vocal in the spontaneity of the playing-field, was one of the few things left that she liked. They could not see her through the screening clematis.

Outside of the class proper, English was allowed for only one half-hour in the day, the last one before evening silence and prayers. Accents from all over the country. But English as spoken by the Dingle girls was like a third language. What they wrote in it would be mostly correct, if stilted; this she knew for she had been given their papers to mark. But when they spoke it they made their own of it, in cadence and lilt and phraseology. It would have been scarcely intelligible to her own urbanised family, she sometimes thought.

Only now and then did she stop and face squarely towards the field; mostly she allowed the mixed noises from it to filter through her think-ing while she walked, hands folded into deep sleeves, face well back in the recess of her veil.

"Clodhoppers, culchies," most surely that would have been Julia's opinion of them. In her mind she could hear that particular daughter's voice, the most incisive in the family, "God, what a life! How can girls *live* this way? It can't be called *living*. They don't know a thing . . . two, three years in this dump, wearing clothes like that—I wouldn't be seen dead in such a freakish get-up."

"Well, they *are* fulfilling a function," Sister Benignus parried, in the safety of the mental juxtaposition, with its emotional detachment from Julia, and purely for the sake of argument since her convictions concerning the matter were null. "They are *good* girls. They will teach the rising young."

"Good?" Julia was contemptuous. "Do you mean good holy or good working?"

"It's a point," answered her mother with an open-mindedness that this mental argument favoured. "Considering it, I would say most likely both; most of them anyway. That is, when 'holy' means observing the rituals of making the sign of the cross before class, before meals; gabbling some automatic noises called prayers; never, never missing Mass; never giving scandal by a, possibly quite sincere, love experiment; sticking to the required observances. Yes, this bunch of girls will probably answer all the holy requirements. *And* are likely to work more or less as is demanded of them; often desperate enough, trying to cover the quota for the Department inspectors. Imagination? Even if they have it they will scarcely have the courage to substantiate it. Imagination is dangerous to religiously established tenets and to be checked at first evidence."

"But what life is it?"

"Depends how you see it. Contempt is arbitrary, and any life can be despised if we want to despise it. Is your sophistication more of an answer?"

"For me at present, no doubt about it; yes. You can have this lot any time."

"In fact, I think," Sister Benignus went on discursively, "there are some among them a bit like yourself but without your heritage of freer thought; these won't answer to the acceptable standard, in all likelihood, but will shape a bit after their own fancy. Sooner or later they bump into the trouble of their own punishing guilt and the censure of the powers that be. Probably the greater bulk of them, the abiders, the holy ones if you like, will make the strongest teachers in the long run. The most consistent. And isn't that what's needed in the country?" Sarcasm, cover for feeling, was gaining ground. She did not want to be disturbed to feeling. She wished no further involvement than the non-involvement of letting time pass. Anyway (in this mental projection of dialogue) Julia did not seem interested sufficiently to answer. Nevertheless her mother persisted in the same strain:

"The wayward Irish need a narrow consistency. Otherwise the growing young might find themselves imbalanced in a horrible jeopardy of experimental living and thinking. Iron strictures are the necessity of mad imaginations. That is a Church axiom. A people of tyranny and cowardice! And of them I am one. Therefore I can mock, criticise, condemn, propound, theorise, to my satisfaction. Not that it avails me or them in any way."

But Julia had left.

A bell signifying the end of recreation sounded from the convent. Not always lady-like the sounds that issued from those teachers-in-the-making at the end of play.

"Raucous," Sister Benignus thought, "and something else. What? What else is it that they are? Animals? Yes. Dogs. Only human dogs. Snarling animals. Teachers in the making. They are putting away the balls, the camogie sticks, the racquets and croquet mallets, these last symbols of a refinement removed from animals. Personified in Mother Evangeline. Belonging to another generation, she is nonplussed by this rough-raw material. The day of the West Briton is definitely finished. She presides only because of the prestige of her seniority. Soon she will be replaced. The Dingle girls will not make croquet-players. Never. Maybe some of the aspiring socialites from other parts will?

"The wallop of a camogie stick; cows massing through a gap in the ditch. My children were like this. Walloping, crowding. Only I relinquished command. Trying for a gentler control in reaction against regimentation, I lost direction; bogged down. Swamped. I was beaten. Their fierce uncontrol triumphed. I have accepted failure. In the end they all went their own ways. I was needed no more. They were gone. Then Alec dead. Often I wished to be dead. Why he first? Was it fair? He left me without any final resolution between us. We never worked the thing out. I think the facade appeared whole. I think so. No one knew. Only the two of us knew the defeat, the problem unsolved. The unbridged islands. It *is* fair that he is dead. He is at least beyond the daily mortification of having a passionless wife, beyond the defeat of my unbelief, the waste of my uncharity. It is I who am, after all, dead. He is at rest. I have really been dead for a very long time. This that I walk about in is a cold clay case."

She walked no further but sat in a wooden alcove, just aware of pelvic stiffness.

"Incipient arthritis," her mind went on. There was no anxiety. "Inherited tendency. It invades more rapidly when the wish to live is absent."

The last prefects had left the field.

"Along the corridors I see them looking at me, these untried girls who have come here—Julia would triumph to hear it said—to have the clamps of dogma tightened about their already straitened thinking. So it was with me; long, long ago, at the very spring the stream was choked never to find a life-broad flow. Only last Sunday I heard Mother Evangeline giving them the weekly Adult Talk: 'Always sit upright in the chair. Never, never lean back in a relaxed manner. A man, seeing you like that, will be bound to have evil thoughts.' And each listening girl instinctively tightens muscles; braces herself afresh against the assault of man, the enemy. Of course later they will laugh—maybe. Silly old Mother Evangeline, they may say. Rubbish, they may think they think. But a poison, nevertheless, stays deep in the centre. It has already done its work to which no intellectualisation can be antidote. That poison was in fact lodged in them already before they came here and Mother Evangeline has added only a probably unnecessary booster to the earlier innoculation against innocent delight in the flesh.

It is well that Alec is gone. Indeed I coldly killed him. Crime of frigidity. I see them looking at me, these gullible girls, wondering at my face. I have at last perfected the mask; its smiling ice is permanent. It pleases me to see the recoil in their faces.

Soon the nuns' bell will ring. I will go to the mechanical prayer, kneel in my stall, the veil hiding my silence. Despising the cant. No word of it all makes me feel less cold. The routine, the order, the cleanliness of this place please me. Four pleasures: the Dingle girls talking Irish and these. But altogether I have five.

There were other things I could have done. Turned to drink. The end is public, shameful. Everyone knows your sottish end. Privacy is a last necessity. Drugs? Worse than drink. More degrading, more confessedly selfish. And I never had money. Taken the offering lovers? And grown daily more dependent, more fearful because older. None of them would have borne with me as did Alec. I could have held no lover; I had nothing to give.

I considered these things. I found no further hold in the outside world. In latter years my inclination had been more and more to retreat. I considered much. Once, they had wanted me here and I would not stay. Eager then, the insidious blights as yet unfelt, I went into the world to breed many years' puzzlements, confusion; and then knew myself barren. Then having lost any further urge to outwardness, I remembered back to this retreat, a place to wait detachedly for the end I had not the courage to make immediate.

I still possessed the things they once wanted from me here, brain, energy—which even if reduced could still be willed to efficient activity. The inner grave of no-belief was coldly secret, inaccessible to priest or mother superior. Confession? Profession of fervency? They did not bother me. I could now tell sinless lies, who had long striven to live to unattainable truth.

It was not difficult to be accepted here. I was a prodigal returned. They were ready to forgive my humble heart and were unsuspicious of deceit. They were glad to refuge the erring widow whose family was fledged and provided for. Had she not also skills they could use, keeping in the convent useful money? They embraced my edifying vocation.

I have felt relief in the changeless days. So then I practised the smile that very soon became a reflex to the rising bell. Now it serves me most usefully. When they speak to me and I am not disposed to conversation, I merely continue to smile and bow my head and pass along. Everyone respects my reserve. I am the widow who has known much sorrow. They forgive my eccentricity.

Only when I play the organ—the fifth pleasure—a slow forgotten warmth sometimes stirs in me, and in the darkened chapel I know my smile is gone and I feel a wetness on my cheeks.

The Wall-Reader

Fiona Barr

"Shall only our rivers run free?" The question jumped out from the cobbled wall in huge white letters, as The People's taxi swung round the corner at Beechmount. "Looks like paint is running freely enough down here," she thought to herself, as other slogans glided past in rapid succession. Reading Belfast's grim graffiti had become an entertaining hobby for her, and she often wondered, was it in the dead of night that groups of boys huddled round a paint tin daubing walls and gables with tired political slogans and clichés? Did anyone ever see them? Was the guilty brush ever found? The brush is mightier than the bomb, she declared inwardly, as she thought of how celebrated among journalists some lines had become. "Is there a life before death?" Well, no one had answered that one yet, at least, not in this city.

The shapes of Belfast crowded in on her as the taxi rattled over the ramps outside the fortressed police barracks. Dilapidated houses, bricked-up terraces. Rosy-cheeked soldiers, barely out of school, and quivering with high-pitched fear. She thought of the thick-lipped youth who came to hijack the car, making his point by showing his revolver under his anorak, and of the others, jigging and taunting every July, almost sexual in their arrogance and hatred. Meanwhile, passengers climbed in and out at various points along the road, manoeuvring between legs, bags of shopping and umbrellas. The taxi swerved blindly into the road. No Highway Code here. As the woman's stop approached, the taxi swung up to the pavement, and she stepped out.

She thought of how she read walls—like tea-cups, she smiled to herself. Pushing her baby in the pram to the supermarket, she had to pass under a motorway bridge that was peppered with lines, some in irregular lettering with the paint dribbling down the concrete, others written with felt-tip pen in minute secretive hand. A whole range of human emotions splayed itself with persistent anarchy on the walls. "One could do worse than be a reader of walls," she thought, twisting Frost's words. Instead, though, the pram was rushed past the intriguing mural with much gusto. Respectable housewives don't read walls!

The "Troubles," as they were euphemistically named, remained for this couple as a remote, vaguely irritating wart on their life. They were simply ordinary (she often groaned at the oppressive banality of the word), middle-class, and hoping the baby would marry a doctor, thereby raising them in their autumn days to the select legions of the upper class. Each day their lives followed the same routine—no harm in that sordid little detail, she thought. It helps structure one's existence. He went to the office, she fed the baby, washed the rapidly growing mound of nappies, prepared the dinner and looked forward to the afternoon walk. She had convinced herself she was happy with her lot, and yet felt disappointed at the pangs of jealousy endured on hearing of a friend's glamorous job or another's academic and erudite husband. If only someone noticed her from time to time, or even wrote her name on a wall declaring her existence worthwhile; "A fine mind" or "I was once her lover." That way, at least, she would have evidence she was having impact on others. As it was, she was perpetually bombarded with it. Marital successes, even marital failures evoked a response from her. All one-way traffic.

That afternoon she dressed the baby and started out for her walk. "Fantasy time" her husband called it. "Wall-reading time" she knew it to be. On this occasion, however, she decided to avoid those concrete temptations and, instead, visit the park. Out along the main road she trundled, pushing the pram, pausing to gaze into the hardware store's window, hearing the whine of the Saracen as it thundered by, waking the baby and making her feel uneasy. A foot patrol of soldiers strolled past, their rifles, lethal even in the brittle sunlight of this March day, lounged lovingly and relaxed in the arms of their men. One soldier stood nonchalantly, almost impertinent, against a corrugated railing and stared at her. She always blushed on passing troops.

The park is ugly, stark and hostile. Even in summer, when courting couples seek out secluded spots like mating cats, they reject Musgrave. There are a few trees, clustered together, standing like skeletons, ashamed of their nakedness. The rest is grass, a green wasteland speckled with puddles of gulls squawking over a worm patch. The park is bordered by a hospital with a military wing which is guarded by an army billet. The beauty of the place, it has only this, is its silence.

The hill up to the park bench was not the precipice it seemed, but the baby and pram were heavy. Ante-natal self-indulgence had taken its toll—her midriff was now most definitely a bulge. With one final push, pram, baby and mother reached the green wooden seat, and came to rest. The baby slept soundly with the soother touching her velvet pink cheeks, hand on pillow, a picture of purity. The woman heard a coughing noise coming from the nearby gun turret, and managed to see the tip of a rifle and a face peering out from the darkness. Smells of cabbage and burnt potatoes wafted over from behind the slanting sheets of protective steel.

"Is that your baby?" an English voice called out. She could barely see the face belonging to the voice. She replied yes, and smiled. The situation reminded her of the confessional. Dark and supposedly anonymous, "Is that you, my child?" She knew the priest personally. Did he identify her sins with his "Good morning, Mary," and think to himself, "and I know what you were up to last night!" She blushed at the secrets given away during the ceremony. Yes, she nervously answered again, it was her baby, a little girl. First-time mothers rarely resist the temptation to talk about their offspring. Forgetting her initial shyness, she told the voice of when the baby was born, the early problems of all-night crying, now teething, how she could crawl backwards and gurgle.

The voice responded. It too had a son, a few months older than her child, away in Germany at the army base at Munster. Factory pipes, chimney tops, church spires, domes all listened impassively to the Englishman's declaration of paternal love. The scene was strange, for although Belfast's sterile geography slipped into classical forms with dusk and heavy rain-clouds, the voice and the woman knew the folly of such innocent communication. They politely finished their conversation, said goodbye, and the woman pushed her pram homewards. The voice remained in the turret, watchful and anxious. Home she went, past vanloads of workers leering out at the pavement, past the uneasy presence of foot patrols, past the church. "Let us give each other the sign of peace," they said at Mass. The only sign Belfast knew was two fingers pointing towards Heaven. Life was self-contained, the couple often declared, just like flats. No need to go outside.

She did go outside, however. Each week the voice and the woman learned more of each other. No physical contact was needed, no face-to-face encounter to judge reaction, no touching to confirm amity, no threat of dangerous intimacy. It was a meeting of minds, as she explained later to her husband, a new opinion, a common bond, an opening of vistas. He disclosed his ambitions to become a pilot, to watching the land, fields and horizons spread out beneath him—a patchwork quilt of dappled colours and textures. She wanted to be remembered by writing on walls, about them that is, a world-shattering thesis on their psychological complexities, their essential truths, their witticisms and intellectual genius. And all this time the city's skyline and distant buildings watched and listened.

It was April now. More slogans had appeared, white and dripping, on the city walls. "Brits out. Peace in." A simple equation for the writer. "Loose talk claims lives," another shouted menacingly. The messages, the woman decided, had acquired a more ominous tone. The baby had grown and could sit up without support. New political solutions had been proposed and rejected, inter-paramilitary feuding had broken out and subsided, four soldiers and two policemen had been blown to smithereens in separate incidents, and a building a day had been bombed by the Provos. It had been a fairly normal month by Belfast's standards. The level of violence was no more or less acceptable than at other times.

One day—it was, perhaps, the last day in April—her husband returned home panting and trembling a little. He asked had she been to the park, and she replied she had. Taking her by the hand, he led her to the wall on the left of their driveway. She felt her heart sink and thud against her. She felt her face redden. Her mouth was suddenly dry. She could not speak. In huge angry letters the message spat itself out,

"TOUT."

The four-letter word covered the whole wall. It clanged in her brain, its venom rushed through her body. Suspicion was enough to condemn. The job itself was not well done, she had seen better. The letters were uneven, paint splattered down from the cross T, the U looked a misshapen O. The workmanship was poor, the impact perfect.

Her husband led her back into the kitchen. The baby was crying loudly in the living-room but the woman did not seem to hear. Like sleepwalkers, they sat down on the settee. The woman began to sob.

Her shoulders heaved in bursts as she gasped hysterically. Her husband took her in his arms gently and tried to make her sorrow his. Already he shared her fear.

"What did you talk about? Did you not realise how dangerous it was? We must leave." He spoke quickly, making plans. Selling the house and car, finding a job in London or Dublin, far away from Belfast, mortgages, removals, savings, the tawdry affairs of normal living stunned her, making her more confused. "I told him nothing," she sobbed, "what could I tell? We talked about life, everything, but not about here." She trembled, trying to control herself. "We just chatted about reading walls, families, anything at all. Oh Sean, it was as innocent as that. A meeting of minds we called it, for it was little else."

She looked into her husband's face and saw he did not fully understand. There was a hint of jealousy, of resentment at not being part of their communication. Her hands fell on her lap, resting in resignation. What was the point of explanation? She lifted her baby from the floor. Pressing the tiny face and body to her breast, she felt all her hopes and desires for a better life become one with the child's struggle for freedom. The child's hands wandered over her face, their eyes met. At once that moment of maternal and filial love eclipsed her fear, gave her the impetus to escape.

For nine months she had been unable to accept the reality of her condition. Absurd, for the massive bump daily shifted position and thumped against her. When her daughter was born, she had been overwhelmed by love for her and amazed at her own ability to give life. By nature she was a dreamy person, given to moments of fancy. She wondered at her competence in fulfilling the role of mother. Could it be measured? This time she knew it could. She really did not care if they maimed her or even murdered her. She did care about her daughter. She was her touchstone, her anchor to virtue. Not for her child a legacy of fear, revulsion or hatred. With the few hours' respite the painters had left between judgement and sentence she determined to leave Belfast's walls behind.

The next few nights were spent in troubled, restless sleep. The message remained on the wall outside. The neighbours pretended not to notice and refused to discuss the matter. She and the baby remained indoors despite the refreshing May breezes and blue skies. Her husband had given in his notice at the office, for health reasons, he suggested to his colleagues. An aunt had been contacted in Dublin. The couple did not answer knocks at the door. They carefully examined the shape and size of mail delivered and always paused when they answered the telephone.

The mini-van was to call at eleven on Monday night, when it would be dark enough to park, and pack their belongings and themselves without too much suspicion being aroused. The firm had been very understanding when the nature of their work had been explained. They were Protestant so there was no conflict of loyalties involved in the exercise. They agreed to drive them to Dublin at extra cost, changing drivers at Newry on the way down.

Monday finally arrived. The couple nervously laughed about how smoothly everything had gone. Privately, they each expected something to go wrong. The baby was fed, and played with, the radio listened to and the clock watched. They listened to the news at nine. Huddled together in their anxiety, they kept vigil in the darkening room. Rain had begun to pour from black thunderclouds. Everywhere it was quiet and still. Hushed and cold they waited. Ten o'clock, and it was now dark. A blustery wind had risen, making the lattice separation next door bang and clatter. At ten to eleven, her husband went into the sitting-room to watch for the mini-van. His footsteps clamped noisily on the floor-boards as he paced back and forth. The baby slept.

A black shape glided slowly up the street and backed into the drive-way. It was eleven. The van had arrived. Her husband asked to see their identification and then they began to load up the couple's belongings. Settee, chairs, television, washing machine—all were dumped hastily, it was no time to worry about breakages. She stood holding the sleeping baby in the living-room as the men worked anxiously between van and house. The scene was so unreal, the circumstances absolutely incredible. She thought, "What have I done?" Recollections of her naivety, her insensibility to historical fact and political climate were stupifying. She had seen women who had been tarred and feathered, heard of people who had been shot in the head, boys who had been knee-capped, all for suspected fraternising with troops. The catalogue of violence spilled out before her as she realised the gravity and possible repercussions of her alleged misdemeanour.

A voice called her, "Mary, come on now. We have to go. Don't worry, we're all together." Her husband led her to the locked and waiting van. Handing the baby to him, she climbed up beside the driver, took back the baby as her husband sat down beside her and waited for the engine to start. The van slowly manoeuvred out onto the street and down the main road. They felt more cheerful now, a little like refugees seeking safety and freedom not too far away. As they approached the motorway bridge, two figures with something clutched in their hands stood side by side in the darkness. She closed her eyes tightly, expecting bursts of gunfire. The van shot past. Relieved, she asked her husband what they were doing at this time of night. "Writing slogans on the wall," he replied.

The furtiveness of the painters seemed ludicrous and petty as she recalled the heroic and literary characteristics with which she had endowed them. What did they matter? The travellers sat in silence as the van sped past the city suburbs, the glare of police and army barracks, on out and further out into the countryside. Past sleeping villages and silent fields, past whitewashed farmhouses and barking dogs. On to Newry where they said goodbye to their driver as the new one stepped in. Far along the coast with Rostrevor's twinkling lights opposite the bay down to the Border check and a drowsy soldier waving them through. Out of the North, safe, relieved and heading for Dublin.

Some days later in Belfast the neighbours discovered the house vacant, the people next door received a letter and a cheque from Dublin. Remarks about the peculiar couple were made over hedges and cups of coffee. The message on the wall was painted over by the couple who had bought the house when it went up for sale. They too were ordinary people, living a self-contained life, worrying over finance and babies, promotion and local gossip. He too had an office job, but his wife was merely a housekeeper for him. She was sensible, down to earth, and not in the least inclined to wall-reading.

The Day of the Christening

Harriet O'Carroll

Mrs. Morrisey got up at six o'clock on the morning of the christening. It was her usual time to get up, she did not feel it a hardship. She could get things to rights better when she had the place to herself. She moved quietly in the kitchen of the sleeping house, taking the marmalade pot, sugar bowl and milk jug from the cupboard to the table. He couldn't complain about his breakfast, at any rate. Since the day after they got married it had been on the table for him at a quarter to eight, day in day out, save only the times she was in having the children. He couldn't complain, but he would. Reason and right had never stopped him doing anything he wanted to do. His allegiance was to the football field and the gathered cronies in the scruffy shadows of the pub. If he had a skinful the night before he would call the sausages raw or burnt, whatever they looked like. Or he would get up at twelve and mutter morosely while he waited for them to be warmed up for him. She didn't listen to what she didn't want to hear. If you weren't going to make a hole in the rock, why bruise your head by banging. She had bruised herself enough in the early days. There was no sense in dwelling on what was past, and beyond cure. For years now she had been too busy to rake over rights and wrongs, and just as well too, because surely she had no judgement.

She had thought her last outrage would have cried to the Lord God Himself, for vengeance. She thought even distant connections would have been enraged to the point of violence. She would not have been surprised at balls of fire and thunderbolts. She thought there might have been boycott, bloodletting and imprisonment. But it turned out instead to be a small matter. There was a court appearance, one headline in a local paper, and a few blows after the pubs had closed. She had seen more trouble over a doped greyhound.

The baby was still asleep, that was one mercy. He was a quiet little fellow so far; he made it through the night. She remembered how she had walked the floor with his mother. It did not seem a week ago. A small squalling nervous thing, she had been, tiny arms akimbo at every rustle, noisy dismay at every disturbance. Mrs. Morrisey thought sometimes she must have walked in her sleep, up and down the narrow space, whispering softly and frantically.

"Hush now give over, off to sleep, baby baby, sleepybys, off to sleep, off to sleep, off to sleep."

She could still feel the fatigue in her bones, head nodding, knees bending, craving and drying and sighing for sleep, whisper fading and trailing, the feeling of a fine wax on her face and the terror in case the three year old would wake too, and the whole night would be gone, neither one settling until daytime was there to be faced again. She had moved then as if to stop would be to die, and she hadn't lost the habit since. She did casual hours at the hotel, serving at winter functions, or cleaning after summer visitors, and she was known as a good worker, an honest woman and an awful talker. Talking was better than thinking any day, and there wasn't a house on the road that did not have its trouble.

"God between us and all harm."

If Morrisey wasn't the best, maybe he wasn't the worst either. If he did not give her a penny, at least he did not knock her about, she could close her ears to his talk, and what was it to her what he did outside the house. She took care not to find out.

She wondered would Rosaleen ever marry now. Who would have her? And why should she? She had the baby. If she could finish her schooling and get some sort of job, wouldn't she be better off the way she was. It was little of her father's money had put the clothes on her back, or the food on her plate. It was all done by her own scrubbing and cleaning and later on the hours at the factory, not enough time in any day. Mrs. Morrisey took the airing racks away from in front of the dead ashes and folded the clothes in tidy single heaps. She had a few things soaking and she would have time to rinse them out and get them on the line before she slipped out to Mass. Sunday, Monday, she had things on the line, chasing all the time to catch up or to get a little work in hand. The mist was on the sloping fields when she went out. It would be a fine Autumn day, a fine day for it anyway, as people said about a wedding or a funeral. It would be a fine day for the christening of her first grandchild.

She took a look in at Rosaleen and the baby before she left. They were both asleep, mother and child, two children. She turned her eyes quickly away from Rosaleen's pallor and the old lines that should have no place on a fourteen-year-old face. She focussed instead on the baby. He was sleeping as though he would never wake, impregnable in his unconsciousness, with that soft serene aura that even the ugliest sleeping baby wears. He was not an ugly little fellow. Thank the Lord God in Heaven, he was all right, at least as far as one could see. No twisted foot, no cleft palate, no deformity had been visited on them. That final horror at least they were spared.

It was three quarters of a mile into town. She often said that if she put her shoes at the gate, they would walk there themselves, so used would they be to the journey. She didn't feel it going in to Mass on a fine morning, but the weary journeys home, laden with the things from the shop, or bone tired after scrubbing someone's floor, or worst of all frantic with worry in case the child left behind was smothering in the cot, these trips were twice as long. The road all seemed uphill, all the steps were an effort. Time and again she had put together enough for a bicycle, and every time there was another call on the money. Now the girls were big enough to carry the messages home for her. Her legs had held out when she needed them.

They usually got away with a short sermon at early Mass. Next month would be November, the month of the dead. She would be ritually reminded of her father, slipping away into childhood and coma and death, and of Morrisey's mother, struggling and straining and hanging on. She took five years to go, moaning, haranguing and tormenting in every clear minute. Mrs. Morrisey found it hard to be edified by the prospect of death. She hadn't time to die. Morrisey too, she thought, was made of some material that would hang on until the bitter end. Like a rock, or a malignant weed, he would last her out. The great trouble with Mass was that it gave her time to think. She said over her beads with determination. A long time ago she used to say in Confession, "I let my thoughts stray in my prayers." Her thoughts had strayed then to pleasure and prospect, eyeing handsome shoulders in the pews ahead. Her thoughts were now threatened with floodtides of resentment. When she saw the schoolmistress at the door, she knew

it was a sign of no ordinary trouble. For ordinary trouble the schoolmistress would have sent for her.

"No point in going over that now," she said to herself. "What's done
is done."

"Lamb of God, who takest away the sins of the world, grant us
peace." It was nearly over, not much more to go.

"Count your blessings" Mrs. Morrisey told herself.

Morrisey at least had given her the four girls, beautiful girls too,
each in her own way. She supposed that her two boys were also blessings. She had fretted over them as much as she ever had over the girls.
They were their father's sons and hard as nails. The girls though, had
carried the load with her, they had seen what needed to be done. A
world that contained Maura, Rita, Rosaleen and Nora could never be
completely black.

In three hours she would be back here for the christening. The baby
would be called Michael and where would he belong? There were those
in the village who thought she should have said nothing, and sent
Rosaleen away. She knew there were some who said it behind her
back, and there were others who said it again and again to her face.

"Yerra Maggie, least said soonest mended. You can't undo what's
done, what do you want to spread it abroad for? Think of the child."

"Rosaleen is my child first."

"Listen here Maggie, what about her schoolmates. You don't expect
her to face them, do you?"

"Better to face them out than to know they're whispering. It's no
use talking, Rosaleen is not going away."

And they finally stopped talking to her face, though she knew that
still the gossip flourished and elaborated. An already cruel and incredible story became even more fantastic and unbelievable, embellished
with the personal style of every teller. It was a cause of shock, a cause
of scandal, a cause of evil glee, a cause of ribald speculation, supposedly
also a cause of compassion and sympathy.

Morrisey said nothing. She had prepared to tell him with feelings
of foreboding and dread, but as the words came out she felt an odd
vindictive glee. The piece of bacon was halfway to his lips when she
said,

"Your fine bucko, Connors has raped our Rosaleen. She is expecting
his kid."

He put down the fork and walked straight out. She sat at the table, head in hands. She looked at the skin on the grease congealing on the plate. To think she had once thought that when she had him away from his miserable taunting old mother, he would soften and grow. What a thick deluded idiot she had been, and still was to have linked her life like that. He wouldn't say a word to her, no more than if she had never spoken. She could as well have climbed the nearest hill and howled the words to the night wind. He would eat and work and drink and fuck and sleep as he had always done and not a thousand years would shake him alive. She heard afterwards of the brawl outside the pub, but not of anything said. The next time she saw Connors he did not show any obvious signs of ill treatment. She turned away her head as if confronted with a nauseating wound.

"Go, you are dismissed, go in peace."

Mass was over, and she would be in time to get back and have breakfast on the table. Rosaleen was filling bottles in the kitchen when she came in.

"He's not stirring yet, Mam. He had a bottle at five o'clock. Four ounces, he took. He should be alright until half nine, and if I give him another at half eleven, he should be alright for the christening."

Rosaleen was already on the old protective treadmill, no way of looking back. She was tied to this small independent life, loving and hating her bondage by turns. She was separated from her age group by maternity as she never could be by sexual knowledge.

The house felt warm and small after the open road. The steam from the kettle was suffocating Mrs. Morrisey. She threw open the small kitchen window.

"I was ever a one for air" she said. "Don't you feel it close, Rosy?"

"I didn't notice it" said Rosaleen. "Will you have some tea if I wet it? No one is moving yet."

Mrs. Morrisey sat and drank tea with her daughter, and told her who was at Mass and what they were wearing and who was prayed for, having died during the week.

"Who would have expected Jimmy Mullen to go like that? He could only be fifty-eight, and him a fine fresh coloured man, wasn't he in past the house to the creamery not much more than a week ago. And not chick nor child to take over that fine place. It will probably go to a nephew if it isn't sold up altogether."

And all the time she talked she wondered how it was that she had never noticed that Rosaleen was pregnant, and had to be told by the schoolteacher. She hadn't found it in her to believe it, and yet was too stunned to deny. That day too, the room had become suddenly hot, the delph and the dresser and the mantlepiece had swam round her, and as they settled, she heard the voice saying,

"I'm afraid you'll have to prepare yourself for a shock. The father is a married man."

"Tell me then, in the name of God."

She couldn't think who it could be, Morrisey's gormless boozing crony was the last to occur to her. The schoolmistress was a strong woman with a fine family. They had stuck to their books, grown up, and taken their degrees. They were married now, or in the Civil Service, settled respectably. She had been in control of the situation all her life. She looked at Mrs. Morrisey with useless sympathy. She felt as if in the presence of terminal illness, words of alleviation were of no avail, the only grim solace lay in outfacing the stony fact. Life would go on, until it ceased.

"I don't think any of her classmates know. She did not really know herself, at least, she was hoping it couldn't be so. She has only the vaguest idea of . . . you know. If it wasn't for the pregnancy I don't suppose anyone would ever have known what went on. She was afraid to say, you see."

"I never saw a thing, myself."

"She started going pale in class. Then I found her being sick one day. After that I kept my eyes open and I finally persuaded her to speak to me."

Mrs. Morrisey still wondered what Rosaleen had said to the teacher. The subject was too thick with rocks, she kept away. To Rosaleen she had said,

"Why did you not tell me?"

"I don't know. What could I say?"

"Do you want to stay at home, or do you want to go away?"

"Oh Mam, I want to stay home."

"That's that so."

So Rosaleen stayed home, and when the child was born, there was no word of bringing him anywhere but home. Morrisey could do what he chose, and he chose to do nothing.

Rosaleen's three sisters and two brothers came to the christening, and Morrisey too stayed on after late Mass. The church was all empty and echoing as the words were said that made the child a Christian. It was done so quickly and it was done for life.

Morrisey wanted his lunch for half past one, at the latest. There was a football match he couldn't miss, but the meat and soup were on the range since before they all went to the Church. The potatoes were peeled, and the cabbage would boil in no time. If he was late itself, thought Mrs. Morrisey, he had not much to complain of, one day in how many years? Rita had the table set, and mercifully the baby settled down again after his experience. Maybe he wouldn't stir until they were all fed. Finally the eight of them were sitting down, and she herself last of all, when the truly unusual and cataclysmic event occurred.

Mrs. Morrisey looked at the two slices of beef and the dark green cabbage, and the brown gravy against the potatoes. Unexpectedly, without precedent, without rhyme or reason she began to cry. The tears fell first, almost before she, or anyone else knew it, then gathering force, great warm heavings spread down through her neck, throat and chest. Her skin throbbed, her face ached, the back of her head felt rigid and hard and the rigidity reached to all her muscles, all her body quivered with spastic, retching sobs, her lungs groaned in the clamour for breath and tears. The family stopped eating and looked at her. It was Maura the eldest girl who took over.

"Come on Mam, come and lie down, I'll see to the rest of the meal. Come and have a little lie down."

There was such a screaming in her brain, such an incredible inferno of noise and feeling, such a jumble of misery, surprise and grief that she wasn't really aware of Maura helping her into bed, of her shoes being eased off, of sheets being pulled up to her chin. Sound multiplied on sound, reverberation of bone-shaking, nerve-destroying, throbbing, thudding and exploding. Noise thudded back from the inside of her skull, flung itself like living water from the walls of the room, enveloped muscle and fibre and cell in a sheet of tumult and catastrophe. Like hail against a window pane, like rocks tumbling down a mountain, like a bursting dam when the last support has gone, her sobs grew in waves and cascades and subsided to grow higher, so that they flowed within and through and around her until the muscles of her feet ached with effort as much as the muscles of her face.

Unaccountably the sobbing ceased and she felt in herself such a sensation of limpid and untrammeled solitude, such an amazing unexperienced felicity, such a peacefulness of power and possibility that she had difficulty in associating the sensation with herself. She seemed to be floating in a warm and gentian sea, flat out upon the blue, below the blue above. Blue above and blue below, and she was warm and free, suspended between them, elemental, passive, powerful. Water stirred in supportive caress, lapping in soft undulations along her pliant limbs.

She stared up at the distant sky, white sea birds were etched far above her and behind them, an infinity. She felt as if the water beneath went as deep as the sky was high, and between them she was suspended in a serene lucent ether. Time was immaterial, she existed there for ever in glorious silence, just herself and the sea, and the quiet distant birds.

But it seemed in a while, as if she were no longer in the sea, or of the sea but walking beside it, walking without object or effort along a high cliff path. It was more as if she had become part of the sky and was attaining this incredible summit by floating through air, or swimming upwards, light and supported. Her path was bordered by tropical creepers, winding up withered trees, and like fountains releasing from their highest point cascades of scarlet blossoms. The flowers were like red stars, blood red and poised and separate. In that extraordinary light, the red was more remarkable than any seen before, a colour to be tasted and felt and smelled as well as seen, and the green was more green, the white more pure and all the colours and sensations were true and perfect beyond conception.

As she looked at that blue dazzling sea, she perceived that it was not, as she had supposed, empty but that surging up from its depths, rising and disappearing were numerous fishes, small red, fluorescent fishes. It was restful to watch them moving and darting. They formed accidental patterns, flitting about in small groups that split and reformed, sometimes one swimming off alone. They were like scattered petals, swimming garlands and posies, gathering around a dark spread-eagled body, floating face up to the sky. She knew it was Morrisey, his pose uncharacteristically relaxed. The fish swarmed round him, multiplying into shoals, hundreds and hundreds of small flashing mites. As she watched, one shoal in a body swooped towards his right hand. She watched them swim away, and the red dye spreading out in the blue. It was scarlet as the fishes at first but soon began to fade and dilute as it spread wider. Then there came another shoal, and a new red sea-cloud poured from the region of his neck. It seemed brighter and thicker, and fish and colour merged as in coloured smoke. The colour seemed to attract more fish because shoals were coming from every direction. More and more fronds of scarlet spiralled through the blue. The dark body had become obscure in the melee of red fishes and red blood.

There was a noise edging in on her total blissful silence. There was a rattle and a voice. Then the rattle was a thin clink and the voice approaching was saying,

"Mam, Mam, are you all right?"

Mrs. Morrisey shook off the mists of sleep clinging implacably around her. Rosaleen was standing with a cup of tea, looking with concern at the rock upon which she relied.

"Oh lovey, you woke me up" said Mrs. Morrisey. "And I was having such a beautiful dream."

Melancholy Baby

Julia O'Faolain

"Ah no?"

"God help us!" Mrs. Kelly sometimes greased gossip with pity. "Aunt Adie HAS NO WOMB!"

Neighbours thrilled. "You're not serious!"

"Had it cut out before her marriage and NEVER TOLD HER HUSBAND!"

"Go on!"

"Cross my heart!"

"And so?"

"The poor man is praying for children to this day and has herself going down making the Nine Fridays for the same Intention! And down my lady goes."

"Gnawing the altar rails with the best!"

"It's hard to understand some people!"

"Ha! She can have the fruits of *my* womb for the asking!" Mrs. Kelly slapped her protuberant belly. "To them that have more shall be given! I do have to laugh!" She took a swig at her pint and guffawed again.

"I hear," said the postmistress, "how she's taking her niece out of the orphanage at last."

Adie lived in a run-down fishing village: a row of grey houses roofed with what might have been shards of solidified winter sea. Hope here was landlocked by the fog which rolled in to settle in the back-yard plots: mild incubators where lettuces grew greasy as seaweed and buckets, left out to shelter rhubarb stalks, rusted red only to be resilvered by snail tracks. Round the front, owners decorated their posts with shells which had once encased flesh as sluggish as their own. She too was grey: eyes, hair, and a dead pellicle of neglected pores which concealed the currents of her blood. But she had energy. When her husband's trade—he was a sign painter—was ruined by the advent of neon, she opened a tearoom and succeeded in selling soda bread and blackberry jam to the odd Lancashire mill-worker on holiday or Christian Brother who paused on that shingly beach. At a window prettified by gingham curtains and geraniums she would sit, with her teeth in, smiling out at them as they alighted from bus or bicycle and draw their attention to the sign painter's last effort in two-tone Celtic script: AUNT ADIE'S COUNTRY TEAS. The promissory legend followed them through their dip in the savage waters of the Irish Sea and drew them back for Teas: Plain at three bob a head or High (with fry) for seven and six. In a backward, discouraged place, she cornered or created what trade there was and soon was selling cigarettes, chocolate bars, home-made sponge-cakes and lavender pincushions to the charmed and hungry Britishers who began to drift in after the war. She had the toughness without the timorousness of her stock. Once, when a GI asked for a room to rest in with his fiancée, she lent him her own and, thrilled by the pound he paid her, begged him to mention her address to friends. He must have forgotten, for no other couple asked for the favour, although she enveigled a number up to look at the view.

"She's a caution!" said Mrs. Kelly, Aunt Adie's char.

"Did jez hear what Aunt Adie's after doing now?"

"That one's a Godless aul rip! If the priest were to hear of it he'd ballyrag her off the altar."

Adie continued to knead soda bread with ardent knuckles and her business boomed. She could do without the esteem of the draggled village women, whose heads were addled by the squalling of their litters, and she was indifferent to the opinions of the ex-sign painter, who had settled into placid redundance. Yet her vigour, having developed the tearooms to their limits, carried her no further. She thought for a while of launching into the pastry business and even found a bakery ready to act as distributor—but she gave up the idea. ("Why work my fingers to the bone while himself sits there on his bum?") Business never became a passion with her. Churchgoing—another favourite filler for lonely women's lives—had no resonance in hers. Like the poised claw of a crane, her affective energies remained in suspense.

Gap-toothed, bravely lipsticked Mrs. Kelly was her companion. "Friend" would not be the word. Mrs. Kelly's own illusions had long

left her as birds leave a contaminated nest. Her husband had drunk
her out of a pub, a house, and the middle class, and now—shiftless
mother of five children whom she was raising on the dole, despising
and despised by all around her—she took her pleasure in savage gossip.
"I do have to laugh." It was from her that the neighbours first heard
of Adie's niece, Gwennie.

"Four years," Mrs. Kelly shook her head at cronies in the pub, "in
the orphanage without Adie as much as paying her a visit! She's only
taking her out now because the nuns won't keep her any longer. The
girl's sixteen."

"Didn't the mother die of consumption?"

"Now you're talking. Adie's frightened silly of disease and of course
the girl herself must be *prone!*" Mrs. Kelly spoke with allusive refinement. "I remember the time when a touch of it in a family was as big
a bar to matrimony as madness. Still, that's no excuse for leaving her
to moulder that long in an institution! What is it but a bloody sweat
shop? The so-called Sisters of Charity run a laundry out of it! Plenty
of unpaid labour!"

"Isn't the girl's father alive?"

"In England. Working in a pub. Sends nothing towards the girl's
keep. Or so Adie says. You couldn't believe daylight outa her!"

Adie went into town alone to meet the girl's bus which would leave
her off, the nuns had written, at Aston Quay. But the green buses
proclaimed only their destination—Dublin—and not their place of
departure, so she began to race round in circles, bumping into the
general ragtag and badgering inspectors. She wasn't even sure she would
recognize the girl whom she hadn't seen since she was twelve. And
why should *she,* she thought as another green bus drew in and swept
to a halt forty yards down the quay, why (she puffed and ran and puffed)
go pelting about like this after other people's brats? Her sister, God rest
her, had married a gom from down the country, a ne'er-do-well. She
panted. The girl wasn't on that bus! Adie had refused to let her sister
have a share of their mother's furniture. "Why throw good money after
bad?" she had reasoned at the time. And how right she had been! Her
sister's husband's brogue had been as thick in his mouth as the dirt
was under his nail! A no-good country gawk! Look at her now having
to take in his daughter! Who was maybe consumptive! She shuddered,
wondering whether she ought to even hug the girl. She had a handkerchief soaked in disinfectant in a plastic container in her purse. "I'll

let *her* kiss me if she wants to," she decided, "then I'll pretend to blow my nose."

A bus drew in and a raggedy crowd of snot-nosed urchins rushed up yelling "porter, porter!" Adie drew away, wary of germs. A louse, she thought, might jump off one of them or a bedbug. An urchin snatched a case from a passenger and, aiming a kick at a rival, jumped clear of the bus. "Taxi, Ma'am?" he yelled at the owner of the case, a girl not much bigger than himself who plunged down the steps, planted one red claw (whose cracked flesh billowed between the joints) on his elbow and with the other landed two noisy slaps on his cheek. "Thief!" she gasped and dragged the suitcase from him. The boy goggled. "Hey, you. . . ." His fist clenched. Aunt Adie recognized her niece, Gwennie.

"I thought I'd die," she told Mrs. Kelly the next day. "I was ready to sink through the ground with mortification. Oh my Godfathers! Only for the bus conductor and the inspector the boys'd have had her clothes off her back! They held them and we had to scuttle off with the suitcase and everyone sniggering at us for a pair of country gawks!"

"Ah! What could she know of the world!" Mrs. Kelly sighed. "Four years in a convent!"

"Kind father to her," sniffed Adie who had intended telling none of this. "We went straight to the Celtic Ice-Cream Parlour. I had to sit down. I was shaking like a leaf. Do you know, I ate two Melancholy Babies and she had a Knickerbocker Glory before either of us said one word!"

These were sundaes and Aunt Adie's predominant passion. ("What's your predominant passion?" the priest had asked her once at a retreat. "Sundaes, father!") Once a week she closed her tearooms and rode to town—twelve miles in the bus—to revel in them. They cost half a crown apiece, which was almost what she charged in her own establishment for tea with scones and a boiled egg. They were her one extravagance, a trochaic trimeter that evoked the syrupy sundae itself: Méll and Cólly Baby. It drew fizzles of saliva to her lips.

Confused by the suitcase rumpus, too outraged to even scold this atrocious niece, Adie, with no more than a "you can leave your case with the cashier," plunged her senses in a well of marshmallow and cool cream. Goblets later, notions which had been clashing in the corners of her shattered mind ("Straight back on the next bus!"—"Ship her to her father in England tonight!") dissolved and withdrew. She looked at the girl who would not meet her eye. Adie's descended to long lyle stockings, lumpy with darns. She recalled the price she had been required to pay for six such pairs. Further up, a belt had been dragged tightly across a discoloured gymslip in an effort to give it shape. A poplin tie was punctured by a pin which bore, impaled and bleeding, a nickel emblem of the Sacred Heart. The girl's hair was wild as overblown furze. A gawk, Adie decided and was depressed. God help us, a poor eedjit. She was not surprised. People from outside County Dublin were half baked. Though they could be sly enough when it suited their book. Country cute. Pale between spiky lashes, the girl's eyes reminded Adie suddenly of the untarred roads to nowhere that she had taken four years before when she went down to bury her sister. The country, smothered in mildewed hedges, had stunk of rotted flax, and Gwennie's freckles struck her then as being the same colour as the little mouldering mounds. The speechless child gave her the willies. Was she a moron, Adie had wondered between shudders at the cold, the lichenous presence of failure and the hens ridden by parasites. Going through her dead sister's duds had crowned it. There was so little to note: the wedding lines, some badly taken snaps, a few cheap medals. Musty smells, clammy oilcloth, a spray of withered twigs stuck in a bottle convinced her that her sister had put up no fight at all, that the last few months must have been nothing but a spineless drift into death and out of her responsibilities. The accumulations of this foolish life got Adie down properly. There was nothing you would take as a present. The poor trumpery would have been cruel as a souvenir. She couldn't get out of the place fast enough. "The nuns," she told the child, "will teach you Domestic Economy. Then you can come and live with me." But she had put off taking her from year to year.

"Well, Miss," Adie nodded impatiently at the goblet smeared with remnants of sundae. "Did that please you?"

"Oh Ma'am," said the girl. "It's gorgeous! I didn't know there was anything *like* that to eat annyplace."

Adie was moved. Contemptuous but moved. The sundaeless dreariness of convent life struck her with a precise pain which was promptly relieved by the knowledge that she, Adie, could now bring happiness to a deprived creature. It was an odd sensation, sad but agreeable. Like crying at a movie. Adie was a great crier. She began to cry now and dried her eyes with the disinfectant-soaked handkerchief which stung the tender flesh of her underlids.

"Oh," she gasped. "Oh!"

"What is it, Ma'am?" Gwennie asked.

"I was thinking of your poor mother," Aunt Adie lied. "Call me 'Aunt Adie.' Everyone does." And she smiled bravely in spite of the sting in her eye. She leaned a cheek towards the girl: "Kiss me," she said recklessly.

"Isn't that life!"

Mrs. Kelly—bulbously pregnant and terrified of twins—rocked with laughter. "Ha! Ha! Ha!" She flung her head so far back that Adie could see the uvula glisten in the moist vaulting of her mouth. "I do have to laugh! Sure, if I had the money to insure against them, I'd be in no need to insure! Ah well," she told Adie, *"you've* never known the meaning of the word 'trouble'! Maybe you'll learn now! *I'd* say there was more than meets the eye in the nuns wanting to get shut of Gwennie! At sixteen she was just beginning to be worth pounds and pounds to them! *Unless* there was something wrong with her health? A delicate girl. . . ."

"She's not 'delicate'!" Aunt Adie shied before the word "TB" and cantered firmly round it. "She *was* sick. Now she's cured."

Mrs. Kelly sighed, soaked cake in her tea and spooned it between her gums. "I suppose I'll lose another tooth with this baby! If I was you, Adie, I'd insure the girl." Chewing, her lips, bunched in an interrupted kiss, moved across her face like a fish form on sand. "Death is an expense! Like birth!" She paused to watch a tick eddy and descend into the grave of Adie's chin. "But you have money. You should take out a life insurance on her." She put an undunked piece of cake in her mouth and drank tea through it. "I'm eating for two," she remarked, "three maybe! When I was a girl we were warned never to kiss consumptives . . ." she considered her teacup, "and never to drink from anything they . . ."

"If that's what's worrying you," Adie snapped, "I keep hers apart! It'd do my business no good," she added, "to have you blabbing all around the village. . . ."

Mrs. Kelly bridled. "Is it *me.* . . ."

Adie wasn't listening. She was remembering former plans for launching into the pastry business. She saw a van gaily painted by the sign-painter carrying AUNT ADIE'S HOME-MADE CAKES AND PASTRIES to the four corners of the county. She and, yes, Gwennie in fur coats eating

Melancholy Babies in the Ice Cream Parlour. Though Gwennie's health. . . . Insurance? She'd see. The gay van blackened mournfully. Adie picked up and stroked the snoring head of her old tabby cat.

"I always slept with me Mammy," Gwennie had told her on her first night. And with horror: "Oh, don't make me sleep alone."

Adie imagined the anaemic pair cuddled in a cocoon of obstinacy and disease. She shoved the cat off her lap. *Sleep* with her in a germy bed indeed!

"You're not serious!" She had scolded. "It's four years since your Mammy died. You didn't sleep with anyone in the convent, did you? Well, did you? Can't you answer me?"

The girl's closed air made Adie's voice sharpen. What was the use of having affection to give if you came up against sullenness? Gwennie looked underhand: a convent Miss. "Well," Adie chivvied. "Well? *Did* you share a bed with anyone?"

Gwennie, a nerve of memory jabbed, let out a shrill giggle. "The nuns ada creased us! One time," she gabbled in a jet of loquacity, "Sister Teresa-of-the-Little-Flower caught two girls in the one bed and kicked them the length of the dorm. They could hardly sit down for a week! She wore men's boots. Mary—she was one of the two girls—said if she ever got a chance when she'd left the place, she'd come back and bust her nose in."

Gwennie stopped as suddenly as she had begun. Her expression—practised perhaps to deceive the eyes of nuns—as moon innocent as before.

"Oh!" said Adie and then: "If you need anything you can call me. I'll leave my door open."

"Okeydoke!"

Later, hearing a window bang in Gwennie's room, Adie came in and found her bundled like a hedgehog: head and all beneath a bristle of blankets. Uncovering the face, she stared a while in puzzlement and with a nagging though indefinite twinge at the vulnerably prominent eyelids: convex and blue veined marbles.

Adie put Gwennie to work in the tearoom and let her keep half the tips—generously, for she was a disastrous waitress. The nuns had discouraged baths and saved soap for the convent laundry, so now Gwennie plunged black-bordered nails in plates of white pudding and tomatoes that she plonked before customers. With a bang. And a sputter. Then pounded downstairs with the heft of a mare in foal.

"My Lord!" Mrs. Kelly said.

"She'll grow out of it," Adie excused her.

Waste energy leaped from the girl. "Ow!" she screamed. "Whoops! I've banged my funnybone! Drat it! Holy Smoke! Whee! Here comes the bride Forty inches wide! I'll never make it with this tray! Look out all! I'm going to slip! Oy! Ow! Saved it!" There was an imbalance about her, an air of risk as she zoomed about like an unguided motor boat. Groans and giggles preceded her as regularly as the engine's throb. But she also made faces at herself in the tearoom mirror; dodged the Goldflake ad printed across its glass, dragging a steel comb through hair which leaped, crackled and came out in handfuls of knots like rutting spiders which she saved to make a bun. She longed to put up her hair, to wear a wide swishing skirt and be grown up. Coiled inside the uncomfortable schoolgirl a woman writhed, about to burst out with the lopsided force of leaves ripping their bud. Half shadowed by the convent still, she alternated:

> I'd like to get you
> On a slow boat to China
> All to myself alo-o-ne.

with:

> Come Holy Ghost send down those beams
> Which sweetly flow in silent streams
> From thy great home abo-o-ove.

"I don't care who sends it," Mrs. Kelly observed, "a bit of silence would be a relief alright."

"Think of living with fifty like that!" Aunt Adie sighed. "Those nuns must have been tough babies."

"Brides of Christ!" said Kelly acidly. "I'd rather have fifty like that any day and no man! Nuns have it easy!"

"Well, no one can say her health hasn't picked up," said Adie, "since she's been with me. I brought her back from death's door!" She was sorry now that she'd taken out the Life Insurance. It was only a waste and after the first quarter she let the payments lapse. "I'm more than a mother to that girl," she told everyone. "It's great to have a bit of youth round the house!" She bought Gwennie nylons—irregulars— for wearing in the tearoom, a plastic nail-brush and semi-heeled shoes.

Gwennie crossed her legs like a stocking advertisement.

"Jeez!" she screamed, "if the nuns could see me now!"

"Do you miss the convent?" Adie asked.

"That dump!"

"Where would you like best to live?"

"Here. Always."

Adie melted. "Listen," she said. "We'll go to town tomorrow to the Royal. They're showing *The Girl He Left Behind Him*."

Gwennie hugged her. The two enjoyed such outings enormously and were seen to giggle ridiculously on the bus. Gwennie was open-mouthed at the promise of her own uncommitment. She bought *The Girl's Crystal* and *Maeve's Own Weekly* with her tips and imagined that because nothing had happened to her yet anything might. Airy as a pingpong ball tossed on a jet of spray, she affected Adie with her excitement.

"More than a mother really, I feel like a *sister* to her," Adie said, "or a girl friend." At one swoop she was fulfilling the roles she had mismanaged until now. The sign painter was not included on any of these trips which began in complicity as the pair sneaked past Mrs. Kelly's hovel. Adie had dropped her old companion, who was suffering from morning sickness and depressed her with complaints.

"That one would put years on you," said she to Gwennie, "she'd cry this year for next year."

In the autumn, when tourists fell off and there was nothing for Gwennie to do in the tearoom, Adie found her a place as nursemaid with a doctor's family who lived a mile up the hill. She was to sleep in so as to be on hand in case the children needed her at night and this, as Adie told her, was to her advantage because it meant she would be spending the winter in a heated house and would have the doctor to keep an eye on her in case she had a relapse. Meanwhile better not mention the consumption. What people didn't know needn't trouble them. Gwennie was to have Sunday afternoons and two evenings a week off to spend with Adie and the two kissed lightly when the doctor came to pick her up with her suitcase. She would be round for supper three nights later.

But she was hardly out the door before Adie began to regret her. It was four months now since the day she had gone to meet her off the bus and she could hardly remember what she had done with herself before the girl's arrival. The autumn fogs had started and clung like grey stoppers at every window. No customers came. Adie mooched round the house, considered pocketing her pride and calling on the neglected Mrs. Kelly, then bit the nose off the sign painter when he told her she was like a hen that has lost its chick.

At three on the day Gwennie was due for supper, Adie was making scones; by six she had cooked a big juicy fry and was beginning to watch the hill road. By seven all the water in the kettle had boiled away and she was in a rage. "Ha!" said she as she filled it up again. "All the trouble I went to! Fat thanks I get!" She put it back on the fire and stared at her waiting table. "Selfishness of the young!" She sighed with jealousy.

Gwennie arrived at seven-thirty. "I had to wash me hair," she explained.

"Very dainty!" sneered her aunt. "You never used to bother! Whom are you trying to please?"

"It'll be no time," said the sign painter, comfortably filling his mouth with sausage, "till she'll have a young man. She's getting to be a fine girl. She'll be walking out in no time."

"Ha!" cried his wife. "She'd have to be weak in the head to look crooked at a man after what she's seen around her. Little good husbands did for me or her mother or Mrs. Kelly."

"Maybe not! Aha! But ye all wanted one! And so will she! I see there's a young fellow working up at your place these nights!" He winked at Gwennie.

She told them the doctor was having a second garage built.

"That's a bricklayer," said the sign painter. "Moonlighting! And it's not all bricklayer's work he's doing there either. I was passing the house the other night and seen where he put in a window and door. He could be put out of the union for that. Doing a carpenter's job. Maybe you should give him the tip to be careful." He grinned at his niece. "Help you get acquainted."

"Don't either of you bother your heads," Aunt Adie advised. "What good did unions ever do *you?*" she asked her husband. "We'da been in a nice pass if we'da been depending on you and unions! God help the women that rely on men! Did jez see where Mrs. Kelly's hubby was taken off with a perforated ulcer? Roaring! I suppose she'll be around here begging louder than ever now. All she gets is the Outdoor Relief. She ran through the dole months ago. It doesn't do you good to think of the troubles of the world. Give us a song Gwennie."

Gwennie sang *I love the dear silver that shines in your hair* and the rest of the evening passed off amiably.

Her next evening off, however, she was so late that when she arrived Adie and the sign painter were sitting down to supper. She came in the door still panting.

"Oho!" the sign painter grinned. "I was just saying to myself, 'tis out courting with the bricklayer you were! We're no company for a young girl. His name," he informed her, "is Mat Mullen."

A rush of distress swept through Aunt Adie and shook her chin as she gobbled fried apple and sausage. She glanced sideways at the sign painter with hatred.

With mild moon eyes and hanging adenoidal jaw, Gwennie explained that she had been to Mrs. Kelly's with some leftover pudding that the doctor's wife had told her she might take. "They had a big party last night and there was lashings of creamy stuff that wouldn't keep," she told Adie. "I knew the Kellys would be glad of it. You never saw such misery," she went on, "the poor kids sitting around on the floor. And it'd make your hands itch to wipe the snot off their noses."

"How fair," said Adie, "you didn't think to offer *me* the pudding?"

Gwennie gave her a look of surprise. "It was only leftovers."

"*Only* leftovers! Very uppity we are these days. Was there sherry in the trifle?"

"Honest to God, Adie, you're making a mountain . . ." begged the sign painter.

"You shut up," Adie told him. "Well, was there?" She knew she sounded wrong, and was upset by this and felt that somewhere underneath she wasn't wrong at all but wronged and must dig to the truth and justify herself with it. "Well?" she harangued.

"I dunno," Gwennie sounded sullen.

"But you gave it to those little fairies of starving brats! Sure that will sicken them. They'll have colic all night and be raising the roof. . . ." Adie flailed about for the right words, flinging wrong ones from her with contempt. She saw Gwennie and the sign painter exchange a glance which seared her. To think of them ganging up on her! She would have liked to embrace Gwennie but the girl's sour puss checked her. It was too late now—or too soon. "Giving presents to strangers," she resumed painfully. "Lady Bountiful no less! And what about your own," she paused, "family? That did so much for you? Brought you back from death's door when you were good for nothing but a sanatorium? Took you into this house and found you work! Is this your thanks?" The girl's sullenness enraged her now. The hangdog look called out for punishment. Gwennie's glance slid crookedly away from her own. Adie wanted to shake or slap her. Anything to get through to her so that she could take her in her arms again. Coddle, restore and love her. My own baby, she thought and groaned: "More fool me!" She could feel spittle bubbling at the corners of her mouth. Her eyes strained, swollen in their sockets. "I'm an ugly old woman and youth is selfish! Well, it's nothing to me. . . . Why should I care?" Gwennie wasn't listening. "Are you listening?" she hissed.

The sign painter walked across the room and closed the door after him. That was as much disapproval as he ever showed.

"Yes Ma'am."

At the "ma'am" Aunt Adie's rage collapsed.

"Sure all I want is your good," she wheedled. "Sure aren't you more than a daughter to me? Who else have I? Who else have you? To think that the one time you had a chance to give something, you preferred. . . ." She was on the right track now. "Not that it's the thing itself I care about but the *thought*. . . ." She paused, losing the thread. Gwennie was listening attentively now. "Don't tell me either that that doctor's wife hasn't given you other presents that you're hiding from me. As if I'd ask you for them! Oh, I'm not the fool I may look! That Limerick lace blouse she used to wear to church—didn't she give you that? Dare you say she didn't? I haven't seen it on her this long time. Maybe you're waiting to give that to Mrs. Kelly too? Or to wear it yourself for your . . . bricklayer?"

"I swear to God," Gwennie began, "she never. . . ."

Aunt Adie raised a hand.

"Don't perjure yourself!"

The next time Gwennie came she brought the blouse. Adie took it casually. "Very nice fit," she said, trying it on. "It'll look snappy with my black suit. She used to have gloves to match," she remembered. "Why don't you ask her for them? One's no good without the other."

"Oh I couldn't *ask* her," Gwennie began to whimper.

Adie turned back to the mirror. "Sure she doesn't know what she has. Spoilt rotten that kind of woman is!"

Pale hair, pale lace confronted her in the glass, cold as spray and remote as an old snap. She knew she was crumbling away Gwennie's affection. As she ruffled the flounces on her chest the glass buttons danced.

"I'll wear it to mass," she said. "In the bus."

Gwennie's hand flew to her mouth. "She'll see you!"

"So what?" said Aunt Adie. "So what? It's mine, isn't it?"

In her blurred vision the lace thickened consistency, became a caul of lard on the sloping shoulder of a leg of lamb.

"So what?" asked the lump of grey cold meat in the mirror, "so what?"

Gwennie wept.

Within a week the doctor's wife found a dozen purloined objects in Gwennie's suitcase. She questioned the girl curiously. None were of value: a few steel butter knives, some napkins, an embroidered pillowcase.

"What could you possibly want with these, Gwennie?" she wondered. "They're hardly saleable you know!"

Gwennie got hysterical and the doctor had to give her a sedative. He agreed with his wife that the girl was a bit unstable and probably unfit to be left in charge of children. When Gwennie and the children wept over this decision they agreed, doubtfully, to give her a second chance.

"Bobby and Clare adore her," Gwennie overheard the doctor's wife say. "I suppose that's what matters. One can't apply one's own standards to these people."

Gwennie retailed all this to Aunt Adie who only laughed. "You don't need them! What do you care?" she said. "Next year we'll start the pastry business and then you'll be your own boss. You won't call the queen your cousin. We'll show them!"

She was not sorry that Gwennie should have fallen out of favour at the big house. With its wood of foreign trees imported by the doctor's grandfather, it filled her with hatred and suspicion. Its view plummetted into the bay beyond the roofs of the village. Its name was haughtily foreign: Bella Vista. Behind high walls topped with broken glass, it sprawled outlandishly and was kin only to a few neighbouring mansions:

Khyber Pass, Miramare, Saint Juan les Pins, where old colonels and retired British civil servants with jaundiced skin chewed the cud of memories as snuffy, no doubt, and as alien as the smell from the eucalyptus leaves which stuck in the gutters and were floated down the hill to the village—a smell which reminded Adie of sick rooms and antiseptic. She cursed herself for ever getting Gwennie the job in that house, cursed it for making the girl independent and for giving her notions. She began to watch sourly on the nights Gwennie was not off and Mat Mullen, the foxy-haired, moonlighting bricklayer, strode up the hill with shouldered hod. He was about twenty-two, with an impudent blue eye and, Gwennie had told her, the mistress sent her out to him with cups of tea and Guinness. Had that one no sense? Or was it deliberate? Adie questioned Gwennie to know did she like him but the girl had grown sly. Ah, she said, he thought too much of himself. How did she know that? Ah, she just did. The secret burst from her:

"He asked me to a dance. In the Town Hall."

"And you said?"

"No."

"I should just think so! The cheek!"

"Ah," regretfully, "I hadn't a decent dress."

Adie contained herself. Next day she went to see the doctor and reproached him for not keeping a sufficiently close eye on Gwennie, an innocent girl. Things improved. The garage was finished and Gwennie, more solicitous than before, bought her aunt presents with her wages and accompanied her twice a week to the movies and Ice Cream Parlour. Adie grumbled because it couldn't be more often but Gwennie said the doctor's wife was too busy with Red Cross work.

"Red Cross my big toe," said Adie. "That one's an ikey lass! Charity, you might tell her, begins at home. If you lie down and make a door mat of yourself you'll be trodden on. Stand up for your rights!"

"Oh," said Gwennie, "I couldn't."

In February—three months after the bricklayer had asked Gwennie to the dance—Adie had occasion to go to the cinema alone. *Frankenstein* which she couldn't bear to miss was showing locally. Gwennie was not off and Adie, returning by dark from the bus stop, was pursued by monsters. Scuttling from street lamp to street lamp, she clawed at the walls which, in places, yielded beneath her fingers with the suspect pliancy of moss. The stretch of road past the doctor's gate was particularly dark. Protruding stucco erections and fanciful battlements reared;

ancient cedars concealed the sky. Beyond them was the sea. On the curve of road below, a line of cars, packed tight like scales on a snake, harboured lovers. Adie, hastening in the dark past the doctor's gate, heard a half smothered, wholly familiar laugh. She whipped round, plunged back. Heedless of doubt, she grabbed the woman's arm and pulled her into the lamplight. It was Gwennie. With the bricklayer. "You . . . yous!" Hysteria choked her. Gwennie wrenched her arm free and ran in. A door creaked shut. The bricklayer disappeared. Adie, who had wasted her ammunition on skirmishes, was foiled of the major battle, disarmed before the true betrayal. She turned away, groping. Below her the closed cars crouched in their ranks. "Sluts!" she muttered at them. "Whores!" She plunged and stumbled, almost fell down the hill, beyond the trees, to where the bay opened wide to the moonlight. "Underhand . . ." she groaned. "Hypocrite!" The words, not quite released, fell back in her throat with the loneliness of a sleeper's moan. "Trailing round lanes . . . !" she spat. Down here, in gardens heavy with winter greenery, artificial pagodas and summer houses shone in a light which ignored the small village house further below, shadowed by the hill's shoulder and dank with its drainings. Leaves clattered. The sea sucked. With head hunched into her shoulders, Adie fled the empty openness of the night and at a swift lope, made for the consoling limits of her own kitchen.

Alone there, later, while the sign painter snored, she sat like Niobe and pondered. On the sly! All these months Gwennie had had nights off that she had not confessed. Red Cross indeed! Adie laughed sourly and caught a hateful glimpse of her own derision in the glass. Gulled! Gulled! That two-faced, simpering trollop had deceived her! *She* had been rationed! Two nights a week for her and how many for the bricklayer? All the sweetness to herself had been a sop thrown to stick in her gullet. To shut her up! Three for him or four? *Five* maybe? Maybe she was off every night! At the suspicion Adie went rigid with pain. What would she not have done for Gwennie! Nights blank as the bay she had just passed stretched despairingly in front of her. After such treachery whom could she ever trust? Adie, who had never smashed a possession deliberately or hardly even wept if not at the movies, sat stifling with unvented misery until, in the small hours of the morning, she dozed off in her chair.

At nine she was ringing the doctor's bell. He came to the door himself. Gwennie had taken the children to the dentist. Adie told him she wanted her niece back. She needed her in the tearooms. He said, coldly, that he thought he had gathered that the girl herself was eager to stay. Seeing his inquisitive stare, Adie tried to settle wisps of hair which she had not combed since the morning before. Her breath catching, she said "Gwennie is under age."

"But she tells me," he said, "that her father is her legal guardian."

Adie broke down at this proof of a fresh conspiracy. "Oh," she sobbed. "To think that I . . . after all, all. . . . Brought her back from death's door! Where's me handkerchief? Oh the hussy. . . . The snake! Asp in my bosom. . . . Oh!"

The doctor sat her down, gave her a glass of something, tried to soothe, talked of the understanding we must all have for the young and how Mat Mullen was a decent young man. At this Adie collected her dignity and walked out of the house. They were all against her. There was no trust.

That morning she denounced Mat Mullen to an officer of the bricklayer's union.

For weeks she did not see Gwennie whose guilty conscience, no doubt of it, was keeping her embuttressed in the doctor's house up the hill. She heard from Mrs. Kelly however that Mat had been given his marching orders and that, as this meant he couldn't work any more in the Republic, he was going to buy a ticket for the other side. Then news came that Gwennie too had given notice. It seemed she would wait for Mat to get a job before joining him. She had written to her father in London and had got an answer. Meanwhile, the two were observed courting on the hill roads where cedars and ilexes lent concealment even in January. By the winter twilight Adie saw them in every couple that passed up or down the road or stood at lookout points above the bay: unidentifiable match-stick figures, pausing by parapets like migrant birds. When business took her to Dun Laoghaire Harbour, she swerved towards the wooden departure pier, to scrutinise the spray-blown, pink-nosed travellers who queued, moving their bundles with intent patience. Gold-braided harbour officials ushered striding gentlemen ahead, and relatives waved despondently from behind a parapet. Gwennie's underhand countenance snuffled beneath every umbrella. Then Adie heard that Mat had indeed gone, that Gwennie had a cold, had pleurisy, had been moved to hospital with TB meningitis. The doctor came and drove Adie in, weeping all the way, in his own car.

At ten that morning, Adie sat, alone among the marble tables of the Ice Cream Parlour, and held a handkerchief to her lips. She had been there an hour when Mrs. Kelly, lean and mangey after her delivery, came in to help her home.

"I couldn't face back alone," Adie told her. "I've been to the hospital. They wouldn't let me see her." She sobbed. "First her mother and now her! And those two men off in England! Her father and the other one! Leaving it all to me. Such a responsibility! Doctor Flynn says there's a new Wonder Drug they could try on her. It costs hundreds of pounds but they'd try it on her as an experiment. Free! How do I know what to say? Maybe they're using her as a guinea pig? What do doctors care for the poor? Have a sundae. No? Ah do! As we're here. I didn't know where else to go. Have a Melancholy Baby. To think she used to love coming here!" Aunt Adie sobbed again lengthily. She dabbed her face. "I suppose I'll be alone at her funeral," she groaned. "Like I was at her mother's. If she dies. He wouldn't tell me what the chances were. A buttoned-up old puss-in-boots that doctor. On and on about how they do their best and the state of medical science and a lot of jawbreakers!" Aunt Adie fell silent, sighed, blew her nose and drew a corner of an envelope from her handbag. Letters protruded: P-R-U-D-E-N. . . . Seeing Mrs. Kelly lean forward, she pushed it back and clamped shut, first the bag, and then her mouth as though it contained a frog which she was afraid might jump out. The frog kicked the inside of her cheeks so that they trembled, and Adie opened her mouth with a pop.

"I went in," she gasped, "and paid up the back payments of the Life Insurance anyway. I'd stopped paying them for a while there when she looked so healthy."

She turned in her chair to call the waitress and ordered a Melancholy Baby for herself and another for Mrs. Kelly. The two women spooned silently into their sundaes.

"God help us but it's a queer world we live in," Mrs. Kelly said, through a spoonful of marshmallow.

"Eat up," Aunt Adie said. "We may as well enjoy it while we're in it."

Pure Invention

Anne Le Marquand Hartigan

The Long Man of Newtown and the Fat Woman of Newtown lived in a house of straw.

It was always collapsing.

Much to the distress of the Long Man and to the satisfaction of the Fat Woman, for she was very beautiful and of a malicious nature.

The Long Man thought all the time how to prevent the house of straw collapsing; for it worried him to think how it upset the Fat Woman, not realising, of course, the deep satisfaction it gave her to be miserable about it; and the even greater satisfaction to see him worrying about it. Even greater her satisfaction was, than her contentment with him in bed, and that was truly great as can be proved by the deep hollow in the center, showing the good use they made of it.

The Long Man spent much weary time drawing up plans and adding up immense sums, which sometimes went up and down, and sometimes went sideways in the most alarming manner. At least they alarmed the Fat Woman, she was deeply suspicious of sums; sideways sums most of all. But she knew their magic could not be strong as they never came to anything.

The Long Man smoked many pipes, filling the room with smoke so the Fat Woman could complain about that too. So her cup of pleasure was pressed down and running over, and she lived her days in true joy as long as the Long Man worked to no avail to make their home more secure.

One morning the Long Man kissed the Fat Woman, oh fondly fondly, and long gazed into her eyes. When they had finished with their kissing and their long gazing, they had not, but sometimes they had to do other things in the morning. The Long Man said, "I am off on a journey."

Now this did not please the Fat Woman at all. She was not in the least bit fond of journeys, particularly when the Long Man went on them. She never went. They made her tired, and besides she might have got thin with all that walking. The Long Man would not have liked that. The Fat Woman was profoundly unhappy because she would have to do all her worrying by herself, and what good was that? She must have her man to worry on, so as to really enjoy it. So this journey business was not a bit to her liking.

However, he seemed extraordinarily set on it. The wailing and the fussing, the little jobs to be done, had no affect whatever. The Long Man whistled to the Wobberly Dog, and set off with many a backward turn to wave to his wife. She was at pains to know whether to bawl and cry, or to blow kisses to him, but neither were any use to her now. The Long Man and the Wobberly Dog had turned into dots on the horizon. They were lucky to live near a horizon, as nearly all horizons have been built on, so you have little opportunity of becoming a dot on one. When going on any self-respecting journey this is essential. The Fat Woman turned with a sigh. She would have had to admit it was a pleased sigh, if she had been thinking about it. She was not thinking about it. She was busily planning who she could take her comforting annoyance to. She was thinking of the Dark Woman. Ordinarily she did not enjoy the Dark Woman's company, but she was a close friend of hers, she met and talked with her quite often as an insurance policy. Not that she really believed that she would need one, but now she did. Also the Dark Woman's husband and the Long Man enjoyed each other's company, and would spend many long evenings together discussing how bad everything was with the land and slowly sucking everlasting pipes.

The insurance policy taken out with the Dark Woman was a listening one. She had forty-two and a half hours, seven minutes and thirty-nine seconds listening to her credit. A firm resolve was settling in the Fat Woman's mind to cash some of it.

The Dark Woman's eyes were set in a yellow face. Now and then she would open these eyes very wide, but the expression would stay the same. She was not a listening woman. The Fat Woman watched the curl of bubbles circle in her coffee cup as she sat listening to the Dark Woman, waiting her moment to cash her credit. In the past she listened to long, Oh-so-long tales of troubles. The Dark Woman had a family; what a family. The Fat Woman thought she was very stupid with her family, after all if they were so troublesome, why hadn't she lost them long ago? She had lost hers the moment she met the Long Man. When she knew, in the first blinding flash of true love, that her life would be spent annoying him. She wet her lips and waited, but the Dark Woman had already got going. A sister of hers was having a breakdown. A brother of hers was unbearably rich. A mother of hers was showering her children with presents. Oh, what an impossible family.

The Fat Woman pounced.

"I had a terrible cold last weekend. . . ." It was not what she meant to say at all. The Dark Woman flashed an accusing look and went on with her own delicious woes. The Fat Woman tried again.

"My man's sums are all coming out red." It was still not what she wanted to say but was better than her last attempt.

The Dark Woman sighed and went on. "But I don't know if it is right for me, meaningful, you know what I mean, you understand?"

The Fat Woman did not know, she did not understand. What is more, down in the bottom part of her stomach was growing, slowly slowly, an anger. "The Long Man has gone on a journey and left me alone."

The Fat Woman had got it out. The Dark Woman's eyes opened wide and for a moment focused on the Fat Woman. "Oh, dear," she said. "That will help you to understand my problem, if I sleep with the inviting stranger it will enlarge my experience and benefit my marriage, don't you agree?"

Now that low-down belly anger in the Fat Woman grew and grew. The Dark Woman was not obeying the rules. She knew, although it was never mentioned, that the Fat Woman had forty-two and a half hours, seven minutes and thirty seconds to her credit. She well knew that in the rules of over-the-kitchen-table talk, that most sacred and everlasting ritual, that mention of your man took precedence over all else. You had right of way. An inviting stranger was important, no doubt, but your man, then death, took precedence over everything.

The Dark Woman's eyes narrowed, she faltered in her speech but on she went. "Ah yes, I understand, but you are a mature woman, you are older than I, you will be able to cope, you are so clever. But me, I'm so sensitive, if something like that happened to me, why, I would be prostrate, I wouldn't rise from my bed, but you, you will . . ."

The Fat Woman did not wait. She stood up. Her chair fell back, she went swiftly from the room, and though she was fat, she moved gracefully, the light of her anger threw a red glow around her and the rooks in the trees looked down and said;

"There goes a real woman."

And did not shit for five minutes.

The Fat Woman went home and shut the door. She took out her broom and did a great sweeping. She took out her mop and she did a great washing. She flapped her duster, and polished and rubbed. The glow from her anger lowered and faded, the glow went into the clean floor and polished furniture. So the whole house gleamed and shone as it had not done for years.

She sat down, the anger gone from her, but with no happiness in her heart at all. She did not mind dust, she could happily leave it. The empty, clean house reflected its nothing back to her.

The Long Man was away one week. Two weeks. Then one Thursday afternoon in the third week, as the rain lashed and the usual ominous drip, drip, started in the back bedroom, in he came, the Wobberly Dog bounding and panting ahead of him. The Fat Woman's heart beat and leapt but she continued to savagely stir the soup.

"My love my love," said the Long Man sweeping her into his arms and kissing her fondly.

"Get out, you awful dog; your footprints all over the floor." The Fat Woman glowered at the Wobberly Dog, who slunk towards the door, tail between her legs, her brown eyes humbling.

The Fat Woman gave himself a cold supper. The supper was hot but she was cold; enquiring stiffly how the journey went. The Long Man didn't seem to notice her coldness and answered her questions cheerfully. Gradually over the third or fourth Guinness she melted a little, and almost let interest seep into her voice, then caught herself out and stiffened again.

"Did you do good business?" she asked. She was not in the least interested but she sounded enthralled.

"Oh yes yes," he murmured tiredly, "very good, very good. They might put my invention, Y.17, into production."

"Did you meet many women?"—Now this did interest her. From her voice you would never have guessed.—

"Oh yes yes," he answered, "many beautiful women."

These answers were not at all to her liking. The first she didn't listen to. The second she heard too much.

"They are thinking of a fancy name for it," said the Long Man, taking a deep suck on his pipe, "The Happy Home Saver, a mad class of a name altogether."

The Fat Woman listened and did not listen, but the fury came on her at the thought that one of his sums might have power, when it should stay with all the others safely on sheets of paper and go nowhere. "That is not a name for anything at all," she snorted, as she whisked away the end of his pudding just before he had finished; but he filled her glass high to the brim while she noisily banged the dishes. So, over the fire, as the Wobberly Dog steamed her wet belly, they drank the soft and dark, eased and warmed.

That night their bed springs sang joyful tunes again.

A week later Mick-The-Post delivered a stiff fat envelope of expensive and creaking paper. It was for the Long Man. He opened it and a cheque fluttered to the ground.

Dear Sir:

I am delighted to inform you that we are able to make use of and develop during the coming months your design for product Y.17, that you outlined to us during your recent visit. While it will mean our company investing considerable capital, our Company Director considers that the company's policy of encouraging talent and ideas, however small, should, whenever possible, be pursued to its etc., etc. . . . .

I enclose a cheque for five hundred pounds. We know you will be proud that a little idea of yours will help our great company prosper for the good of all mankind etc., etc. . . . .

"Five hundred pounds," the Fat Woman gasped.

"Yes. They are going to develop it exactly as I imagined it," said the Long Man with a smile of real satisfaction.

"From one of your sums?" said the Fat Woman.

"Yes," he said.

"A sideways sum?"

He was laughing and laughing because his good idea was going to be made. But the Fat Woman grumbled because it was hateful to her that his magic could be so potent. She could not understand it at all.

"And now I've just got one too," said the Dark Woman, eyeing the Fat Woman over her cup of tea. "Everyone in the village is getting one."

The Fat Woman was cross. She wanted one, but really, it would only have been useful to her to have had it before the Dark Woman had one. Now, half the fun would have gone out of it. If and when she did get one the Dark Woman would pester her with good advice and help, when the real pleasure would be, if she could give that advice to her.

"It's a marvellous new invention," said the Dark Woman. She knew she was on a winning streak.

"You sound like a television ad," said the Fat Woman sourly. "More tea dear?" she said, in an attempt to stop the flow of self-satisfaction.

At that moment a large vehicle swept up to the door, making the house shake and bounce. There purred a car, as long as the building itself, pale silver outside, pale blue inside, and a pale female with amazing yellow hair sat beside a small man with a fat cigar. The small man bounced out of the car. The Fat Woman did not trust women with yellow hair.

The visitor pumped the hand of the Long Man, who had gone out to meet him. The two women watched from the window.

"Hallo hallo old boy," pump pump, "just down for the weekend." Pump pump, wink wink. The yellow woman yawned. "Just popped in to see how's tricks," pump pump.

The Long Man rescued his hand. "Do come in, you're very welcome."

"Oh no no old man, the boss said to look you up. To tell you you're not to forget to drop in and see us next time you have any little ideas, we might be able to help again, you know. Yes, it is a nice car. Yes, business has been good."

The Long Man lit a pipe.

"Very well really, all things considered, some of our products have turned up trumps. Yes yes your little Y.17 among them, not so little, no, you're right, could say that, ha ha, you could say business is booming. You really could. Well. Must push on, regards to the lady wife." Pump pump.

Clip, swish, demure purr, and the silver vision curved into somewhere else.

The two women returned to their cups for support. The Long Man came into the kitchen puffing his pipe and accepting a cup of tea.

"Now," continued the Dark Woman, wishing to return to her area of conquest, "this wonderful new invention, 'The Happy Home Saver,' and it's so true, so true, you must get one dear, it cleans everything like a dream, it could change your life." The Dark Woman looked smugly at the cobwebs on the kitchen windows.

The Fat Woman started. Her eyes swivelled onto her husband. She felt such horror that the voice that came out of her was not hers at all. "Invention," she said. "Happy Home Saver," she growled.

The Long Man smiled at her wreathed in smoke.

The Fat Woman jumped up. "I wouldn't want any old invention to keep my house cleaner," she said, looking knives at the Long Man. She swung over to the window and pushed it open, flapping angrily at the smoke. Outside the rain had begun to lash the grass and trees, they bent and struggled in the sudden onslaught. The Fat Woman stared at the wetness. His magic had a small bit of power only. Five hundred pounds? That was nothing at all. From the back room came a familiar song, drip, drip, drip, the leak in the roof. This sound caused pleased aggravation in the heart of the Fat Woman, as she continued with vigor to wave her arms at the smoke from the Long Man's pipe; and then she realised, with much annoyance, that she was content.

The Intruders

Rita Kelly

Irish was always somewhat virginal. Prayers, poems, and Mass for St Patrick's Day. Shamrocks pinned to the full of our gymslips, crowding to greet the priest at the convent gate—*Dia duit, 'Athair. Fáilte romhat 'Athair*. And after communion and the sweet homily on the dear little snakes, we hymned mellifluously in the Saint's own sanctified language, *Aspal Mór na hÉireann*. Not a trace of the asp in *aspal*, though we hissed the *rs* with what we had been taught to be a Celtic sibilance which seemed to refute the claim for Patrick vis-à-vis the snakes. But *An tAthair* just smiled, or rather pulled his thick lips into that ingratiating grin which he seemed to adopt for us and for the good Sisters— *Bail ó Dhia orthu*. The sly glances across the aisle, row upon row, exposing quick teeth to a companion in our secret tiger's yawn, a glint of fang, before spitting out the regulated *rs* of the final verse.

The confessional was ideally makeshift so that *An tAthair* could hold our hands or touch our cheeks, part of the perks, as well as an invaluable practice for our oral examinations and the more seemingly *outré* the sin the more contact afforded. It was all so innocuous. *Sea, a chroí . . . inis dom arís . . . Beannacht Dé ort, a thaisce . . . agus ortsa, a Athair*. The *diabhal* never arose, there was no place for him in such an atmosphere. He did find mention, more than seemed necessary at times, in the conversation-pieces of the prescribed prose. But that was all native, and the *diabhal* had some kind of unexplained precedence in those Gaeltacht places. However, the word must be noted with its genitive form, but no one ever used it in an essay, and it was considered un-nice for conversation.

Even the Man who came with the *Fáinne* never used it. But then he never said much anyway, his brand of Irish was like himself: meagre and balding. The nun showed pain as he slurred his *rs*, making a whore of the slender endings. He wore an outsize *Fáinne*, gold and glistening, we got little silver ones, and the nun thought it would be a nice idea if he himself attached them to our gymslips when we had paid the money and said the necessary few words. He seemed a little worried at first, but the juniors encouraged him by their underdevelopment. He poked his way through us seniors, and some of us indeed were a handful, placing the *Fáinne* gingerly on the palpitating cleft. Privately we called him the Fanny Man, in public *An tUasal Ó Riain*. He began to teach us Irish dancing, at least that way he could keep us at a distance. We could dance already better than he could, but the nun felt, well after all he must be tolerated for the language, and he is doing his best, poor man. But he never got further than the "Siege of Ennis," *ar aghaidh 's ar gcúl ad infinitum*. So the nun talked him out of that, and he tried to talk her into camogie, and the amount of Irish to be learned from the rules. We tried it, broke some hurley-sticks, slashed some ankles, and gave it up, throwing the boots, which he had supplied at a reduced cost, into a press.

But his department appointed him to another town. We held a collection, bought him the new Irish Dictionary, a senior composed the dedication, she had thoroughly grasped the subjunctive mood and liked using it; a junior did the calligraphy in the antique script, where the M looks like a rake and there is a profusion of dots over everything. He came to give thanks, big the honour, not small the sorrow on leaving us, hope at God, hope at himself that we would all become in our mothers fecund and Irish, now that we were in our nice girls. He left many *sláns* at us, and we put many with him. Hope, of course, being at us, that everything would rise with him. What a hope.

Then there was the school-tour to the Gaeltacht, it was really the science department's idea, and they were not very interested in this Irish thing. Archimedes' principle, they felt, is simply the same as *Prionsabal Archiméid*, something to be taught year in, year out. One clear diagram is more impressive than four pages of writing, so no need to be awkward about this language business, it is all so irrelevant anyway in the interest of science.

The bus travelled for hours. Even the juniors wearied of waving at young men on tractors. There were miles of sheep coming out of the indistinction, grazing, scurrying along mountain-paths, and slowly disappearing. Finally, the sea, and a secluded foreshore. Not a native in sight. We killed some jellyfish, put sea-anemones *in vitro* and watched them purple against the sun. We collected some clammy shells as the tide receded, noting the precise spot of the discoveries on our diagrams. Just one starfish, which we killed and dropped in stinking formalin for further study. Armfuls of *Fucus spiralis* and *vesiculosus*, enough wrack to manure a potato-patch. Then we had tea and sandwiches among the rocks. But no swimming, because the bus-driver had us in full view despite his newspaper. Any kind of exposure in a public place was not the norm, it was even immodest to roll back the sleeves of our blouses. We came home with sand in our stockings, and hardly believing that the Gaeltacht was merely an acrid smell, a garage and a pub huddled together at intervals, bearing the sign *Tigh Mhicí Sheáin Pheaits* or *Tigh Pheaits Sheáin Mhicí* in most garish colouring; more sheep, a donkey or two, fatigue, and a sunset beyond imagination. We stopped in a village, and we all marched into the local convent to wash our hands. The bus jerked off again, casting an ungainly shadow until the light eked itself out of the sky. We disembarked at midnight, and the kitchen nun brought us warm milk and two plain biscuits to bring the Gaeltacht to an end.

Those who could not afford France went to this Gaeltacht during the summer, and brought their bicycles. They never brought back much, or so it seemed, other than harmless little stories about getting punctures in Irish, brushes with boys at the *céilí*, bullocks in fields, or the fact that their periods always came just when he said he'd see them on the beach. They picked up a phrase or two, so that they prefixed the most banal statement with *Craidhps, an dtuigeann tú bhfuil's agat*, everything was *go cinnte dearfa* and happened in the *cianta cairbreacha* until the first hint of winter, hockey, and all was forgotten.

Then Cóilín came to produce our play, or rather rescue it. We had been doing so badly at the festivals that our drama-mistress became desperate, and word passed quickly round that a real native had come.

He was so—what we had not expected—sophisticated, a dark well-clipped beard, sunbrowned fingers slender and sensitive. Sea green eyes, a soft look in them, or was it mocking? No one called him an *tUasal*, quietly we said Cóilín, or else manoeuvered the vocative out of the sentence. To our great surprise we understood every word he spoke, his *r* was slender too, but subtly different, gently rippled, he didn't hiss. His speech was so distinct that all the difficult genitive-endings were clear, yet not unduly emphasized. And what he said always seemed significant, said with a desire to impart his feelings or elicit yours.

At once the play was the thing. So unlike our *comhrá* sessions when we attempted to outdo each other in knitting together a patchwork of readymade bits of speech and idiom, and groped for a conversational structure in which to display them. And our *comhrá* pieces were always *cúrsaí reatha*, running affairs, and the weather. We were expected to be cognisant with pollution, education, religion, violence, party politics and lunar expeditions. We exhibited numerous nebulous ideas which were merely media clichés translated, and we shouldn't have cared in the least if everything connected with *cúrsaí reatha*, running affairs, found itself on a lunar expedition of no return. We had words for everything, spaceships, contraceptives, referenda, hijackings and abortions, all neatly underlined, giving declension, gender, person, number and case. But Cóilín simply never talked about these things. It was odd.

We heard him entranced, yet uneasy. His Irish was not just a language, in a curious way it was himself. Vibrant under one's gymslip. With him, none of us flashed our secret tiger's yawn across the class, except one of the denser girls who was surprised when it was not returned.

Then something happened to the play, it was no longer an excuse for a romp, and all about a bird and a tinker. It became something serious, interesting and slightly puzzling. We began to hear it and feel it, even into the girl's part Cóilín infused a life, a tone of voice, a character—she could be one of us in our private selves. One was slightly shocked to realise that one was really such an exuberant little tinker.

Then you changed too. Things were no longer so flippant, no longer a cause for adolescent giggling. Silences had meaning and import. Minute gestures of eye, of facial muscle. An ease and a reserve, a liveliness untainted by exaggeration or blatancy. You grew rather pensive, tended to avoid the after-tea chirrupy chatter and boisterous jump about. How attractive the outer garden by the river became. Those May evenings, the flit of wing through the plumtrees, their delicate blossom, not white, not red, so shortlived, from the moment of tenuous appearance to the touch of rust. This year you would not pick the fruit.

You'd be far from the eager hands which would pack it into a pillow-cover and hide it until midnight. Half-eaten plums flying across the beds, too much eaten too soon, and an overtired attempt to bring the feast to a climax. Passing the climax without knowing it and reaching a chaos of legs, nightdresses and stunted screams, until someone sees or imagines a light in the corridor, panic, and the feast deflates itself and all are supremely glad to sleep. No one comes, breathing becomes regular and soft, the dormitory is pervaded by a smell of crushed plums, childishly sweet. . . .

You did hear a footstep, and Cóilín comes. Through the trees to where you are sitting on a discarded pew. You know that he ought to be at his tea, and you are embarrassed at finding yourself alone with him, it has never happened before, and there are so many mistakes that you could make, especially in the relative form.

His greeting is so natural, and though he must have said it many times to many people, it seems as if he had just composed it. He sits. He would. Now he can watch you, he talks on, the words are understandable in themselves, but the way they are combined and placed together gives something else not so readily understood, and the tone, difficult to name. It is friendly and easy, a little enthusiastic, but more.

You can see his hands, the vital fingers, the face is a blur of beard just out of focus; yes, *caint* is feminine so the adjective is aspirated. He says *drámaíocht* in the genitive, and *réalaíocht*. Must check, does it mean stars or reality? Those idioms, he could be saying one thing and meaning another, he probably is doing that. And very ordinary words have, well, have other meanings, which he must know though you do not. Of course, *nádúr* is first declension, stupid, politely he pretends not to notice. Politeness, or pretense?

You continue, trying to think less about grammatical distinctions. While you think about language, its links and articles, he has all the time possible to think of other things, to shape and dominate the conversation, push it this way and that, and worst of all, observe your difficulties and reactions. You have time for nothing except an endless and breathless debate on gender—so much depends on gender—you risk losing the primary meaning of his sentences, catch the beginning and the end of phrases, surmise the rest, of course you are doomed to make a faux pas, to blurt out *ó sea, sea* when it ought to be a decided negative. The whole thing begins to sound impossible, artificial. Why not admit defeat, excuse your Irish, surely he would go away rather than speak English. What was that? "Am I boring you?" he said, and you answer automatically in Irish, turn, face him and get through at least three full-length sentences without a tremor. Now he falters, or seems to, his smile is so . . . and you quickly turn away. He continues, but the tone has changed, searching for words, or is he? And you finish a sentence for him, he repeats your addition, weighs it, accepts it as inevitably correct in the context. Is it a method for putting you at your ease, by seeming to adopt your problem of incoherence? Who knows.

He speaks of the drama-mistress, and says very flatly that she is *dóighiúil*, that could mean that he finds her "good-looking," or it could mean "generous," he does not insinuate which, but he must mean "good-looking," after all the juniors have a crush on her, then he asks if you agree with him, you can only say "perhaps," that is *b'fhéidir*. Now he praises her Irish. That needles you and you say if it were all that good why did she have to send into the wilds for him, and why was the play such a flop before his coming. He smiles, you are looking at him now, and notice the slight raising of an eyebrow. And you smile too, you are beginning to feel . . . but you can't be sure. He makes some joke about drama and mistresses and laughs, but its actual meaning is lost on you, and there is something disturbing about his laughter.

He rises, moves with deliberation towards one of the trees, turns, poses at an angle, hand on the bark, allowing his body to compose itself in contrast to the erect tree-trunk. A branch ruffles his hair and you notice, too suddenly, the tightness of his trousers. Now you don't know where to look, then you fix on the back of the school, like all town houses from the rear, it appears rather shabby. You imagine every room, every nook, know where every window opens, how much of the garden and river can be seen. Yet, it seems to distance, the desks, the chalk-dust, the waxed floors.

He is close by you again, sweet smelling, must be some male de-odorant. He asks, can we be seen, and you say why, what matter and you are aware of grammar again. He is not thinking of kissing you is he? And you focus on his beard and blush. If only he would and . . . but he is talking about the river, yes, why not you think, over the stile, into the wilderness of osiers.

You run, and you know it's reckless, he is there right behind you on the stile, you pause, his hand touches yours, so close, you feel your nipples stiffen, and he says, *amach leat* just into your ear, and you are over.

Running blindly through the osiers you rip a stocking, what matter, even the trickle of blood on your skin, he is trying to get ahead of you. On and on through the heavy smell of mud and weed, jumping stumps of trees, through a tangle of undergrowth, squelching from footfall to footfall. He sits on a tree-stump, you return, stand over him unsteadily, quick, flushed breathing, shreds of phrases mocking and urging. And you are off again dragging him by the hand, you stumble and fall into a swamp of flowering-reeds, the blackamoors, feel the dampness seep through your blouse, and along your thighs, he simply looks down and laughs.

You are up, ignoring the mud and the wet, you pull up a blackamoor and explode it on his head, the brown flower-dust showers into his hair and beard—*I dtigh diabhail leat!* The phrase lingers. He is ruffling his hair to brush off the clinging particles, he pauses, and comes to help remove the mud from your blouse, and as he extends his hands you feel your throat constrict, and through a sticky spittle you shoot phrases out, you drag them up out of some boiling confusion, red and hot. The intent and fluency of them surprises you for a second merely. He seems to recognise the breathless, perspiring and fierce attack. Your Irish is charged as it never was before. He grins. You turn.

From the stile the school looks strange, foreign. A light is switched on in the study, how small, how distant, and the eagerness to put on your house-shoes, take your seat, and sink into the atmosphere of little noises, whispers, and pen-scratches, has suddenly deserted you. You are outside in a hint of dew and a fading light.

Naming the Names

Anne Devlin

Abyssinia, Alma, Bosnia, Balaclava, Belgrade, Bombay.

It was late summer—August, like the summer of the fire. He hadn't rung for three weeks.

I walked down the Falls towards the reconverted cinema: "the largest second-hand bookshop in the world," the billboard read. Of course it wasn't. What we did have was a vast collection of historical manuscripts, myths and legends, political pamphlets, and we ran an exchange service for readers of crime, western and paperback romances. By far the most popular section for which Chrissie was responsible, since the local library had been petrol bombed.

I was late when I arrived, the dossers from St. Vincent de Paul hostel had already gone in to check the morning papers. I passed them sitting on the steps every working day: Isabella wore black fishnet tights and a small hat with a half veil, and long black gloves even on the warmest day and eyed me from the feet up; Eileen who was dumpy and smelt of meths and talcum powder looked at everyone with the sad eyes of a cow. Tom was the thin wiry one, he would nod, and Harry, who was large and grey like his overcoat, and usually had a stubble, cleared his throat and spat before he spoke. Chrissie once told me when I started working there that both of the men were in love with Isabella and that was why Eileen always looked so sad. And usually too Mrs. O'Hare from Spinner Street would still be cleaning the brass handles and finger plates and waiting like the others for the papers, so that she could read the horoscopes before they got to the racing pages. On this particular day, however, the brasses had been cleaned and the steps were empty. I tried to remember what it had been like as a cinema,

93

but couldn't. I only remember a film I'd seen there once, in black and white: A *Town like Alice*.

Sharleen McCabe was unpacking the contents of a shopping bag on to the counter. Chrissie was there with a cigarette in one hand flicking the ash into the cap of her Yves St. Laurent perfume spray and shaking her head.

She looked up as I passed: "Miss Macken isn't in yet, so if you hurry you'll be all right."

She was very tanned—because she took her holidays early—and her pink lipstick matched her dress. Sharleen was gazing at her in admiration.

"Well?"

"I want three murders for my granny."

I left my coat in the office and hurried back to the counter as Miss Macken arrived. I had carefully avoided looking at the office phone, but I remember thinking: I wonder if he'll ring today?

Miss Macken swept past: "Good morning, ladies."

"Bang goes my chance of another fag before break," Chrissie said.

"I thought she was seeing a customer this morning."

Sharleen was standing at the desk reading the dust-covers of a pile of books, and rejecting each in turn:

"There's only one here she hasn't read."

"How do you know?"

"Because her eyes is bad, I read them to her," Sharleen said.

"Well there's not much point in me looking if you're the only one who knows what she's read."

"You said children weren't allowed in there!" she said pointing to the auditorium.

"I've just given you permission," Chrissie said.

Sharleen started off at a run.

"Popular fiction's on the stage," Chrissie called after her.

"Children! When was that wee girl ever a child!"

"Finnula, the Irish section's like a holocaust! Would you like to do something about it. And would you please deal with these orders."

"Yes, Miss Macken."

"Christine, someone's just offered us a consignment of Mills and Boon. Would you check with the public library that they haven't been stolen."

"Righto," sighed Chrissie.

It could have been any other day.

Senior: Orangeism in Britain and Ireland; Sibbett: Orangeism in Ireland and Throughout the Empire. Ironic. That's what he was looking for the first time he came in. It started with an enquiry for two volumes of Sibbett. Being the Irish specialist I knew every book in the section. I hadn't seen it. I looked at the name and address again to make sure. And then I asked him to call. I said I thought I knew where I could get it and invited him to come and see the rest of our collection. A few days later, a young man, tall, fair, with very fine dark eyes, as if they'd been underlined with a grey pencil, appeared. He wasn't what I expected. He said it was the first time he'd been on the Falls Road. I took him round the section and he bought a great many things from us. He was surprised that such a valuable collection of Irish historical manuscripts was housed in a run-down cinema and said he was glad he'd called. He told me that he was a historian writing a thesis on Gladstone and the Home Rule Bills, and that he lived in Belfast in the summer but was at Oxford University. He also left with me an extensive booklist and I promised to try to get the other books he wanted. He gave me his phone number, so that I could ring him and tell him when something he was looking for came in. It was Sibbett he was most anxious about. An antiquarian bookseller I knew of sent me the book two weeks later, in July. So I rang him and arranged to meet him with it at a café in town near the City Hall.

He was overjoyed and couldn't thank me enough, he said. And so it started. He told me that his father was a judge and that he lived with another student at Oxford called Susan. I told him that I lived with my grandmother until she died. And I also told him about my boyfriend Jack. So there didn't seem to be any danger.

We met twice a week in the café after that day; he explained something of his thesis to me: that the Protestant opposition to Gladstone and Home Rule was a rational one because Protestant industry at the time—shipbuilding and linen—was dependent on British markets. He told me how his grandfather had been an Ulster Volunteer. I told him my granny's stories of the Black and Tans, and of how she once met de Valera on a Dublin train while he was on the run disguised as an old woman. He laughed and said my grandmother had a great imagination. He was fascinated that I knew so much history; he said he'd never heard of Parnell until he went to Oxford. And he pronounced "Parnell" with a silent "n," so that it sounded strange.

By the end of the month, the café owner knew us by sight, and the time came on one particular evening he arrived before me, and was sitting surrounded by books and papers, when the owner remarked, as the bell inside the door rang:

"Ah. Here's your young lady now."

We blushed alarmingly. But it articulated the possibility I had constantly been pushing to the back of my mind. And I knew I felt a sharp and secret thrill in that statement.

A few hours later, I stood on tiptoe to kiss him as I left for my bus—nothing odd about that. I often kissed him on the side of the face as I left. This time however I deliberately kissed his mouth, and somehow, the kiss went on and on and on; he didn't let me go. When I stepped back on to my heels again I was reeling, and he had to catch me with his arm. I stood there staring at him on the pavement. I stammered "goodbye" and walked off hurriedly towards the bus-stop. He stood on in the street looking after me—and I knew without turning round that he was smiling.

"Sharleen. *Murder in the Cathedral* is not exactly a murder story," Chrissie was saying wearily.

"Well, why's it called that then?"

"It's a play about—" Chrissie hesitated—"martyrdom!"

"Oh."

"This is just too, too grisly," Chrissie said, examining the covers. "Do they always have to be murders? Would you not like a nice love story?"

"She doesn't like love stories," Sharleen said stubbornly. "She only likes murders."

At that moment Miss Macken reappeared: "You two girls can go for tea now—what is that smell?"

"I can't smell anything," Chrissie said.

"That's because you're wearing too much scent," Miss Macken said. She was moving perfunctorily to the biography shelving, and it wasn't until I followed her that I became aware of a very strong smell of methylated spirits. Harry was tucked behind a newspaper drinking himself silly. He appeared to be quite alone.

"Outside! Outside immediately!" Miss Macken roared. "Or I shall have you forcibly removed."

He rose up before us like a wounded bear whose sleep we had disturbed, and stood shaking his fist at her, and, cursing all of us, Isabella included, he ran out.

"What's wrong with him?"

"Rejection. Isabella ran off with Tom this morning, and didn't tell him where she was going. He's only drowning his sorrows," Chrissie said. "Apparently they had a big win yesterday. Eileen told him they'd run off to get married. But they've only gone to Bangor for the day."

"How do you know this?"

"Eileen told Mrs. O'Hare and she told me."

"What kind of supervision is it when you two let that man drink in here with that child wandering around?" Miss Macken said, coming back from seeing Harry off the premises.

We both apologized and went up for tea.

There was little on the Falls Road that Mrs. O'Hare didn't know about. As she made her way up and down the road in the mornings on her way to work she would call in and out of the shops, the library, the hospital, until a whole range of people I had never met would enter my life in our tea room by eleven o'clock. I knew that Mr. Quincey, a Protestant, from the library, had met his second wife while burying his first at the City Cemetery one Saturday morning. I knew that Mr. Downey, the gatehousekeeper at the hospital, had problems with his eldest daughter and didn't like her husband, and I was equally sure that thanks to Mrs. O'Hare every detail of Chrissie's emotional entanglements were known by every ambulance driver at the Royal. As a result, I was very careful to say as little as possible in front of her. She didn't actually like me. It was Chrissie she bought buns for at tea time.

"Oh here! You'll never guess what Mrs. McGlinchy at the bakery told me—" she was pouring tea into cups, but her eyes were on us. "Wait till you hear—" she looked down in time to see the tea pouring over the sides of the cup. She put the teapot down heavily on the table and continued: "Quincey's being transferred to Ballymacarrett when the library's reopened."

"Och you don't say?"

"It's the new boss at Central—that Englishwoman. It's after the bomb."

"But sure that was when everybody'd gone home."

97

"I know but it's security, you know! She doesn't want any more staff crossing the peace line at night. Not after that young—but wait till you hear—he won't go!"

"Good for him."

"He says he's been on the Falls for forty years and if they transfer him now they might as well throw the keys of the library into the Republican Press Centre and the keys of the Royal Victoria Hospital in after them."

"He's quite right. It's ghettoization."

"Yes, but it's inevitable," I said.

"It's not inevitable, it's deliberate," said Chrissie. "It's exactly what the crowd want."

"Who?"

"The Provos. They want a ghetto: the next thing they'll be issuing us with passes to come and go."

"Security works both ways."

"You're telling me."

After that Chrissie left us to go down to the yard to renew her suntan. Mrs. O'Hare watched her from the window.

"She'd find the sun anywhere, that one." She turned from the window. "Don't take what she says too much to heart. She's Jewish, you know. She doesn't understand."

I was glad when she went. She always felt a bit constrained with me. Because I didn't talk about my love life, as she called it, like Chrissie. But then I couldn't. I never really talked at all, to any of them.

The room overlooked the rooftops and back yards of West Belfast. Gibson, Granville, Garnet, Grosvenor, Theodore, Cape, Kasmir.

Alone again I found myself thinking about the last time I had seen Jack. It was a long time ago: he was sitting at the end of the table. When things are not going well my emotions start playing truant. I wasn't surprised when he said:

"I've got an invitation to go to the States for six months."

I was buttering my toast at the time and didn't look up.

"I'm afraid I'm rather ambivalent about this relationship."

I started battering the top of my eggshell with a spoon.

"Finn! Are you listening?"

I nodded and asked: "When do you go?"

"Four weeks from now."

I knew the American trip was coming up.

"Very well. I'll move out until you've gone."

I finished breakfast and we spoke not another word until he dropped me at the steps of the bookshop.

"Finn, for God's sake! Get yourself a flat somewhere out of it! I don't imagine I'll be coming back." He said: "If you need any money, write to me."

I slammed the car door. Jack was always extremely practical: if you killed someone he would inform the police, get you legal aid, make arrangements for removing the body, he'd even clear up the mess if there was any—but he would never, never ask you why you did it. I'd thrown milk all over him once, some of it went on the floors and walls, and then I ran out of the house. When I came back he'd changed his clothes and mopped up the floor. Another time I smashed all the dinner dishes against the kitchen wall and locked myself in the bathroom, when I came out he had swept up all the plates and asked me if I wanted a cup of tea. He was a very good journalist, I think, but somehow I never talked to him about anything important.

Because Mrs. Cooper from Milan Street had been caught trying to walk out with sixteen stolen romances in a shopping bag and had thrown herself on the floor as if having a heart attack, saying: "Oh holy Jay! Don't call the police. Oh holy Jay, my heart," Chrissie forgot to tell me about the phone call until nearly twelve o'clock.

"Oh, a customer rang, he wanted to talk to you about a book he said he was after. Sibbett. That was it. You were still at tea." She said, "I told him we were open to nine tonight and that you'd be here all day."

For three weeks he hadn't rung. I only had to pick up the phone and ring him as I'd done on other occasions. But this time I hoped he would contact me first.

"Is something wrong?" Chrissie said.

"I have to make a phone call."

After that first kiss on the street, the next time we met I took him to the house, about ten minutes' walk from the park.

"When did you say your granny died?" he asked, looking with surprise around the room.

"Oh, ages ago. I'm not very good at dates."

"Well, you don't appear to have changed much since. It's as if an old lady still lived here."

He found the relics, the Sacred Heart pictures and the water font strange. "You really ought to dust in here occasionally," he said, laughing. "What else do you do apart from work in the bookshop?"

"I read, watch television. Oh, and I see Jack," I said quickly, so as not to alarm him.

"Good Lord. Would you look at that web; it looks like it's been there for donkeys!"

A large web attaching itself in the greater part to the geraniums in the window had spread across a pile of books and ended up clinging heavily to the lace curtains.

"Yes. I like spiders," I said. "My granny used to say that a spider's web was a good omen. It means that we're safe from the soldiers!"

"It just means that you never open the curtains!" he said, laughing. Still wandering around the small room he asked: "Who is that lady? Is she your grandmother?"

"No. That's Countess Markievicz."

"I suppose your granny met her on a train in disguise—as an old man."

"No. But she did visit her in prison."

He shook his head: "The trouble with you—" he began, then suddenly he had a very kind look in his eyes. "You're improbable. No one would ever believe me." He stopped, and began again. "Sometimes I think—" he tapped me on the nose—"you live in a dream, Finn."

And then he kissed me, and held me; he only complained that I was too quiet.

It was nine thirty when I left the building and shut it up for the night: Miss Macken had offered to drop me home as she was leaving, but I said I'd prefer to walk. There were no buses on the road after nine because a few nights before a group of youths had stoned a bus passing Divis flats, and the bus driver was hurt. The whole day was a torment to me after that phone call and I wanted to think and walk.

When I got to the park I was so giddy that I didn't care whether he came or not. My stomach was in a knot—and I realized it was because I hadn't eaten all day. The summer was nearly over—I only knew that soon this too would be over. I had kept my feelings under control so well—I was always very good at that, contained, very contained—so well, that I thought if he even touched me I'd tell him—Oh run! Run for your life from me! At least I didn't tell him that I loved him or anything like that. Was it something to be glad about? And suddenly there were footsteps running behind me. I always listened for footsteps. I'd walked all through those streets at night but I had never been afraid until that moment.

I suddenly started to run when a voice called out:

"Finn! Wait!" It was his voice.

I stopped dead, and turned.

We stood by the grass verge.

"Why didn't you ring me?" I asked, listlessly, my head down in case he saw my eyes.

"Because I didn't think it was fair to you."

"Fair?"

"Because, well—"

"Well?"

"I'm in England and you're here. It's not very satisfactory."

"I see."

"Look, there's something I should tell you. It's—Susan's been staying with us for the last three weeks."

"I see."

I couldn't possibly object since we both were supposed to have other lovers, there was no possibility of either of us complaining.

"But we could go to your place now if you like."

I was weakening. He stooped to kiss me and the whole business began as it had started. He kissed me and I kissed him and it went on and on.

"I was just getting over you," I said, standing up.

"I didn't know there was anything to get over. You're very good at saying nothing."

And before I could stop myself I was saying: "I think I've fallen in love with you."

He dropped his head and hardly dared look at me—he looked so pained—and more than anything I regretted that statement.

"You never told me that before," he said.

"I always felt constrained."

He began very slowly: "Look, there is something I have to say now. I'm getting married at the end of the summer." And more quickly. "But I can't give you up. I want to go on seeing you. Oh don't go! Please listen."

It was very cold in the park. I had a piercing pain in my ear because of the wind. A tricolour hung at a jaunty angle from the top of the pensioner's bungalow, placed there by some lads. The Army would take it down tomorrow in the morning. The swings, the trees and grass banks looked as thoroughly careworn as the surrounding streets.

Lincoln, Leeson, Marchioness and Mary, Slate, Sorella and Ward.

I used to name them in a skipping song.

The park had been my playplace as a child, I used to go there in the mornings and wait for someone to lead me across the road, to the first gate. Sometimes a passer-by would stop and take my hand, but most times the younger brother of the family who owned the bacon shop would cross with me.

"No road sense!" my grandmother used to say. "None at all."

In the afternoon he would come back for me. And I remember—

"Finn, are you listening? You mustn't stop talking to me, we could still be friends. I love being with you—Finn!"

I remember standing in the sawdust-filled shop waiting for him to finish his task—the smooth hiss of the slicing machine and the thin strips of bacon falling pat on to the greaseproof paper.

I began to walk away.

"Finn. I do love you." He said it for the first time.

I pulled up the collar of my coat and walked home without looking back.

It should have ended before I was so overcome with him I wept. And he said: What's wrong and took me and held me again.

It should have ended before he said: "Your soul has just smiled in your eyes at me—I've never seen it there before."

Before. It should have ended before. He was my last link with life and what a way to find him. I closed my eyes and tried to forget, all vision gone, only sound left: the night noises came.

The raucous laughter of late-night walkers; the huddle of tomcats on the backyard wall: someone somewhere is scraping a metal dustbin across a concrete yard; and far off in the distance a car screeches to a halt: a lone dog barks at an unseen presence, the night walkers pause in their walk past—the entry. Whose is the face at the empty window?—the shadows cast on the entry wall—the shape in the darkened door-way—the steps on the broken path—who pulled that curtain open quickly—and let it drop?

I woke with a start and the sound of brakes screeching in my ears—as if the screech had taken on a human voice and called my name in anguish: Finn! But when I listened, there was nothing. Only the sound of the night bells from St. Paul's tolling in the distance.

I stayed awake until daybreak and with the light found some peace from dreams. At eight o'clock I went out. Every day of summer had been going on around me, seen and unseen, I had drifted through those days like one possessed.

Strange how quickly we are reassured by ordinariness: Isabella and Tom, Harry and Eileen, waiting on the steps. And Mrs. O'Hare at the counter with her polishing cloth, and Miss Macken discussing her holiday plans with Chrissie. Externally at least, it could have been the same as the day before, yesterday—the day before I left him in the park. But I saw it differently. I saw it in a haze, and it didn't seem to have anything to do with me.

"The body was discovered by bin-men early this morning," Miss Macken said. "He was dumped in an entry."

"Oh, Finn, it's awful news," said Chrissie, turning.

"It's the last straw as far as I'm concerned," Miss Macken said.

"Mr. Downey said it's the one thing that turned him—he'll not be back to the Royal after this."

"We knew him," Chrissie said.

"Who?"

"That young man. The one who looked like a girl."

"The police think he was coming from the Falls Road," Miss Macken said.

"They said it was because he was a judge's son," said Chrissie.

"The theory is," said Miss Macken, "that he was lured there by a woman. I expect they'll be coming to talk to us."

"Aye, they're all over the road this morning," said Mrs. O'Hare.

"Where are their bloody black flags today?" said Chrissie with tears in her eyes. "Where are their bloody black flags today?"

At lunch time they came.

"Miss McQuillen, I wonder?"

A noisy row between Isabella and Eileen distracted me—Eileen was insisting that Isabella owed her five pounds.

"Miss McQuillen, I wonder if you wouldn't mind answering a few questions?"

"How well did you know . . . ?"

"When did you last see him?"

"What time did you leave him?"

"What exactly did he say?"

"Have you any connections with . . . ?"

Osman, Serbia, Sultan, Raglan, Bosnia, Belgrade, Rumania, Sebastopol.

The names roll off my tongue like a litany.

"Has that something to do with Gladstone's foreign policy?" he used to laugh and ask.

"No. Those are the streets of West Belfast."

Alma, Omar, Conway and Dunlewey. Dunville, Lady and McDonnell.

Pray for us. (I used to say, just to please my grandmother.) Now and at the hour.

At three o'clock in the afternoon of the previous day, a man I knew came into the bookshop. I put the book he was selling on the counter in front of me and began to check the pages. It was so still you could hear the pages turn: "I think I can get him to the park," I said.

Eileen had Isabella by the hair and she stopped. The policeman who was writing—stopped.

Miss Macken was at the counter with Chrissie, she was frowning— she looked over at me, and stopped. Chrissie suddenly turned and looked as well in my direction. No one spoke. We walked through the door on to the street.

Still no one spoke.

Mrs. O'Hare was coming along the road from the bread shop, she raised her hand to wave and then stopped.

"Quickly," the policeman said. "Headquarters. Turn the car."

"But we're due in Hastings Street at two," his driver said.

"Do as I say."

Harry had just tumbled out of the bookies followed by Tom.

They were laughing. And they stopped.

We passed the block where the babyclothes shop had been, and at the other end the undertakers: everything from birth to death on that road. Once. But gone now—just stumps where the buildings used to be—stumps like tombstones.

"Jesus. That was a thump in the stomach if ever I felt one," one policeman said to the other.

Already they were talking as if I didn't exist.

There were four or five people in the interview room.

A policewoman stood against the wall. The muscles in my face twitched. I put my hand up to stop it.

"Why did you pick him?"

"I didn't pick him. He was chosen. It was his father they were after. He's a judge."

"They?"

"I. I recognized the address when he wrote to me. Then he walked in."

"Who are the others? What are their names?"

"Abyssinia, Alma, Balaclava, Balkan."

"How did you become involved?"

"It goes back a long way."

"Miss McQuillen. You have a captive audience!"

"On the fourteenth of August 1969 I was escorting an English journalist through the Falls: his name was Jack McHenry."

"How did you meet him?"

"I am coming to that. I met him on the previous night, the thirteenth; there was a meeting outside Divis flats to protest about the police in the Bogside. The meeting took a petition to Springfield Road police station. But the police refused to open the door. Part of the crowd broke away and marched back down to Divis to Hastings Street police station and began throwing stones. There was trouble on the road all night because of roaming gangs. They stoned or petrol bombed a car with two fire chiefs and burned down a Protestant showroom at the bottom of Conway Street. I actually tried to stop it happening. He was there, at Balaclava Street, when it happened. He stopped me and asked me if I'd show him around the Falls. He felt uneasy being an Englishman and he didn't know his way around without a map. I said I'd be happy to."

"Were you a member of an illegal organization?"

"What organization? There were half a dozen guns in the Falls in '69 and a lot of old men who couldn't even deliver the *United Irishman* on time. And the women's section had been disbanded during the previous year because there was nothing for them to do but run around after the men and make the tea for the Ceilies. He asked me the same question that night, and I told him truthfully that I was not—then.

"On the evening of the fourteenth we walked up the Falls Road, it was early, we had been walking around all day, we were on our way back to his hotel—the Grand Central in Royal Avenue—he wanted to phone his editor and give an early report about events on the road. As we walked up the Falls from Divis towards Leeson Street, we passed a group of children in pyjamas going from Dover Street towards the flats. Further up the road at Conway Street a neighbour of ours was crossing the road to Balaclava Street with his children; he said he was taking them to Sultan Street Hall for the night. Everything seemed quiet. We walked on down Leeson Street and into town through the Grosvenor Road: the town centre was quiet too. He phoned his paper and then took me to dinner to a Chinese restaurant across the road from the hotel. I remember it because there was a false ceiling in the restaurant, like a sky with fake star constellations. We sat in a velvet alcove and there were roses on the table. After dinner we went back to his hotel and went to bed. At five o'clock in the morning the phone rang. I thought it was an alarm call he'd placed. He slammed down the phone and jumped up and shouted at me: 'Get up quickly. All hell's broken loose in the Falls!'

"We walked quickly to the bottom of Castle Street and began to walk hurriedly up the road. At Divis Street I noticed that five or six shops around me had been destroyed by fire. At Divis flats a group of men stood, it was light by this time. When they heard that Jack was a journalist they began telling him about the firing. It had been going on all night they said, and several people were dead, including a child in the flats. They took him to see the bullet holes in the walls. The child was in a cot at the time. And the walls were thin. I left him there at Divis and hurried up the road to Conway Street. There was a large crowd there as well, my own people. I looked up the street to the top. There was another crowd at the junction of Ashmore Street—this crowd was from the Shankill—they were setting fire to a bar at the corner and looting it. Then some of the men began running down the street and breaking windows of the houses in Conway Street. They used brush handles. At the same time as the bar was burning, a number of the houses at the top of the street also caught fire in Conway Street. The crowd were throwing petrol bombs in after they broke the windows. I began to run up towards the fire. Several of the crowd also started running with me.

"Then I noticed for the first time, because my attention had been fixed on the burning houses that two turreted police vehicles were slowly moving down the street on either side. Somebody shouted: 'The gun turrets are pointed towards us!' And everybody ran back. I didn't. I was left standing in the middle of the street, when a policeman, standing in a doorway, called to me: 'Get back! Get out of here before you get hurt.'

"The vehicles were slowly moving down Conway Street towards the Falls Road with the crowd behind them, burning houses as they went. I ran into the top of Balaclava Street at the bottom of Conway Street where our crowd were. A man started shouting at the top of his voice: 'They're going to fire. They're going to fire on us!'

"And our crowd ran off down the street again.

"A woman called to me from an upstairs window: 'Get out of the mouth of the street.' Something like that.

"I shouted: 'But the people! The people in the houses!'

"A man ran out and dragged me into a doorway. 'They're empty!' he said. 'They got out last night!' Then we both ran down to the bottom of Balaclava Street and turned the corner into Raglan Street. If he hadn't been holding me by my arm then that was the moment when I would have run back up towards the fires."

"Why did you want to do that? Why did you want to run back into Conway Street?"

"My grandmother lived there—near the top. He took me to Sultan Street refugee centre. 'She's looking for her granny,' he told a girl with a St. John's Ambulance armband on. She was a form below me at school. My grandmother wasn't there. The girl told me not to worry because everyone had got out of Conway Street. But I didn't believe her. An ambulance from the Royal arrived to take some of the wounded to the hospital. She put me in the ambulance as well. It was the only transport on the road other than police vehicles. 'Go to the hospital and ask for her there,' she said.

"It was eight o'clock in the morning when I found her sleeping in a quiet room at the Royal. The nurse said she was tired, suffering from shock and a few cuts from flying glass. I stayed with her most of the day. I don't remember that she spoke to me. And then about six I had a cup of tea and wandered out on to the road up towards the park. Jack McHenry was there, writing it all down: 'It's all over,' he said. 'The Army are here.' We both looked down the Falls, there were several mills that I could see burning: the Spinning Mill and the Great Northern, and the British Army were marching in formation down the Falls Road. After that I turned and walked along the Grosvenor Road into town and spent the night with him at his hotel. There was nowhere else for me to go."

I was suddenly very tired; more tired than on the day I sat in her room watching her sleep; more tired than on the day Jack left; infinitely more tired than I'd ever been in my life. I waited for someone else to speak. The room was warm and heavy and full of smoke. They waited. So I went on.

"Up until I met Jack McHenry I'd been screwing around like there was no tomorrow. I only went with him because there was no one else left. He stayed in Belfast because it was news. I never went back to school again. I had six O-levels and nothing else."

"Is that when you got involved?"

"No, not immediately. My first reaction was to get the hell out of it. It wasn't until the summer of '71 that I found myself on the Falls Road again. I got a job in the new second-hand bookshop where I now work. Or did. One day a man came in looking for something: 'Don't I know you?' he said. He had been a neighbour of ours at one time. 'I carried your granny out of Conway Street.' He told me that about eleven o'clock on the night of August fourteenth, there were two families trapped at the top of Conway Street. One of them, a family of eight, was escorted out of their house by a policeman and this man. Bottles and stones were thrown at them from a crowd at the top of the street. The policeman was cut on the head as he took the children out.

The other family, a woman, with her two teenage daughters refused to leave her house because of her furniture. Eventually they were forced to run down the back entry into David Street to escape. It was she who told him that Mrs. McQuillen was still in the house. He went back up the street on his own this time. Because the lights in our house were out he hadn't realized there was anyone there. He got scared at the size of the crowd ahead and was going to run back when he heard her call out: 'Finn! Finn!' He carried her down Conway Street running all the way. He asked me how she was keeping these days. I told him that she had recently died. Her heart gave up. She always had a weak heart.

"A few weeks later Jack took me on holiday to Greece with him. I don't really think he wanted me to go with him, he took me out of guilt. I'd rather forced the situation on him. We were sitting at a harbour café one afternoon, he was very moody and I'd had a tantrum because I found out about his latest girlfriend. I got up and walked away from him along the harbour front. I remember passing a man reading a newspaper at another café table, a few hundred yards along the quay. I saw a headline that made me turn back.

" 'The Army have introduced internment in Belfast,' I said.

"We went home a few days later and I walked into a house in Andersonstown of a man I knew: 'Is there anything for me to do?' I said. And that was how I became involved."

"And the man's name?"

"You already know his name. He was arrested by the Army at the beginning of the summer. I was coming up the street by the park at the time, when he jumped out of an Army Saracen and ran towards me. A soldier called out to him to stop, but he ran on. He was shot in the back. He was a well-known member of the Provisional IRA on the run. I was on my way to see him. His father was the man who carried my grandmother out of Conway Street. He used to own a bacon shop."

"Did Jack McHenry know of your involvement?"

"No. He didn't know what was happening to me. Eventually we drifted apart. He made me feel that in some way I had disappointed him."

"What sort of operations were you involved in?"

"My first job was during internment. Someone would come into the shop, the paymaster, he gave me money to deliver once a week to the wives of the men interned. The women would then come into the shop to collect it. It meant that nobody called at their houses, which were being watched. These were the old Republicans. The real movement was re-forming in Andersonstown."

"And the names? The names of the people involved?"

"There are no names. Only places."

"Perhaps you'll tell us the names later."

When they left me alone in the room I began to remember a dream I'd had towards the end of the time I was living with Jack. I slept very badly then, I never knew whether I was asleep or awake. One night it seemed to me that I was sitting up in bed with him. I was smoking, he was writing something, when an old woman whom I didn't recognize came towards me with her hands outstretched. I was horrified; I didn't know where she came from or how she got into our bedroom. I tried to make Jack see her but he couldn't. She just kept coming towards me. I had my back against the headboard of the bed and tried to fight her off. She grasped my hand and kept pulling me from the bed. She had very strong hands, like a man's, and she pulled and pulled and I struggled to release my hands. I called out for help of every sort, from God, from Jack. But she would not let go and I could not get my hands free. The struggle between us was so furious that it woke Jack. I realized then that I was dreaming. He put his hands on me to steady me: "You're having a fit. You're having a fit!" he kept saying. I still had my eyes closed even though I knew I was awake. I asked him not to let me see him. Until it had passed. I began to be terribly afraid, and when I was sure it had passed, I had to ask him to take me to the toilet. He never asked any questions but did exactly what I asked. He took me by the hand and led me to the bathroom where he waited with me. After that he took me back to bed again. As we passed the mirror on the bedroom door I asked him not to let me see it. The room was full of mirrors, he went round covering them all up. Then he got into bed and took my hand again.

"Now please don't let me go," I said. "Whatever happens don't let go of my hand."

"I promise you. I won't," he said.

But I knew that he was frightened.

I closed my eyes and the old woman came towards me again. It was

my grandmother; she was walking. I didn't recognize her the first time
because—she had been in a wheelchair all her life.

She reached out and caught my hands again and the struggle between
us began: she pulled and I held on. She pulled and I still held on.

"Come back!" Jack said. "Wherever you are, come back!"

She pulled with great force.

"Let go of me!" I cried.

Jack let go of my hand.

The policewoman who had been standing silently against the wall all
the time stepped forward quickly. When I woke I was lying on the
floor. There were several people in the room, and a doctor.

"Are you sure you're fit to continue?"

"Yes."

"What about the names?"

"My father and grandmother didn't speak for years: because he married my mother. I used to go and visit him. One night, as I was getting
ready to go there, I must have been about seven or eight at the time,
my grandmother said, 'Get your father something for his birthday for
me'—she handed me three shillings—'but you don't have to tell him
it's from me. Get him something for his cough.'

"At the end of Norfolk Street was a sweet shop. I bought a tin of
barley sugar. The tin was tartan: red and blue and green and black.
They wrapped it in a twist of brown paper. I gave it to my mother
when I arrived. 'It's for my Daddy for his birthday in the morning.'

"From whom?"

"From me."

"Can I look?"

"Yes."

"She opened the paper: 'Why, it's beautiful,' she said. I remember
her excitement over it. 'He'll be so pleased.' She seemed very happy.
I remember that. Because she was never very happy again. He died of
consumption before his next birthday."

"Why did you live with your grandmother?"

"Because our house was too small."

"But the names? The names of the people in your organization?"

"Conway, Cupar, David, Percy, Dover and Divis. Mary, Merrion,

111

Milan, McDonnell, Osman, Raglan, Ross, Rumania, Serbia, Slate, Sorella, Sultan, Theodore, Varna and Ward Street."

When I finished they had gone out of the room again. Only the policewoman remained. It is not the people but the streets I name.

The door opened again.

"There's someone to see you," they said.

Jack stood before me.

"In God's name, Finn. How and why?"

He wasn't supposed to ask that question. He shook his head and sighed: "I nearly married you."

Let's just say it was historical.

"I ask myself over and over what kind of woman are you, and I have to remind myself that I knew you, or I thought I knew you, and that I loved you once."

Once, once upon a time.

"Anything is better than what you did, Finn. Anything! A bomb in a pub I could understand—not forgive, just understand—because of the arbitrariness of it. But—you caused the death of someone you had grown to know!"

I could not save him. I could only give him time.

"You should never have let me go!" I said, for the first time in ten years.

He looked puzzled: "But you weren't happy with me. You didn't seem very happy."

He stood watching for a minute and said: "Where are you, Finn? Where are you?"

And getting no answer he said: "May your God forgive you."

The door closed. An endless vista of solitude before me, of sleeping and waking alone in the dark—in the corner a spider was spinning a new web. I watched him move from angle to angle. An endless confinement before me and all too soon a slow gnawing hunger inside for something—I watched him weave the angles of his world in the space of the corner.

Once more they came back for the names, and I began: "Abyssinia, Alma, Balaclava, Balkan, Belgrade, Bosnia," naming the names: empty and broken and beaten places. I know no others.

Gone and going all the time.

Redevelopment. Nothing more dramatic than that: the planners are our bombers now. There is no heart in the Falls these days.

"But the names? The names of the people who murdered him? The others?"

"I know no others."

The gradual and deliberate processes weave their way in the dark corners of all our rooms, and when the finger is pointed, the hand turned, the face at the end of the finger is my face, the hand at the end of the arm that points is my hand, and the only account I can give is this: that if I lived for ever I could not tell: I could only glimpse what fatal visions stir that web's dark pattern, I do not know their names. I only know for certain what my part was, that even on the eve, on such a day, I took him there.

Amnesty

Maeve Kelly

Every June when the peel were running, the sister was at the boat slip before seven in the morning. She moored the flat-bottomed craft to the one rotting post at the pier. The brother heaved out the sacks of fish, and rowed back to the island. She waited for the 7:15 bus. When it pulled up beside her the bus conductor said "Good catch?" and she either nodded or shook her head crossly. Not one word did she utter on the journey to town and the Fish Merchant. Nobody knew that the grimness of her silence was simply a necessary part of her life. It was her preparation for the tussle over pennies per pound with the Fish Merchant. This way she stored her mental energies, drew on her strength of will so that he might not "best" her. In the old days when calves were sold at the street fairs she had gone into training in the same way. The steely core of her will was not to be softened by pleasant talk of weather or crops or children. People who knew her were wise enough to leave her alone. They said, tolerantly, that after all what could you expect from a poor creature whose every day was spent in the company of a deaf mute. The brother had been born that way. Still, others said, it wouldn't hurt her to bid you the time of day at least. And how was it that on the way back from town she was all beams and friendly talk, like a long-playing record. You couldn't stop her. It was true. The bus conductor on the return journey could vouch for that.

"And wouldn't we all smile and talk," he said, "if we had the same bagful of money." And that only a fraction of what had been left in the bank.

Over the years, the mainlanders, by conjecture and rumour, built

114

up a picture for themselves of a woman who only smiled when she had money in her fist, of two strange islanders whose days were passed in silence and incomprehension. The mainlanders were not hostile to the sister. They pitied her and had regard for the way she cared for the dependent brother. They admired her energy and diligence in work. But who could be warmly friendly with such odd people? At times a farmer counting his cattle along the estuary shore would hear the sister's voice amplified by the water between them, as she talked to herself. It was strange to hear the words floating across, disembodied, and it was hard to put sense or meaning to them. She was once heard singing the Agnus Dei on a Sunday morning although it was many years since either the brother or herself had been to Mass. "Lamb of God, Who takest away the sins of the world, have mercy on us; Lamb of God, Who takest away the sins of the world, have mercy on us; Lamb of God, Who takest away the sins of the world, grant us peace." It was quite likely she sang it as a hymn of praise to her own flock of sheep. No one could imagine the sister petitioning God or man for anything, not even for peace.

When the peel were running they fished at the turn of the tide, she handling the boat, he watching the currents, signalling sharply with his arms when she was to turn, throwing out the great empty net. When it was too heavy for him, they both hauled in the shimmering young salmon, baulked of their urge to spawn, and emptied them onto the bottom of the boat. Some seasons the results were poor. That meant less fertiliser for the stony island, less carrying power for its cattle and sheep. The island parched easily. In dry summers it showed brown and singed when the mainland farms kept their glossy green. They never ventured out in rough weather, although they were occasionally caught by a storm. When that happened they hauled in the nets, fish or no fish, and headed for the nearest landing place. Where they fished, the river widened into the estuary and the cross winds were treacherous. Several foolhardy sailing boats were capsized or had their occupants thrown into the water by a suddenly swinging boom. But the brother and sister knew the river well. He in particular knew all its secret recesses, where the swans nested, where the mallard came to feed. In hard winters when the mud was frozen to silver and the river reflected the lavender and pink of evening skies, he would lie on his stomach in ditch or reedy bank, watching his breath vaporise as he waited for the wild geese to come in and feed. Although he could not hear their haunting lamenting cry, his heart would pound with excitement when they arrowed in and he felt the crack of his gun in the tissues of his own body. The sister was proud of his hunting skill and would clap him on the back when he brought home two rabbits, and pointed his forefinger triumphantly to tell her he'd got them with the one shot. His hunting was an expression of his masculinity but at the same time he had his sister's thrifty soul and he always killed for the pot. He never brought back a bird or beast disintegrating with the blast of pellets, so torn that the feathers could not be plucked neatly. And he would not do what tourists did—massacre birds when the weather had been bad for so long that they were starved into docility. He spat in contempt at the sight of such meanness.

The beauty of the island sometimes made the sister's eyes dreamy with wonder. Unlike people who are peasants by nature even if they are bred in the heart of a city, she took time to look at the shapes and colours of stones, at the rock plants adorning their hosts with varying hues of leaf and flower for each season, at the wild roses wreathing their way through love-locked hedges. Visitors came from the continent or England or America, with romantic notions of island life. She had once been offered big money for the island. If the bidder had tried to seduce her she could not have been more offended. "The cheek of it," she declared. "A stranger! The nerve of it. Looking to take the island off me. They can buy the whole country, but they won't buy my island." And she became even more possessive of it, appreciating its shape, the way it turned its cliff face to the rising sun so that the rocks sparkled in the morning, the way the hedges threw giant shadows onto the fields in early autumn evenings.

There was an ancient burial mound on the island, rising hump-backed near their house. Archaeologists came on a Sunday expedition with a group of town enthusiasts to look at it and make notes. She discouraged a repetition of the visit. It didn't matter if the mound was the property of the nation. It was on her island. No curiosity boxes would come peeking at her house, oohing and aahing at it, saying "How quaint. How charming. How adorable." She had to hide the brother from them. He had a habit of grinning foolishly at everyone so that they thought he was an idiot and treated him accordingly. That she would not allow. She scolded him for acting that way, but he grinned at her, screwing his finger into his forehead in mock madness and laughed his giggling, hiccoughing way. There were other times when he resented being frowned on and he scowled back at the mouth making angry shapes at him. Then he would go to the mound, picking at its protruding stones, grunting angrily. "Complaining about me to the dead," she thought. But if it gave him comfort, what of it? The ghosts of a thousand years could have no sting left. Maybe they liked being complained to. It was better than nothing. If the dead are not invoked they are deader than dead. A strange thought came to her. Was that why he was born? To be companion to the forgotten dead? And why was I born? To care for the companion to the forgotten dead? It was no more futile than any other occupation, she thought. For all occupations not geared to immediate need seemed futile to the sister. She had little more than contempt for the bus load of mainlanders, gossiping their way to the town shops. Spending their money on foolish dispensables. Clothes. She had the same coat for thirty years. Her skirts were made by a tailor in the town who also made the rough tweed suits the brother wore. In warm weather she sported a suit of the same material with a pink cotton blouse, her one concession to colour.

The peel were running hard this year. Prices came down because of the glut, but the full sacks gave her a feeling of accomplishment. The Fish Merchant's man was waiting at the bus stop near the shop, ready to lift off the bulging sacks. The Fish Merchant himself came out to greet her, rubbing his hands together to control his greed or to clear off the sweat between the two palms or to erase the smell of gutted fish before he took hers. She allowed him this brief familiarity but withdrew her hand from his at the first quick touch. His money will do me. Let him keep his handshaking for others like himself who value money for its own sake, never for the new net it might buy, or the maiden heifer or the sack of flour against the winter's greed. They began to haggle immediately.

"Can't sell them. No sale. No sale. Too many altogether," he told her. "You can put them in that big freezing place you have," she said, "and keep them for the Christmas parties your swanky customers give."

"Listen," he said. "The people who buy young salmon are just like you and me. They look for good value."

"And you'll give it to them, I suppose," she sniffed.

"Who else? Who else?" He spread his hands wide showing how vulnerably honest he was.

I know you, she thought. Full of town cunning. You'd take the eye out of my head and come back for the other one.

"Six shillings a pound," she said firmly.

"Six shillings! Six shillings!" He was shocked at her avarice. "Thirty pence for a pound. That's £2.40 for an eight-pounder."

"Don't try conning me with that new money. I can multiply with the best of them."

He grinned to himself. She looked suspiciously at him. He had a greasy fishmonger's mind. He caught the look and seized his slight advantage. "Why don't you go and buy yourself a new hat today? Or one of those nice new dresses the ladies all wear now."

Is he mocking me? She peered at his two big sleepy grey eyes. New customers were codded into thinking their blankness meant innocence and were afraid to hurt his feelings by watching the scales when he threw the fish in. "Lovely day, missus." His smile was a lure away from the quick deceiving hands. The smile and the eyes were of heaven. But not the voice, thought the sister. The voice has the gravelly meanness of your soul.

"Three shillings. Fifteen pence. That's all I can do for you now. Bring them somewhere else if you like." He turned his back on her. And she was caught. Filled with an old and terrible humiliation.

She was a young girl again, sent in to market with the new potatoes, her mother's bitter warning ringing in her ears. "Not a penny less than that, mind. Don't come back with less." It was the year of the war, 1939. The end of the hungry 'thirties when Dev had tried not to pay the British the land annuities on the re-possession of Irish farms and the British put an embargo on Irish cattle. At least the island could use the resources of the river, which was more than the mainlanders could do, but they all suffered the poverty of the time. Nineteen hundred and thirty-nine was the end of everything and the beginning of everything. It was the year her father and eldest brother were drowned.

At the market there was soft talk and grinning men, hands stretching hungrily for a good bargain. "You're a lovely girsha, God bless you. And are you the only one at home? You should have a pretty dress to wear." The market full—sweat, smells, laughing, teasing, arguing. "You should have a pretty dress to wear." Tinker talk. Was he a tinker? White teeth in a brown face and blue eyes laughing like the river on a sky blue day. "New potatoes. New potatoes," she called faintly, hoping he wouldn't hear, hoping he was deaf like her brother. But no. Not deaf and dumb. For then he'd never be able to say nice things to her.

"You're a lovely girl." All the old women. "Ah go on, love. Give us a bargain now. Such a lovely girl you are. Throw in a few for luck. There, good girl. Good girl. God bless you." Turning his back on her. Whistling between his teeth, laughing at her clumsy selling, laughing at the way she was cajoled out of her potatoes and paid little more than the price of the seed.

"Why don't you buy yourself a nice dress? A pretty girl like you should wear pretty clothes." Oh the madness of a June day, the last year of the hungry 'thirties. She took his hand and fell into the clamour of the town. In another world was the quiet island and the threatening river, and the plaintive curlew. But the town received the river. It swallowed up the river, wrapped itself around her, cosseted her with bridges, arched in loveliness. It twisted round her curves, locked her into canals, buried her in slobland. It taunted her with garbage, sent the gulls screaming while they scavenged. It used her and abused her, then turned its back upon her when angry and swollen she beat at its doors.

It was late that mad June day, when the sister rode out of town on her bicycle, her cheeks the colour of the new pink dress, her eyes blazing with memories of a squandered day, her pockets and baskets empty. Her mouth still tasted the ice cream and the kisses, the kisses and the ice cream, the ginger ale and kisses, the kisses and the ginger ale. Her heart fluttered like a pigeon caught between her ribs. At the pier the brother was waiting anxiously with the boat. He mouthed at her fussily, but she laughed and showed him her new dress. He touched it delightedly, rubbed the material between his fingers, traced with his small finger the pattern of butterflies and flowers, the lace edging on the collar and bodice. He let his breath out in wonder, then counted on his fingers, gesticulating at her to know how much money she had brought home. She shrugged. Ooh. He sucked in his breath and clapped a hand over his mouth. Only then did she understand the calamity. Not once in the whole lovely day had she anticipated her homecoming. Wearily she climbed into the boat and let him drag the bicycle in after her. The tide was ebbing and she let him push the boat by himself, over the mud, until it eased into the water. Mumbling angrily, he took the oars.

The sister never forgave her mother for the stinging slap on her face and for the name she called her. She forgave her the ranting and wailing and mourning over the wasted day, the baskets of new potatoes gone and nothing to replace them. But she never forgave the slap or the word. She never forgave the priest's visit and his soft but accusing questioning. And she never forgot the mother's hard looks at her in the months that followed, or the relief in her eyes when the flesh fell off her and she grew thin. Flat as a board she had remained for the rest of her life. The brother, although he rescued the dress and coaxed her, imploring her with big eyes and hands to wear it for him, could not soften the humiliation. That was the birth of her steel core.

To the Fish Merchant's back she said, "I'll take my fish and I'll empty them into the docks." He turned and she deliberately began to drag the first sack along the pavement. A boy came up. "Sell us a fish, missus?" "I'll give you one," she said, "if you run around town and let everyone know I'm selling salmon at fifty pence apiece."

"Stop, stop," shouted the Fish Merchant. "I was only joking. I'll give you five bob." She ignored him. "Six. Six. I'll give you the six."

"You're too late," she said, "you're too late."

"I'll have the Guards on you," he frothed. "It's not legal."

"You do that," she glared, "and you'll never get another of my salmon."

"There are others," he said. "You're not the only crazy eejit fishing on the river."

"I know the others," she answered. "Some nights when the peel are running they'll be slopping pints in a public house and you'll be waiting a long time for your silver kings."

"Isn't seven enough for you so?" He was pathetic in defeat. But she needed him too. "You can afford it," she said. "And remember not to drive me too hard the next time. I'll take seven today and we'll start afresh tomorrow. Or will you want them tomorrow?"

"Bring them in as usual," he said sourly, turning away from the blazing eyes. One day, he thought in satisfaction, the old hag will kill herself with work.

The sister was exhausted. She had come straight in off the river. They had started fishing at four. She smiled grimly. It had been a profitable night. She crossed the street to the bank, ignoring the frantic horns and infuriated drivers. At the bank she stopped for a fraction of a second before hurrying by. She walked past the country shop where they sold boots and thick trousers and check shirts. At Regina's boutique she stood and gazed in at the mannequins who stared haughtily over her head with their plastic eyes, their nylon hair brightly blonde or seductively red, their slender limbs thrown elegantly forward, their hands curving in a gesture of disdain. A faint smile dimmed the fire in her eyes. A faint hungry tenderness warmed her. She hurried inside. The salesgirls looked at her, sure she would turn around when she realised she was in the wrong shop.

"I want a pink dress," she said, "with flowers and things on it."

"Is it for yourself?" one of them asked, coolly surprised.

"Who else?" she replied. "Myself of course. One of those maxis if you please. I don't hold with people showing off their ugly knees and thighs. And mine," she glared defiantly at their exposed legs, "are no worse than most." That'll stop their sniggering, she thought.

"Lady Muck come to town," muttered one, but the kinder of the two came forward. "Let me help you." The rails of dresses were dazzling. "Lovely, aren't they?" smiled the girl.

"Lovely, lovely, lovely," said the sister. "Have you e'er a one with butterflies on it?"

"I don't think so," said the girl. They searched in vain.

"Butterflies and flowers I want," said the sister. The girl thought for a moment. "Why don't you buy a butterfly brooch and wear it with a flower dress? Would that do?"

"It's an idea. You're a clever one to think it. I'll take that dress if it's the right size."

"Well it's my size," the girl said doubtfully. The sister looked at her round limbs and curving breasts and sighed.

"I used to be that size once, and that shape. And I'd say my size is the same."

The girl put the dress into a white bag with the word REGINA printed in blue and a silver crown over the R. At a nicknack shop the sister bought a plastic butterfly which she placed in the bag with the dress. She had a cup of coffee in the hotel before doing the rest of her shopping and caught the bus home at midday.

The brother was waiting as usual. His eyes gleamed with excitement when he saw the bag. "A new dress I got. For myself." He giggled and pointed to himself, shaking his head. He could read her lips but a lot of the time she didn't bother facing him or was in too much of a hurry. "It's a pink one. And look." She brought out the butterfly brooch. He held it in his palm as if it was a real one ready to lift its wings for flight. His eyes grew sad. She knew he was remembering the June day. She gave him a new pipe and some dainty cut tobacco in a box. He pulled

121

at the oars joyously and they turned for the island. Turf smoke was rising from the chimney straight up to the blue sky. The river was like a looking glass, cut easily by oars. The island was an emerald rising from its blue setting. The brother was making his happy noise sounds. His singing. On the upland fields the sheep were scattered like white beetles. In the meadow the grass was almost seeding.

The sister knew only the one kind of defeat and that had nothing to do with ideas. If she was a country woman conquered by town, she did not know it. If she was provincial conquered by Dublin she did not know that either. If she was old Gael defeated by foreign money and foreign customs she knew nothing at all of that. Defeat was ill health, hunger, the loss of the island, death. Yet she had smelled defeat at the turn of the Fish Merchant's back. The pink dress was not now a rent flag thrown on a burial mound. It was a song of triumph, a declaration of peace. "I'll wear it to Mass on Sunday," she said. "And I'll pray for Ma's soul."

Forgiveness was a sweetness that smoothed out lines and quenched burning looks. It eased her drying bones and lifted the corners of her mouth.

A Family Picnic

Ita Daly

Mary Johnson opened her eyes to a room filled with yellow sunshine. Although the curtains were drawn, they hardly affected the light, for they were made of such thin stuff. In fact, they were not made of curtain material at all but of some summer dress material that her mother had bought at a sale in Clerys years ago when Mary was very small. They had been very carefully lined, however, and so hung properly. If Mary wished to get out of bed and walk across the still cold linoleum, she would see her mother's careful hand-stitching all around the inside of the curtains. They had never been able to afford a machine, so curtains had to be made by hand, sheets mended; even when Mary and her brothers were children, dresses and shirts had been hand sewn.

Mary stretched and yawned. Then she jumped out of bed, rushed over to the window and tore the curtains apart. The room was transfused with a strange luminosity. It was no longer her room with its shabby familiarity. It had become an abstraction in brightness and warmth. She stretched once more and, picking up the ends of her nightdress, stood on her toes and danced round and around in the sun. She danced her way to the window and collapsed in front of it, resting her chin on the ledge. She looked out into the garden. A cat sat licking itself, half in shade, half in sunlight. A white butterfly fluttered around a dog-daisy before coming to rest on its yellow middle. The cat looked at it for a moment and then, indifferently, went back to cleaning its whiskers.

"We're going on a picnic today," sang Mary, "a pic-nic, pic-nic, pic-nic." The words died away and faded into the heat of the morning outside. It was all so incredibly still.

Down in the kitchen, her father sat, stolidly eating his egg. Her mother bustled around, polishing his shoes, drinking a cup of tea, distractedly trying to think of the million and one things that had to be done. You couldn't leave a house, not even for a day, without seeing to so many things first. Still, it was a nice day for their outing.

"Morning Ma, Morning Daddy." Mary sat down beside her father. She poured herself a cup of tea but then jumped up again and leaned across to the window. "Let's open it," she said. "Why don't you open it and let in all that sunshine. You're missing it."

Her father grunted, but didn't move away as the sashless window banged open and warmth wafted into the little room. He continued to scrape at his egg-shell in silence.

"No, no egg, Ma. I couldn't. You know I never eat eggs when it's this hot. I'll tell you what—hard-boil it and we'll take it with us. Then it won't be wasted."

Reluctantly her mother put the egg back into the saucepan and onto the gas stove.

"I wish you would, Mary. I wish you'd eat properly," she said. "People like you who do so much brain work, they need proper nourishment. You'll end up with a nervous break-down if you go on like that. People do, you know, when they don't eat properly."

"Now, mother, we've had all this out before. You know I'm perfectly capable of dealing with my job—it's not all that taxing. You just think because I'm the only woman there that I must be killed trying to keep up. Anyway, I'm on holidays as from today. No brain work for a fortnight."

Her mother smiled at her. Indeed she *was* able to keep up. Brains to burn. Always had. And what a lovely girl she was. Her girl. Always happy. She had never caused her parents a day's worry in her life. Not like the other two. Not like them. But she mustn't think of them today. They were all going on a picnic and the sun was shining. And if she didn't hurry they'd be late.

"Hurry up, Daddy, and finish your breakfast," she said, taking the tea-pot away. "We'll have to be off soon."

They bundled into the little car, squeezing parcels and shopping bags where they could. Mr. Johnson had to bend his head in the back, the roof was so low. "God," he said, "these seats would skin you— they're scorching." Mary laughed at him. "Stop complaining, Daddy. Think of Ma and myself with no trousers to protect us."

124

Her mother sat beside her, rigid and straight-backed. She didn't think she'd ever feel at home in a car. Maybe it was because they'd never had one themselves. But Mary was great with the lifts. She never let you walk anywhere.

The road seemed still asleep as they set out. Nothing moved in the sun. The little houses lay dusty and still. No one was about, except for a few children, and even they hung limply over railings. It was already too hot to play.

"Now, we're not going to the sea. I've decided against it." Mary's voice was imperious. "It will be horrible on a day like this. All the trippers will be out in force, and nothing but mothers, babies and transistors everywhere. It would ruin the day. But I know just the place and I won't tell you. I'll keep it as a surprise. You just won't believe it when we get there. It is absolutely beautiful—much better than a crowded beach. I can't wait to show you."

Mary's mother looked a little wistful. She had been hoping that Mary would say they'd go to the sea. It was years since she'd been to the seaside. Not since Mary and the others were small. Then on a good Sunday she used to take them all off, with bottles of milk and sandwiches, and they'd spend the whole day on the beach. Mary used to love it in those days. How she used to enjoy paddling, screaming and running away from the big waves. And Daddy loved to have the house to himself. He'd go to bed with the papers. "I'll have a bit of peace and quiet now," he used to say. Still Mary was probably right. It would be very noisy and crowded today. She supposed it was because she herself so seldom went out, so seldom saw anybody except the family, that she liked a bit of noise and excitement. But Mary was right. And she was taking after her father in that respect.

They drove through the city streets. You could almost see the heat rising from the pavements. The odd messengerboy who passed looked as if he must fall off his bike, so slowly, slowly did he turn the pedals. People dragged their feet, knowing it was going to be another scorcher. Would this heatwave never end? As they crossed over O'Connell Bridge, the water of the river seemed to have completely dried up. All that remained was a sort of oozy brown mud. They closed the car windows against the rancid smell of decay.

"Didn't I tell you," said Mr. Johnson, from behind. "This weather is unnatural. We were never meant to have heat like this in Ireland. Look at that river, and the smell of it."

Mary looked in the driving mirror and shook her head at him. "You're starting again, Daddy," she said. "You know perfectly well the Liffey always stinks to high heaven. We need more sunshine here, not less. People open up in the sun. We bloom—don't we, Ma? We're blooming at this very minute."

They opened the windows again and sat back. Nobody said anything. It was too hot for talking. Besides, there was no need to talk: the happiness was palpable inside the little car. Mary's father forgot about the Liffey. Suddenly he could see them all, sitting there on their way to the picnic—blooming. They were like geraniums on the kitchen window-sill at home. The words Mary thought up—the ideas she got. Blooming.

Soon they were out in the country, travelling along a narrow road. There were tall thick hedges on each side, their tops far taller than the roof of the car. The light was coming to them as through a filter—a cool, green filter. How restful it was after the glare of the streets. Eye muscles could relax, eyes could open fully once again and gaze at all that greenery. Mary felt as if she could drink it. They could not see the countryside beyond the hedges; they were enclosed in a dark green tunnel that went on and coolly on. Occasionally the sunlight came through and dazzled them for a second. It was nice to be reminded that outside, just beyond the trees, the sun was blazing fiercely down.

"Now," said Mary, "you must both close your eyes, and don't open them till the car stops. No cheating, Daddy. I've a great surprise for you."

The car stopped and Mr. and Mrs. Johnson opened their eyes and the three of them looked out together. They had pulled up beside an iron gate. The gate was bolted, but beside it was a turnstile. And beyond the turnstile, stretching out in front of them, was a huge, green field. It lay there, amazingly even and flat, and intensely green. They had never seen a field as green before. It was like an enormous table-cloth spread out for them. There were splashes of yellow here and there where little clumps of buttercups grew. In one corner, resting in the shade of some oaks, three or four red cows lay, chewing lazily. And, right at the edge of the field, as if across an emerald piazza, the still soaring ruins of a Gothic monastery rose into the sky. Beyond the monastery, through one of the arched doorways, they could see something shining in the sunlight. Could it be—it must be—a river.

They started across the field, silent and in single file. Awe-struck, one or other of them stumbled occasionally as their eyes discovered some new wonder. They made their way through the ruined cloisters, the gravel crunchy under their feet. "We'll explore it later, but first we'll find a place to eat," said Mary, leading them round the back. Her father smiled as he looked around him. "Begod, but these monks knew where to live—what?"

The ground sloped to the river and the river curved round the monastery, almost like a moat. There was no shade of any kind, only the long shadows cast by the ruined buildings. They sat down against the wall, glad of the comparative coolness, but feeling the warmth of the old stone against their backs. Mrs. Johnson, despite the fortnight of drought, spread rugs beneath them, and warned them against rheumatism. "That river is like tinfoil," said Mr. Johnson, and indeed, it shone so brightly that it hurt your eyes to look at it. Beyond, the land stretched flat and treeless, not a house in sight anywhere. The silence enfolded them, and the low regular murmur from the river only served to emphasise the stillness of the day.

"I wonder could you drink that water? It makes me thirsty just to look at it," Mr. Johnson asked.

"No water for you today," replied Mary. "I've something much better. Now leave it all, Ma, I'll do the unwrapping. This is still part of the surprise, you know. I've gone to a lot of trouble over the picnic— I always think they can be miserable affairs if you don't do them properly."

As she talked, she began to draw things out from the various bags. The table-cloth was unfolded and spread on the grass. It too caught the sun. "It looks like a white house in Andalucia,"—Mary had been to Spain the previous summer. Glasses, plates, knives and forks were all spread out. Mrs. Johnson thought that she had never seen a picnic like this before. What were the glasses for? And how did you eat sandwiches with a knife and fork?

"No soggy sandwiches for us," said Mary, unwrapping a chicken. Then she took out a long package and began to undo it. Layer after layer of paper, cardboard, straw were peeled off, and a slim bottle of wine at last emerged. "Ice cold," she said, "I got the man in the shop to keep it in the fridge till the last minute, and then I insulated it like this myself." She laughed across at her mother. "Don't worry, Ma, I didn't forget you." She took out a flask. "Tea. Good strong tea, and all for yourself—Daddy and I'll have the wine." She spread out everything on the table-cloth in front of them. The skin of the chicken was brown and crisp and there were red tomatoes and golden oranges and a potato salad in a creamy mayonnaise sauce.

Mary served the three of them. Gratefully, her mother drank some tea. How refreshing tea was on a day like this—much better than any of those cold drinks. And certainly a lot better than wine. Wine always made her thirsty and gave her a headache. But this tea—she could drink the whole flask and no bother. She poured some more into her cup and looked across at her daughter and husband. She didn't want to talk; just to sit there and feel the happiness seeping into her body. She hadn't felt like this for years. All her aches and worries seemed to have disappeared, and sitting there in that green field she felt like a girl again. She lay back in the sunshine. She remembered her own home. She remembered the times she used to bring bottles of tea and currant bread to her father and brothers as they worked on the hay during the long summer days. Sometimes, if the weather had been very bad, she would have to help too, but mostly, with five brothers her father had plenty of labour, and all she had to do was bring the tea out to them at one and again at five. They'd all sit down in the meadow together, with the smell of the new-mown hay drugging their senses. They'd eat and drink and talk a little, and her father would give her a penny sometimes, for all her hard work, as he said. Tea and bread had never tasted the same since. The very taste of the world had changed. Those summer dreams had never been fulfilled; not that she could remember what it was she had dreamt, sitting beside her father and brothers in the sweet-smelling meadow. But she remembered the magic, the surging excitement as the world opened up before her; the aching happiness as she stood on the threshold of adventure and romance.

Foolishness. Such foolishness. The world had not opened up. It had shrunk, until it was encompassed by a small terrace house in the south suburbs of Dublin. Her husband was a man who came home in the evenings, too tired to talk. He sat in his shirt sleeves before the fire and read the evening paper, nodding over it, until at about half nine or ten he would drag himself to bed. This tiredness increased as the years went on, and when he retired from his job, five years ago, she thought he must have lost the habit of speech. And the boys—her two sons, where were they now? She had no idea.

But today the magic had come back. Today, she was a girl again.

"I think I'll get Mary to do my hair for me next week," she mused. "And Daddy and myself should go away for a few days when Mary is on holidays. It would do him good. But he looks well—how well he looks today. A handsome man. What a marvellous day."

"Hey, Ma, wake up. You're miles away from us. Daddy and I are going to rinse these plates out in the river. Your day off. Mustn't do anything at all." What a strange woman her mother was, always going off into some dream world of her own. Mary remembered even as a child, her mother's eyes would sometimes stop seeing her and she would be off somewhere else. This used to infuriate her—that she couldn't follow where her mother went. But now she liked it. She liked this dream mother who seemed so much younger than herself in many ways. Her mother would always have that vulnerable air about her, she realised, looking back at her sitting there, playing with a blade of grass.

Mary handed her father a plate which she had just rinsed. How he had enjoyed himself today. He reminded her of when she was young, and he would take her to Mass on Sunday, holding her hand tightly, and telling her stories of his own childhood. Her parents. She felt close to them again; today they were a family.

They felt so tired when they began to prepare for the journey home. The sun was still shining, although it was after five o'clock. The car, which Mary had parked in the shade, was cool as they sat into it. What an effort it was to keep one's eyes open, listening to the throb of the engine. "Hey, Ma," Mary said, "say something or I'll fall asleep over the wheel." But the conversation petered out, as they sat there enjoying the sensation of tired, relaxed bodies, moving imperceptibly with the motion of the car. If only the journey could go on and on forever.

Back in the house, Mrs. Johnson said she would make some more tea for them. "No thanks," said Mary, "I couldn't eat or drink another thing. I think I'll go up to bed, even though it's still early. I can read for a while." Her mother kissed her. "Do, Mary," she said, "off you go, you must be tired. What a marvellous day. Daddy and I certainly enjoyed ourselves." She paused. "You're so good to us, such a good daughter." Quickly she turned her face away and began to busy herself with the crockery.

Mary didn't say good-night and she didn't look at them. She ran up the narrow stairs and into her room. Closing the door behind her she walked over to the window. The sky was darkening outside and in the distance she thought she could hear the first rumblings of thunder. She placed her car keys on the dressing table and noticed that she was still holding the little posy she had gathered earlier. Wild woodbine and scarlet poppies. Already they were beginning to wither.

Outside, the garden was now in complete darkness. Firmly she drew the curtains together and switched on the light. The day was over.

Made in Heaven

Maura Treacy

No. There was neither smell nor sound nor sight of fish frying. Three speckled trout he had caught the evening before in an unpremeditated sortie, his first in years, on the preserved waters of the Crainsfort demesne.—You never lost it: he crooned his admiration to himself and lingered for another look before he tucked the newspaper around them and laid them on the floor of the van.

He was asleep before Rose came home, and since she was asleep when he was going out to work, he left a note for her, instructing her in the blandest terms he could command in the knack of gutting trout. Now he found his note, folded over and over and burnt at one end, lying in an ashtray. The kitchen was empty. The kettle was not boiling. It hadn't even been filled. He heard the occasional soft fall of unhurried footsteps on the bedroom floor above him. "Rose!" He called her again, but it was more a lamentation than a summons and only he heard it. He searched his pockets for a match to light the gas. He put on the kettle, reached for the pan but left it where it was and went in search of the trout. He tried the fridge and every press, and stripped at last of all illusion, he opened the back door. The dented chassis of a Hillman Hunter which he had long since pillaged of everything for which he might find a use or a buyer, mouldered in the long grass, a scene of neglect to which he customarily blinded himself. From the houses on either side he heard in stereo effect the same radio commercial; whiffs of cooking flirted for recognition; plates and cutlery clinked on a table; a saucepan clanged on a draining board.

His emergence disturbed three cats who were gathered around his overturned rubbish-bin. The fattest of them, new to the neighbour-

131

hood, darted for cover. The others, though tensed for flight, gnawed ravenously up to the last minute. They saw him grab the lid, swing it, and even as it hurtled across the yard and crashed into the side of the car, they were safely on the far side and sorting the spoils they had grabbed. Tim looked down at the mangled remains of the smallest trout. Scraps of newspaper still clung to it. He held his breath to quell the storm of rage, frustration and hunger that threatened to rip apart the fabric of his reason. He went inside and slammed the door and at the sound the new cat came back to her pickings.

Rose's influence on him, it seemed to Tim, amounted to three layers deposited over the years on his consciousness; and it was only at odd moments when in a wishful, aggrieved mood he began chipping away at the accretions of more recent times, that he would glimpse again that first phase and realise the tender, undefended innocence of it all.

Eleven years ago there he was drowning in happiness, laughing with Rose at the extent and diversity of her ineptitude, still chortling over her mistakes as he recounted them at home. "Lord save us, Timmy," his mother would chide him, "you'd want to get something right to eat, whatever else. You can't do a day's work on shop cakes and tea. It's not what you were used to in this house, I can tell you." She would find more and more excuses for Tim to call home, and no matter the hour, she would cook something for him. She disregarded her other daughter-in-law, her eldest son's wife, who would clump around the kitchen, tidying, dusting and polishing everything around her feasting brother-in-law, until he was an isolated blot on the immaculate face of the kitchen. Tim's clear blue unselfconscious eyes would, from time to time, deplore the lack of appeal she had for him as she loomed above him and flicked a dead fly off the windowsill, looking at him as if he'd be the next to go.

Nine years ago his mother had died suddenly.

He sat at the table one evening in early summer and waited for Rose to present him with his supper. He kept his face turned towards the window and looked at the houses on the far side, with their laboriously cultivated flower gardens. Many of the tenants grew vegetables in the plots at the back and a few of them kept hens. Many of the houses had Bed And Breakfast signs of wrought-iron or wood erected at the front gate. Mrs. Nagle, three doors down, kept four lodgers and provided dinners every day for several non-residents. Her next door neighbour was a dressmaker. All the while he contemplated the enterprise of his neighbours he was aware of Rose foostering at the new gas-cooker behind him. The television set was in the corner at the other end of the table. In the blank screen he could see her reflection and, dim though it was, it conveyed the essence of her incompetence. More than the mess she was creating and the awkward inexperienced way she approached the most elementary tasks, what really goaded him was her attitude, her refusal to see the importance of what she had to do, her barely-contained giddiness. At any moment her whim of pandering to him was liable to break up. She'd make a brazen childish face behind his back and stick out her tongue at him. She might start giggling or she could throw a tantrum and tell him to go to hell and get his own tea and what was more to take that cooker back to wherever he had got it, she didn't want a heap of metal taking up space. His imagination zig-zagged over the range of possible reactions, not one of which he would wish to precipitate. He tried to close his mind to her methods, to spirit himself forward to the moment when she would set his supper before him. But even as he lured his thoughts through meandering paths of emollient reasoning the pan of gravy hissed, suddenly, viciously, like a nest of vipers disturbed. At the same instant an egg hit the floor and splashed open. Rose scrabbled after it with a spoon. He saw the covert look she darted in his direction as she did so and he jettisoned all his extenuating arguments. "Sufferinjaysus, woman," he roared as he threw down the knife and fork. "Could you not fry a simple bloddy egg, even. Look at that for a mess, you . . . you slob-brachaun." He caught his breath and waited for the sky to fall in. "Go, clean it up this instant, before I . . ." Still crouching, she scuttled out by him to the scullery. She brought back a dish-cloth and lobbed it down on the whole broken egg. His stomach surged. A thousand images crashed together in his mind—his mother in a similar moment scooping up the broken egg, putting it in the gallon for the hens, wiping the floor clean in a few smooth strokes, washing her hands and resuming her work—memories of the first two years of marriage unclouded by responsibility. He remembered Rose, one sunny bank-holiday morning, sitting outside on the low wall of the garden. She had been wearing a yellow dress and white sandals. Young and carefree, she chatted with the older women from the houses on either side. He recalled the feeling he had had at that moment, seeing himself suddenly as part of the backbone of hard-working men which sustained this cosy community of laughing, idle women. And then there was the unarticulated decline of the past few weeks.

In the instant in which he raised his hand and bore it down so that it slapped the side of her head and he felt the high cheekbone, the cool rim of her ear, the smooth hard stone of the ear-ring and a strand of her hair under his fingers, he was borne up by a surge of pride. He'd make her change her ways, learn to cook and sew and keep the house as other women did. She couldn't stay young for ever, she must know that; and her looks would fade. The honeymoon was over. A new phase was about to begin, one that could be just as good in its own way. As he drew his hand away from her face, he thought of this as a benediction on her, the stroke on the cheek that confirmed her, fitted her for a new mature role. He felt a kind of serene sanctity flow through him. They'd buy a cookery book. He'd ask Nick's wife for some of his mother's recipes. Mrs. Kearns next door would help Rose through the early stages. He'd be patient and together they'd go forward.

She was still kneeling and he reached down to raise her up. She looked up at him. Her face was pale and taut with a kind of spirituality. "Rose, girl," he said, "this is only the beginning. . . ." Before his eyes, the colour flowed back into her face. Slowly she straightened up, pushing his helping hands off her arms. "Tim Effing Dunphy," she whispered, almost to herself, as if she had difficulty in recognising him. She repeated it in her most refined enunciation. He gaped at her and she flicked his face with the egg-smeared cloth which had been already wet and filthy. She flicked it again and he backed away and she came towards him, flicking it in his face, left and right, in short vicious insulting swipes as they two-stepped around the room until he stumbled back against the cabinet. Despite his shielding arms, she slapped him around the head and neck while he tried not to absorb the smell and smear of the cloth. He was helpless and her words were like a message meant for someone else. "If you think you can start knocking me around . . ."

"But, Rose, for the love o' . . ." But as he tried to correct her misunderstanding of his intentions, a corner of the cloth trailed across his mouth and he buried his face in the crook of his arm.

"You lousy little rat you."

He managed to slink away into the scullery and close the door between them. When all was quiet, he moved out. In the mirror beside the window he looked at his defiled face and his eyes regarded their reflection as if they would never close again.

That was the beginning of the second phase, an era of mutinous silences broken by frequent bickering, some violence and rare interludes of harmony. But the trend of their relationship was downward until at some stage it had come to rest on a plateau of mutual ironic toleration. From there it could lift off for brief flights, when they lost sight of the disparity of their expectations and shared moments of near happiness, but it had found its permanent base to which it always returned. He might have left her but Damien had been born then and he could not bear to go. A year later Val was born. And yet, it seemed to him in retrospect that apart from the gratifying fact of their existence, the children had made little difference to his life. As often as not he came home to find that they had been left into someone else's house to be minded. In the early days he would rush out to fetch them home immediately until he came to appreciate the exigencies of their presence and then he began to postpone it until he had had his supper, and then until he had read the evening paper or until he had seen the news on television. And besides, he had begun to resume the jobs he used to take on before he had married, working at night, servicing cars, repairing machinery for farmers.

Rose was leading the life that amused and occupied her as before. Her mother lived six doors away, a gaudy widow who got up late and sat around until evening in a vivid patterned dressing-gown, renewing her lipstick whenever she saw anyone passing who might call in on the way back from the shops. She dyed her hair and painted her nails, though that alone would not have antagonised him. She smoked constantly and had a nerve-racking cough which she had refined to such a degree and accompanied with such a cascade of heavily-scented handkerchiefs that healthy people felt crude and green in her presence.

Tim had a poor opinion of the circle of women with whom Rose and her mother mixed. They were people of no property, of no ambition, who yet managed to live comfortable unhurried lives. They spent their days drinking tea and talking in each other's houses, playing cards, breaking off at a moment's notice to make unurgent trips to one town or another to back a horse, see a fashionable wedding, play Bingo or attend an auction, though not to buy; or be the first to enter any newly opened shopping centre, church or lounge bar. They were ready and waiting to turn out to witness a crash, a fire or a row, or get the autograph of a famous person. They committed so little time or effort to what other people considered to be the moral obligations of a working day that they could lavish it instead on the fringe events, activities which amused them and gave them something to talk about, to relate to their work-bound neighbours. To Tim's mind there was something immoral and unwomanly about such an idle, frivolous style of living which he could not reconcile with his own traditional, inbred and instinctive expectation. Young women were decorative and irresponsible and if they were not they depressed him. But he expected them to develop as a matter of course into mature women who were useful and busy, and if face, figure and personality survived the process, that was a bonus one had no right to expect.

Tim drank the scalding tea with careful slurps. Leaving the cup on the table beside him, he groped for his slice of bread and cheese. In his other hand he held a paperback novel open. The road outside was quiet again. A moment before it had swarmed with schoolchildren hurrying back after lunch and there were still a few stragglers. He sat sideways in his chair at the window so that the light fell across his left shoulder onto the page, which was the method his revered schoolmaster used to prescribe. Thus he bandaged and soothed his raw nerves. Even so, he still registered every sound of Rose's footsteps in the room above and sometimes he had to re-read a sentence or a whole paragraph. The bedroom door had opened.—What the hell did you do with the trout? . . . Another door closed; she had gone into the bathroom. There were paragraphs he was going to read again, either way, when he had finished, and as he read one of these his chewing slowed down. His finger would creep in from outside the book and bend the corner of the page. Sometimes it turned down easily as it had been done before and Tim would smirk to himself. Sometimes the page he was about to mark looked as if it had never been touched before and that worried him a little. The bathroom door opened.—That was a grand way you fried the trout . . . . She was back in the bedroom again. Someday the wardrobe would topple over, the way she chucked at that door instead of turning the handle. Sometimes a page was dog-eared and he had found nothing in it so he'd go over it again, combing it for something, a new term maybe that he hadn't heard before. This worried him too, that there might still be something he didn't even know he didn't know. The radio music grew louder as Rose carried the transistor down the stairs. He moved slightly in his chair.—Tell us, did you by any chance see a couple of trout I left in last night. They were in a bit of newspaper. I thought you might fry them for the dinner. . . . The music rose and fell, cleared and blurred, as in moving the radio its direction and position changed. That grated on his nerves too.

He rubbed his fingers on his trouser leg and turned a page as Rose came into the kitchen. She left the radio on the edge of the table and it blared and rasped beside his ear. His eyes skidded over the printed page and he gnawed a crust of bread. She was searching for something under the cushions. He adjusted the radio until the sound cleared.

"That's better," she said agreeably.

"It isn't beyond you to put it right yourself, is it?" he said. And since it had long been his policy to let her be responsible for the first volley, she was surprised. She lifted her head as she stooped over the armchair and looked side-ways at him, just like a grazing pony, he thought. She raised her fine eyebrows and he knew that look of broad-minded, patient amusement. But she was dressed for going out and hadn't time to spare. "Oh, you're better at that kind of thing," she wheedled in a routine way. As she searched along the mantelpiece, she looked at her face in the mirror. Her make-up was perfect and she was pleased with her new scent. From her mother and her cronies she had picked up hackneyed, ill-fitting tips on how to handle him. She was too lazy to modify the general rules to suit him and thus he, who felt he could have borne almost any trial, was wounded in his most vulnerable aspect, his pride in his own individuality. Among all the women he had met there had been one or two who, in Rose's place, would surely have recognised his unique worth, and his bruised mind would delve into plangent daydreams of a re-union with one or other of them.

"Is your tea all right?" she asked suddenly.

"Why wouldn't it be?" Under his breath he added, "When you didn't make it."

"What's that you said?"

"Nothing," he said, rustling a page as he turned it. "I said what could be wrong with it, that's all."

"Hah?" she said, going on to search the other chairs. Already she had lost the trend of what he was saying. If he confused himself too, then in retrospect he wouldn't seem so unarguably a coward. All the time he kept his eyes fixed on the book. Three times they had zigzagged over the same few lines. Sometimes they settled as pointlessly as flies on one word but in the context of his own thoughts it would seem foreign and meaningless. Somewhere perhaps such words were used, but only by people who were free and unattached and had no belittling personal difficulties. A man couldn't use a word like piquant, say, then turn around and in the next breath abuse his wife. "Did you see any sign of a cigarette lighter?" she asked at last. "Ettie thinks she might have left it here yesterday." "Was that ould harpy in here again? No, I didn't. Though someone seems to have done a deal of tidying-up." "If you're referring to that . . . parcel," she said, "you can guess where you'll find it. Such a disgusting . . . phew. Don't bring them in here anymore, if you want a quiet life." She had given up the search and was straightening her slacks and jacket. "And that's a filthy old book you're reading. Make sure you put it some place Damien and Val can't get at it. You may forget the top of the cistern. They're able to climb, you know."

When she was leaving he said Good-bye and have a good time. He switched off the radio, put aside his book and sat very still. When he judged she had reached her mother's house he got up and put the pan on the gas-ring. He reached the door in time to take the parcel from the child he had sent up to the town. He gave him twenty pence for himself and said he hoped he wouldn't get into trouble at school. Back in the kitchen, he tucked a tea-towel into the waist band of his trousers. He surveyed the kitchen. He whistled as he moved into action, opening and closing cupboards and drawers, to fetch a plate, a knife and fork, pepper and salt. While the fat was heating on the pan he had opened the parcel, spread the steak on the table and pounded it with a wooden spoon. He had two onions ready, peeled and sliced. Now as he stood by the pan, poised to turn the steak, he looked out at the cool sunny day. He thought over the work he had to do for the rest of the day. And afterwards he would be going out to see Nick. His wife had phoned him; she wanted to have his opinion of a second-hand car Nick was going to buy for her, instead of the new one she wanted. A feeling of self-sufficiency expanded gently within him and bore him up.

Sister Imelda

Edna O'Brien

Sister Imelda did not take classes on her first day back in the convent but we spotted her in the grounds after the evening Rosary. Excitement and curiosity impelled us to follow her and try to see what she looked like, but she thwarted us by walking with head bent and eyelids down. All we could be certain of was that she was tall and limber and that she prayed while she walked. No looking at nature for her, or no curiosity about seventy boarders in gaberdine coats and black shoes and stockings. We might just as well have been crows, so impervious was she to our stares and to abortive attempts at trying to say "Hello, Sister."

We had returned from our long summer holiday and we were all wretched. The convent, with its high stone wall and green iron gates enfolding us again, seemed more of a prison than ever—for after our spell in the outside world we all felt very much older and more sophisticated, and my friend Baba and I were dreaming of our final escape, which would be in a year. And so, on that damp autumn evening when I saw the chrysanthemums and saw the new nun intent on prayer I pitied her and thought how alone she must be, cut off from her friends and conversation, with only God as her intangible spouse.

The next day she came into our classroom to take geometry. Her pale, slightly long face I saw as formidable, but her eyes were different, being blue-black and full of verve. Her lips were very purple, as if she had put puce pencil on them. They were the lips of a woman who might sing in a cabaret, and unconsciously she had formed the habit of turning them inward, as if she, too, was aware of their provocativeness. She had spent the last four years—the same span that Baba and I had spent in the convent—at the university in Dublin, where she studied languages. We couldn't understand how she had resisted the temptations of the hectic world and willingly come back to this. Her spell in the outside world made her different from the other nuns; there was more bounce in her walk, more excitement in the way she tackled teaching, reminding us that it was the most important thing in the world as she uttered the phrase "Praise be the Incarnate World." She began each day's class by reading from Cardinal Newman, who was a favorite of hers. She read how God dwelt in light unapproachable, and how with Him there was neither change nor shadow of alteration. It was amazing how her looks changed. Some days, when her eyes were flashing, she looked almost profane and made me wonder what events inside the precincts of the convent caused her to be suddenly so excited. She might have been a girl going to a dance, except for her habit.

"Hasn't she wonderful eyes," I said to Baba. That particular day they were like blackberries, large and soft and shiny.

"Something wrong in her upstairs department," Baba said, and added that with makeup Imelda would be a cinch.

"Still, she has a vocation!" I said, and even aired the idiotic view that I might have one. At certain moments it did seem enticing to become a nun, to lead a life unspotted by sin, never to have to have babies, and to wear a ring that singled one out as the Bride of Christ. But there was the other side to it, the silence, the gravity of it, having to get up two or three times a night to pray and, above all, never having the opportunity of leaving the confines of the place except for the funeral of one's parents. For us boarders it was torture, but for the nuns it was nothing short of doom. Also, we could complain to each other, and we did, food being the source of the greatest grumbles. Lunch was either bacon and cabbage or a peculiar stringy meat followed by tapioca pudding; tea consisted of bread dolloped with lard and occasionally, as a treat, fairly green rhubarb jam, which did not have enough sugar. Through the long curtainless windows we saw the conifer trees and a sky that was scarcely ever without the promise of rain or a downpour.

She was a right lunatic, then, Baba said, having gone to university for four years and willingly come back to incarceration, to poverty, chastity, and obedience. We concocted scenes of agony in some Dublin hostel, while a boy, or even a young man, stood beneath her bedroom window throwing up chunks of clay or whistles or a supplication. In our version of it he was slightly older than her, and possibly a medical student, since medical students had a knack with women, because of studying diagrams and skeletons. His advances, like those of a sudden storm, would intermittently rise and overwhelm her, and the memory of these sudden flaying advances of his would haunt her until she died, and if ever she contracted fever, these secrets would out. It was also rumored that she possessed a fierce temper and that, while a postulant, she had hit a girl so badly with her leather strap that the girl had to be put to bed because of wounds. Yet another black mark against Sister Imelda was that her brother Ambrose had been sued by a nurse for breach of promise.

That first morning when she came into our classroom and modestly introduced herself, I had no idea how terribly she would infiltrate my life, how in time she would be not just one of those teachers or nuns but rather a special one, almost like a ghost who passed the boundaries of common exchange and who crept inside one, devouring so much of one's thoughts, so much of one's passion, invading the place that was called one's heart. She talked in a low voice, as if she did not want her words to go beyond the bounds of the wall, and constantly she stressed the value of work both to enlarge the mind and to discipline the thought. One of her eyelids was red and swollen, as if she was getting a sty. I reckoned that she overmortified herself by not eating at all. I saw in her some terrible premonition of sacrifice which I would have to emulate. Then, in direct contrast, she absently held the stick of chalk between her first and second fingers, the very same as if it were a cigarette, and Baba whispered to me that she might have been a smoker when in Dublin. Sister Imelda looked down sharply at me and said what was the secret and would I like to share it, since it seemed so comical. I said, "Nothing, Sister, nothing," and her dark eyes exuded such vehemence that I prayed she would never have occasion to punish me.

November came and the tiled walls of the recreation hall oozed moisture and gloom. Most girls had sore throats and were told to suffer this inconvenience to mortify themselves in order to lend a glorious hand in that communion of spirit that linked the living with the dead. It was the month of the Suffering Souls in Purgatory, and as we heard of their twofold agony, the yearning for Christ and the ferocity of the leaping flames that burned and charred their poor limbs, we were asked to make acts of mortification. Some girls gave up jam or sweets and some gave up talking, and so in recreation time they were like dummies making signs with thumb and finger to merely say "How are you?" Baba said that saner people were locked in the lunatic asylum, which was only a mile away. We saw them in the grounds, pacing back and forth, with their mouths agape and dribble coming out of them, like melting icicles. Among our many fears was that one of those lunatics would break out and head straight for the convent and assault some of the girls.

Yet in the thick of all these dreads I found myself becoming dreadfully happy. I had met Sister Imelda outside of class a few times and I felt that there was an attachment between us. Once it was in the grounds, when she did a reckless thing. She broke off a chrysanthemum and offered it to me to smell. It had no smell, or at least only something faint that suggested autumn, and feeling this to be the case herself, she said it was not a gardenia, was it? Another time we met in the chapel porch, and as she drew her shawl more tightly around her body, I felt how human she was, and prey to the cold.

In the classroom things were not so congenial between us. Geometry was my worst subject, indeed, a total mystery to me. She had not taught more than four classes when she realized this and threw a duster at me in a rage. A few girls gasped as she asked me to stand up and make a spectacle of myself. Her face had reddened, and presently she took out her handkerchief and patted the eye which was red and swollen. I not only felt a fool but felt in imminent danger of sneezing as I inhaled the smell of chalk that had fallen onto my gym frock. Suddenly she fled from the room, leaving us ten minutes free until the next class. Some girls said it was a disgrace, said I should write home and say I had been assaulted. Others welcomed the few minutes in which to gabble. All I wanted was to run after her and say that I was sorry to have caused her such distemper, because I knew dimly that it was as much to do with liking as it was with dislike. In me then there came a sort of speechless tenderness for her, and I might have known that I was stirred.

"We could get her defrocked," Baba said, and elbowed me in God's name to sit down.

That evening at Benediction I had the most overwhelming surprise. It was a particularly happy evening, with the choir nuns in full soaring form and the rows of candles like so many little ladders to the golden chalice that glittered all the more because of the beams of fitful flame. I was full of tears when I discovered a new holy picture had been put in my prayer book, and before I dared look on the back to see who had given it to me, I felt and guessed that this was no ordinary picture from an ordinary girl friend, that this was a talisman and a peace offering from Sister Imelda. It was a pale-blue picture, so pale that it was almost gray, like the down of a pigeon, and it showed a mother looking down on the infant child. On the back, in her beautiful ornate handwriting, she had written a verse:

> Trust Him when dark doubts assail thee,
> Trust Him when thy faith is small,
> Trust Him when to simply trust Him
> Seems the hardest thing of all.

This was her atonement. To think that she had located the compartment in the chapel where I kept my prayer book and to think that she had been so naked as to write in it and give me a chance to boast about it and to show it to other girls. When I thanked her next day, she bowed but did not speak. Mostly the nuns were on silence and only permitted to talk during class.

In no time I had received another present, a little miniature prayer book with a leather cover and gold edging. The prayers were in French and the lettering so minute it was as if a tiny insect had fashioned them. Soon I was publicly known as her pet. I opened the doors for her, raised the blackboard two pegs higher (she was taller than other nuns), and handed out the exercise books which she had corrected. Now in the margins of my geometry propositions I would find "Good" or "Excellent," when in the past she used to splash "Disgraceful." Baba said it was foul to be a nun's pet and that any girl who sucked up to a nun could not be trusted.

About a month later Sister Imelda asked me to carry her books up four flights of stairs to the cookery kitchen. She taught cookery to a junior class. As she walked ahead of me, I thought how supple she was and how thoroughbred, and when she paused on the landing to look out through the long curtainless window, I too paused. Down below, two women in suede boots were chatting and smoking as they moved along the street with shopping baskets. Nearby a lay nun was on her knees scrubbing the granite steps, and the cold air was full of the raw smell of Jeyes Fluid. There was a potted plant on the landing, and Sister

Imelda put her fingers in the earth and went "Tch tch tch," saying it needed water. I said I would water it later on. I was happy in my prison then, happy to be near her, happy to walk behind her as she twirled her beads and bowed to the servile nun. I no longer cried for my mother, no longer counted the days on a pocket calendar until the Christmas holidays.

"Come back at five," she said as she stood on the threshold of the cookery kitchen door. The girls, all in white overalls, were arranged around the long wooden table waiting for her. It was as if every girl was in love with her. Because, as she entered, their faces broke into smiles, and in different tones of audacity they said her name. She must have liked cookery class, because she beamed and called to someone, anyone, to get up a blazing fire. Then she went across to the cast-iron stove and spat on it to test its temperature. It was hot, because her spit rose up and sizzled.

When I got back later, she was sitting on the edge of the table swaying her legs. There was something reckless about her pose, something defiant. It seemed as if any minute she would take out a cigarette case, snap it open, and then archly offer me one. The wonderful smell of baking made me realize how hungry I was, but far more so, it brought back to me my own home, my mother testing orange cakes with a knitting needle and letting me lick the line of half-baked dough down the length of the needle. I wondered if she had supplanted my mother, and I hoped not, because I had aimed to outstep my original world and take my place in a new and hallowed one.

"I bet you have a sweet tooth," she said, and then she got up, crossed the kitchen, and from under a wonderful shining silver cloche she produced two jam tarts with a crisscross design on them where the pastry was latticed over the dark jam. They were still warm.

"What will I do with them?" I asked.

"Eat them, you goose," she said, and she watched me eat as if she herself derived some peculiar pleasure from it, whereas I was embarrassed about the pastry crumbling and the bits of blackberry jam staining my lips. She was amused. It was one of the most awkward yet thrilling moments I had lived, and inherent in the pleasure was the terrible sense of danger. Had we been caught, she, no doubt, would have had to make massive sacrifice. I looked at her and thought how peerless and how brave, and I wondered if she felt hungry. She had a white overall over her black habit and this made her warmer and freer, and caused me to think of the happiness that would be ours, the laissez-faire if we were away from the convent in an ordinary kitchen doing something easy and customary. But we weren't. It was clear to me then that my version of pleasure was inextricable from pain, that they existed side by side and were interdependent, like the two forces of an electric current.

"Had you a friend when you were in Dublin at university?" I asked daringly.

"I shared a desk with a sister from Howth and stayed in the same hostel," she said.

But what about boys? I thought, and what of your life now and do you long to go out into the world? But could not say it.

We knew something about the nuns' routine. It was rumored that they wore itchy wool underwear, ate dry bread for breakfast, rarely had meat, cakes, or dainties, kept certain hours of strict silence with each other, as well as constant vigil on their thoughts; so that if their minds wandered to the subject of food or pleasure, they would quickly revert to thoughts of God and their eternal souls. They slept on hard beds with no sheets and hairy blankets. At four o'clock in the morning while we slept, each nun got out of bed, in her habit—which was also her death habit—and chanting, they all flocked down the wooden stairs like ravens, to fling themselves on the tiled floor of the chapel. Each nun—even the Mother Superior—flung herself in total submission, saying prayers in Latin and offering up the moment to God. Then silently back to their cells for one more hour of rest. It was not difficult to imagine Sister Imelda face downward, arms outstretched, prostrate on the tiled floor. I often heard their chanting when I wakened suddenly from a nightmare, because, although we slept in a different building, both adjoined, and if one wakened one often heard that monotonous Latin chanting, long before the birds began, long before our own bell summoned us to rise at six.

"Do you eat nice food?" I asked.

"Of course," she said, and smiled. She sometimes broke into an eager smile, which she did much to conceal.

"Have you ever thought of what you will be?" she asked.

I shook my head. My design changed from day to day.

She looked at her man's silver pocket watch, closed the damper of the range, and prepared to leave. She checked that all the wall cupboards were locked by running her hand over them.

"Sister," I called, gathering enough courage at last—we must have some secret, something to join us together—"what color hair have you?"

We never saw the nuns' hair, or their eyebrows, or ears, as all that part was covered by a stiff white wimple.

"You shouldn't ask such a thing," she said, getting pink in the face, and then she turned back and whispered, "I'll tell you on your last day here, provided your geometry has improved."

She had scarcely gone when Baba, who had been lurking behind some pillar, stuck her head in the door and said, "Christsake, save me a bit." She finished the second pastry, then went around looking in kitchen drawers. Because of everything being locked, she found only some castor sugar in a china shaker. She ate a little and threw the remainder into the dying fire, so that it flared up for a minute with a yellow spluttering flame. Baba showed her jealousy by putting it around the school that I was in the cookery kitchen every evening, gorging cakes with Sister Imelda and telling tales.

I did not speak to Sister Imelda again in private until the evening of our Christmas theatricals. She came to help us put on makeup and get into our stage clothes and fancy headgear. These clothes were kept in a trunk from one year to the next, and though sumptuous and strewn with braiding and gold, they smelled of camphor. Yet as we donned them we felt different, and as we sponged pancake makeup onto our faces, we became saucy and emphasized these new guises by adding dark pencil to the eyes and making the lips bright carmine. There was only one tube of lipstick and each girl clamored for it. The evening's entertainment was to comprise scenes from Shakespeare and laughing sketches. I had been chosen to recite Mark Antony's lament over Caesar's body, and for this I was to wear a purple toga, white knee-length socks, and patent buckle shoes. The shoes were too big and I moved in them as if in clogs. She said to take them off, to go barefoot. I realized that I was getting nervous and that in an effort to memorize my speech, the words were getting all askew and flying about in my head, like the separate pieces of a jigsaw puzzle. She sensed my panic and very slowly put her hand on my face and enjoined me to look at her. I looked into her eyes, which seemed fathomless, and saw that she was willing me to be calm and obliging me to be master of my fears, and I little knew that one day she would have to do the same as regards the swoop of my feelings for her. As we continued to stare I felt myself becoming calm and the words were restored to me in their right and fluent order. The lights were being lowered out in the recreation hall, and we knew now that all the nuns had arrived, had settled themselves down, and were eagerly awaiting this annual hotchpotch of amateur entertainment. There was that fearsome hush as the hall went dark and the few spotlights were turned on. She kissed her crucifix and I realized that she was saying a prayer for me. Then she raised her arm as if depicting the stance of a Greek goddess; walking onto the stage, I was fired by her ardor.

Baba could say that I bawled like a bloody bull, but Sister Imelda, who stood in the wings, said that temporarily she had felt the streets of Rome, had seen the corpse of Caesar, as I delivered those poignant, distempered lines. When I came off stage she put her arms around me and I was encased in a shower of silent kisses. After we had taken down the decorations and put the fancy clothes back in the trunk, I gave her two half-pound boxes of chocolates—bought for me illicitly by one of the day girls—and she gave me a casket made from the insides of match boxes and covered over with gilt paint and gold dust. It was like holding moths and finding their powder adhering to the fingers.

"What will you do on Christmas Day, Sister?" I said.

"I'll pray for you," she said.

It was useless to say, "Will you have turkey?" or "Will you have plum pudding?" or "Will you loll in bed?" because I believed that Christmas Day would be as bleak and deprived as any other day in her life. Yet she was radiant as if such austerity was joyful. Maybe she was basking in some secret realization involving her and me.

On the cold snowy afternoon three weeks later when we returned from our holidays, Sister Imelda came up to the dormitory to welcome me back. All the other girls had gone down to the recreation hall to do barn dances and I could hear someone banging on the piano. I did not want to go down and clump around with sixty other girls, having nothing to look forward to, only tea and the Rosary and early bed. The beds were damp after our stay at home, and when I put my hand between the sheets, it was like feeling dew but did not have the freshness of outdoors. What depressed me further was that I had seen a mouse in one of the cupboards, seen its tail curl with terror as it slipped away into a crevice. If there was one mouse, there were God knows how

147

many, and the cakes we hid in secret would not be safe. I was still unpacking as she came down the narrow passage between the rows of iron beds and I saw in her walk such agitation.

"Tut, tut, tut, you've curled your hair," she said, offended.

Yes, the world outside was somehow declared in this perm, and for a second I remembered the scalding pain as the trickles of ammonia dribbled down my forehead and then the joy as the hair-dresser said that she would make me look like Movita, a Mexican star. Now suddenly that world and those aspirations seemed trite and I wanted to take a brush and straighten my hair and revert to the dark gawky somber girl that I had been. I offered her iced queen cakes that my mother had made, but she refused them and said she could only stay a second. She lent me a notebook of hers, which she had had as a pupil, and into which she had copied favorite quotations, some religious, some not. I read at random:

> Twice or thrice had I loved thee,
> Before I knew thy face or name.
> So in a voice, so in a shapeless flame,
> Angels affect us oft . . .

"Are you well?" I asked.

She looked pale. It may have been the day, which was wretched and gray with sleet, or it may have been the white bedspreads, but she appeared to be ailing.

"I missed you," she said.

"Me too," I said.

At home, gorging, eating trifle at all hours, even for breakfast, having little ratafias to dip in cups of tea, fitting on new shoes and silk stockings, I wished that she could be with us, enjoying the fire and the freedom.

"You know it is not proper for us to be so friendly."

"It's not wrong," I said.

I dreaded that she might decide to turn away from me, that she might stamp on our love and might suddenly draw a curtain over it, a black crepe curtain that would denote its death. I dreaded it and knew it was going to happen.

"We must not become attached," she said, and I could not say we already were, no more than I could remind her of the day of the revels and the intimacy between us. Convents were dungeons and no doubt about it.

From then on she treated me as less of a favorite. She said my name sharply in class, and once she said if I must cough, could I wait until class had finished. Baba was delighted, as were the other girls, because they were glad to see me receding in her eyes. Yet I knew that the crispness was part of her love, because no matter how callously she looked at me, she would occasionally soften. Reading her notebook helped me, and I copied out her quotations into my own book, trying as accurately as possible to imitate her handwriting.

But some little time later when she came to supervise our study one evening, I got a smile from her as she sat on the rostrum looking down at us all. I continued to look up at her and by slight frowning indicated that I had a problem with my geometry. She beckoned to me lightly and I went up, bringing my copybook and the pen. Standing close to her, and also because her wimple was crooked, I saw one of her eyebrows for the first time. She saw that I noticed it and said did that satisfy my curiosity. I said not really. She said what else did I want to see, her swan's neck perhaps, and I went scarlet. I was amazed that she would say such a thing in the hearing of other girls, and then she said a worse thing, she said that G. K. Chesterton was very forgetful and had once put on his trousers backward. She expected me to laugh. I was so close to her that a rumble in her stomach seemed to be taking place in my own, and about this she also laughed. It occurred to me for one terrible moment that maybe she had decided to leave the convent, to jump over the wall. Having done the theorem for me, she marked it "100 out of 100" and then asked if I had any other problems. My eyes filled with tears, I wanted her to realize that her recent coolness had wrought havoc with my nerves and my peace of mind.

"What is it?" she said.

I could cry, or I could tremble to try to convey the emotion, but I could not tell her. As if on cue, the Mother Superior came in and saw this glaring intimacy and frowned as she approached the rostrum.

"Would you please go back to your desk," she said, "and in future kindly allow Sister Imelda to get on with her duties."

I tiptoed back and sat with head down, bursting with fear and shame. Then she looked at a tray on which the milk cups were laid, and finding one cup of milk untouched, she asked which girl had not drunk her milk.

"Me, Sister," I said, and I was called up to drink it and stand under the clock as a punishment. The milk was tepid and dusty, and I thought of cows on the fairs days at home and the farmers hitting them as they slid and slithered over the muddy streets.

For weeks I tried to see my nun in private; I even lurked outside doors where I knew she was due, only to be rebuffed again and again. I suspected the Mother Superior had warned her against making a favorite of me. But I still clung to a belief that a bond existed between us and that her coldness and even some glares which I had received were a charade, a mask. I would wonder how she felt alone in bed and what way she slept and if she thought of me, or refusing to think of me, if she dreamed of me as I did of her. She certainly got thinner, because her nun's silver ring slipped easily and sometimes unavoidably off her marriage finger. It occurred to me that she was having a nervous breakdown.

One day in March the sun came out, the radiators were turned off, and, though there was a lashing wind, we were told that officially spring had arrived and that we could play games. We all trooped up to the games field and, to our surprise, saw that Sister Imelda was officiating that day. The daffodils in the field tossed and turned; they were a very bright shocking yellow, but they were not as fetching as the little timid snowdrops that trembled in the wind. We played rounders, and when my turn came to hit the ball with the long wooden pound, I crumbled and missed, fearing that the ball would hit me.

"Champ . . ." said Baba, jeering.

After three such failures Sister Imelda said that if I liked I could sit and watch, and when I was sitting in the greenhouse swallowing my shame, she came in and said that I must not give way to tears, because humiliation was the greatest test of Christ's love, or indeed *any* love.

"When you are a nun you will know that," she said, and instantly I made up my mind that I would be a nun and that though we might never be free to express our feelings, we would be under the same roof, in the same cloister, in mental and spiritual conjunction all our lives.

"Is it very hard at first?" I said.

"It's awful," she said, and she slipped a little medal into my gym-frock pocket. It was warm from being in her pocket, and as I held it, I knew that once again we were near and that in fact we had never severed. Walking down from the playing field to our Sunday lunch of mutton and cabbage, everyone chattered to Sister Imelda. The girls milled around her, linking her, trying to hold her hand, counting the various keys on her bunch of keys, and asking impudent questions.

"Sister, did you ever ride a motorbicycle?"

"Sister, did you ever wear seamless stockings?"

"Sister, who's your favorite film star—male?"

"Sister, what's your favorite food?"

"Sister, if you had a wish, what would it be?"

"Sister, what do you do when you want to scratch your head?"

Yes, she had ridden a motorbicycle, and she had worn silk stockings, but they were seamed. She liked bananas best, and if she had a wish, it would be to go home for a few hours to see her parents and her brother.

That afternoon as we walked through the town, the sight of closed shops with porter barrels outside and mongrel dogs did not dispel my refound ecstasy. The medal was in my pocket, and every other second I would touch it for confirmation. Baba saw a Swiss roll in a confectioner's window laid on a doily and dusted with castor sugar, and it made her cry out with hunger and rail against being in a bloody reformatory, surrounded by drips and mopes. On impulse she took her nail file out of her pocket and dashed across to the window to see if she could cut the glass. The prefect rushed up from the back of the line and asked Baba if she wanted to be locked up.

"I am anyhow," Baba said, and sawed at one of her nails, to maintain her independence and vent her spleen. Baba was the only girl who could stand up to a prefect. When she felt like it, she dropped out of a walk, sat on a stone wall, and waited until we all came back. She said that if there was one thing more boring than studying it was walking. She used to roll down her stockings and examine her calves and say that she could see varicose veins coming from this bloody daily walk. Her legs, like all our legs, were black from the dye of the stockings; we were forbidden to bathe, because baths were immoral. We washed each night in an enamel basin beside our beds. When girls splashed cold water onto their chests, they let out cries, though this was forbidden.

After the walk we wrote home. We were allowed to write home once a week; our letters were always censored. I told my mother that I had made up my mind to be a nun, and asked if she could send me bananas when a batch arrived at our local grocery shop. That evening, perhaps as I wrote to my mother on the ruled white paper, a telegram arrived which said that Sister Imelda's brother had been killed in a van while on his way home from a hurling match. The Mother Superior announced it, and asked us to pray for his soul and write letters of sympathy to Sister Imelda's parents. We all wrote identical letters, because in our first year at school we had been given specimen letters for various occasions, and we all referred back to our specimen letter of sympathy.

Next day the town hire-car drove up to the convent, and Sister Imelda, accompanied by another nun, went home for the funeral. She looked as white as a sheet, with eyes swollen, and she wore a heavy knitted shawl over her shoulders. Although she came back that night (I stayed awake to hear the car), we did not see her for a whole week, except to catch a glimpse of her back, in the chapel. When she resumed class, she was peaky and distant, making no reference at all to her recent tragedy.

The day the bananas came I waited outside the door and gave her a bunch wrapped in tissue paper. Some were still a little green, and she said that Mother Superior would put them in the glasshouse to ripen. I felt that Sister Imelda would never taste them; they would be kept for a visiting priest or bishop.

"Oh, Sister, I'm sorry about your brother," I said in a burst.

"It will come to us all, sooner or later," Sister Imelda said dolefully.

I dared to touch her wrist to communicate my sadness. She went quickly, probably for fear of breaking down. At times she grew irritable and had a boil on her cheek. She missed some classes and was replaced in the cookery kitchen by a younger nun. She asked me to pray for her brother's soul and to avoid seeing her alone. Each time as she came down a corridor toward me, I was obliged to turn the other way. Now Baba or some other girl moved the blackboard two pegs higher and spread her shawl, when wet, over the radiator to dry.

I got flu and was put to bed. Sickness took the same bleak course, a cup of hot senna delivered in person by the head nun, who stood there while I drank it, tea at lunchtime with thin slices of brown bread (because it was just after the war, food was still rationed, so the butter was mixed with lard and had white streaks running through it and a faintly rancid smell), hours of just lying there surveying the empty dormitory, the empty iron beds with white counterpanes on each one, and metal crucifixes laid on each white, frilled pillow slip. I knew that she would miss me and hoped that Baba would tell her where I was. I counted the number of tiles from the ceiling to the head of my bed, thought of my mother at home on the farm mixing hen food, thought of my father, losing his temper perhaps and stamping on the kitchen floor with nailed boots, and I recalled the money owing for my school fees and hoped that Sister Imelda would never get to hear of it. During the Christmas holiday I had seen a bill sent by the head nun to my father which said, "Please remit this week without fail." I hated being in bed causing extra trouble and therefore reminding the head nun of the unpaid liability. We had no clock in the dormitory, so there was no way of guessing the time, but the hours dragged.

Marigold, one of the maids, came to take off the counterpanes at five and brought with her two gifts from Sister Imelda—an orange and a pencil sharpener. I kept the orange peel in my hand, smelling it, and planning how I would thank her. Thinking of her I fell into a feverish sleep and was wakened when the girls came to bed at ten and switched on the various ceiling lights.

At Easter Sister Imelda warned me not to give her chocolates, so I got her a flashlamp instead and spare batteries. Pleased with such a useful gift (perhaps she read her letters in bed), she put her arms around me and allowed one cheek to adhere but not to make the sound of a kiss. It made up for the seven weeks of withdrawal, and as I drove down the convent drive with Baba, she waved to me, as she had promised, from the window of her cell.

In the last term at school, studying was intensive because of the examinations which loomed at the end of June. Like all the other nuns, Sister Imelda thought only of these examinations. She crammed us with knowledge, lost her temper every other day, and gritted her teeth whenever the blackboard was too greasy to take the imprint of the chalk. If ever I met her in the corridor, she asked if I knew such and such a thing, and coming down from Sunday games, she went over various questions with us. The fateful examination day arrived and we sat at single desks supervised by some strange woman from Dublin. Opening a locked trunk, she took out the pink examination papers and distributed them around. Geometry was on the fourth day. When we came out from it, Sister Imelda was in the hall with all the answers, so that we could compare our answers with hers. Then she called me aside and we went up toward the cookery kitchen and sat on the stairs while she went over the paper with me, question for question. I knew that I had three right and two wrong, but did not tell her so.

"It is black," she said then, rather suddenly. I thought she meant the dark light where we were sitting.

"It's cool, though," I said.

Summer had come; our white skins baked under the heavy uniform, and dark violet pansies bloomed in the convent grounds. She looked well again, and her pale skin was once more unblemished.

"My hair," she whispered, "is black." And she told me how she had spent her last night before entering the convent. She had gone cycling with a boy and ridden for miles, and they'd lost their way up a mountain, and she became afraid she would be so late home that she would sleep it out the next morning. It was understood between us that I was going to enter the convent in September and that I could have a last fling, too.

Two days later we prepared to go home. There were farewells and outlandish promises, and autograph books signed, and girls trudging up the recreation hall, their cases bursting open with clothes and books. Baba scattered biscuit crumbs in the dormitory for the mice and stuffed all her prayer books under a mattress. Her father promised to collect us at four. I had arranged with Sister Imelda secretly that I would meet her in one of the summerhouses around the walks, where we would spend our last half hour together. I expected that she would tell me something of what my life as a postulant would be like. But Baba's father came an hour early. He had something urgent to do later and came at three instead. All I could do was ask Marigold to take a note to Sister Imelda.

> Remembrance is all I ask,
> But if remembrance should prove a task,
> Forget me.

I hated Baba, hated her busy father, hated the thought of my mother standing in the doorway in her good dress, welcoming me home at last. I would have become a nun that minute if I could.

I wrote to my nun that night and again the next day and then every week for a month. Her letters were censored, so I tried to convey my feelings indirectly. In one of her letters to me (they were allowed one letter a month) she said that she looked forward to seeing me in September. But by September Baba and I had left for the university in Dublin. I stopped writing to Sister Imelda then, reluctant to tell her that I no longer wished to be a nun.

In Dublin we enrolled at the college where she had surpassed herself. I saw her maiden name on a list, for having graduated with special honors, and for days was again sad and remorseful. I rushed out and bought batteries for the flashlamp I'd given her, and posted them without any note enclosed. No mention of my missing vocation, no mention of why I had stopped writing.

One Sunday about two years later, Baba and I were going out to Howth on a bus. Baba had met some businessmen who played golf there and she had done a lot of scheming to get us invited out. The bus was packed, mostly mothers with babies and children on their way to Dollymount Strand. We drove along the coast road and saw the sea, bright green and glinting in the sun, and because of the way the water was carved up into millions of little wavelets, its surface seemed like an endless heap of dark-green broken bottles. Near the shore the sand looked warm and was biscuit-colored. We never swam or sunbathed, we never did anything that was good for us. Life was geared to work and to meeting men, and yet one knew that mating could only lead to one's being a mother and hawking obstreperous children out to the seaside on Sunday. "They know not what they do" could surely be said of us.

We were very made up; even the conductor seemed to disapprove and snapped at having to give change of ten shillings. For no reason at all I thought of our makeup rituals before the school play and how innocent it was in comparison, because now our skins were smothered beneath layers of it and we never took it off at night. Thinking of the convent, I suddenly thought of Sister Imelda, and then, as if prey to a dream, I heard the rustle of serge, smelled the Jeyes Fluid and the boiled cabbage, and saw her pale shocked face in the months after her brother died. Then I looked around and saw her in earnest, and at first thought I was imagining things. But no, she had got on accompanied by another nun and they were settling themselves in the back seat nearest the door. She looked older, but she had the same aloof quality and the same eyes, and my heart began to race with a mixture of excitement and dread. At first it raced with a prodigal strength, and then it began to falter and I thought it was going to give out. My fear of her and my love came back in one fell realization. I would have gone through the window except that it was not wide enough. The thing was how to escape her. Baba gurgled with delight, stood up, and in the most flagrant way looked around to make sure that it was Imelda. She recognized the other nun as one with the nickname of Johnny who taught piano lessons. Baba's first thought was revenge, as she enumerated the punishments they had meted out to us and said how nice it would be to go back and shock them and say, "Mud in your eye, Sisters," or "Get lost," or something worse. Baba could not understand why I was quaking, no more than she could understand why I began to wipe off the lipstick. Above all, I knew that I could not confront them.

"You're going to have to," Baba said.

"I can't," I said.

It was not just my attire; it was the fact of my never having written and of my broken promise. Baba kept looking back and said they weren't saying a word and that children were gawking at them. It wasn't often that nuns traveled in buses, and we speculated as to where they might be going.

"They might be off to meet two fellows," Baba said, and visualized them in the golf club getting blotto and hoisting up their skirts. For me it was no laughing matter. She came up with a strategy: it was that as we approached our stop and the bus was still moving, I was to jump up and go down the aisle and pass them without even looking. She said most likely they would not notice us, as their eyes were lowered and they seemed to be praying.

"I can't run down the bus," I said. There was a matter of shaking limbs and already a terrible vertigo.

"You're going to," Baba said, and though insisting that I couldn't, I had already begun to rehearse an apology. While doing this, I kept blessing myself over and over again, and Baba kept reminding me that there was only one more stop before ours. When the dreadful moment came, I jumped up and put on my face what can only be called an apology of a smile. I followed Baba to the rear of the bus. But already they had gone. I saw the back of their two sable, identical figures with their veils being blown wildly about in the wind. They looked so cold and lost as they hurried along the pavement and I wanted to run after them. In some way I felt worse than if I had confronted them. I cannot be certain what I would have said. I knew that there is something sad and faintly distasteful about love's ending, particularly love that has never been fully realized. I might have hinted at that, but I doubt it. In our deepest moments we say the most inadequate things.

One Word

Juanita Casey

I am not a cruel woman, cried Miss Judith Dannaher. I love God's animals! But if I catch one of those bloody asses in my garden again I'll break all their bloody legs, Lord save us, like sticks for me fire.

Miss Dannaher kicked her own ass in the chest, and felt some measure of relief.

It was all his fault, that whoring Jimmy, roaring off at all hours of the day and night and attracting the rest of his outlaw band off the sand dunes and into her domains.

The times she had to go after the limb of Satan too, looking all over the place and up the roads for him when he broke his hobbles and was away with the nine others of his unspeakable tribe.

The nine belonged to various neighbours around, but having either broken out or been turned away, the nine lived off their wits and other people's gardens and occasionally would be caught up and press-ganged into work again for a few hours.

The long ears of them would scissor together at Miss Judith Dannaher's approach, the rain dropping off their thick pelts and pearling their whiskers as they hunched beneath the few shrubs and thorns around the Maiden's Tower, and she dare not utter the murder within her lest the whole lot take fright and whisk off up the road again. Only when it rained could she catch the wretched Jimmy with any ease, as all the asses were loth to move out from the shelter of the bushes.

Once she had him though. O once she had him. I'll knock shite out of yez, she'd choke hoarsely and mentally murder him all over in various delightful ways until she got him home, when knock shite out of him she did.

158

Sunshine on the other hand meant that long, soul-destroying saunter behind them all, pretending she didn't really want Jimmy at all and was just out for her health. Apoplexy quietly swelled within her as they moved step to her step, just in front, just out of grab, with their black tricorne eyes looking back at her and their tails demurely switching. By the Holy God, she would clench. By the Holy God . . .

Two or three interesting hours could pass thus in gentle ambulation, while bees visited clover and cinquefoil and campion, and the breeze curled the frills of the asses' manes and caressed her hissing brow.

But if there was a wind, then goodbye to the asses and goodbye to Jimmy as they carolled and brayed, bucked and buffeted each other in a mad race to the sea, an ancient, disturbing spirit under their matted hides, and the wildness of swift Asia in their changed eyes. They became, for a short day, the inheritors of ruined Nineveh, the swift ones of Nimrod, the fierce runners of the deserts. Along the strand, matching strides with the waves, wheeling to confront the walker on the sands with the long, burning stare over the civilisations to their green time before men.

When the sea-grasses hummed and whistled and when the winds came, they lifted their scarred and heavy heads. They were the inheritors of the Khamsin and the Sirrocco. They were the Seers.

On these days, the wind also got into Miss Judith Dannaher's head, and she gave up and went to bed with a fierce migraine, which pounded and drummed as though all Jimmy's four hooves were, for once, kicking hell out of her.

With the occasional and begrudging help of the ever-reluctant Jimmy, Miss Judith Dannaher tilled the soil of her few acres, saved a little frantic hay, moved her hens' houses around her own cabin in an uproar of hens, oaths, and the total disarray of both herself and Jimmy, carted a variety of useful and useless agricultural products about, buried the cart and Jimmy at intervals beneath vast, steaming dollops of cow manure, and the same trio went shopping with the odour of sanctity adhering with the bits of straw to all three.

On these expeditions, Miss Judith Dannaher tugged, beat, swore, kicked, and wished the most interesting amendments upon the creeping Jimmy, but on the return journey nothing could hold him as he tore for home and freedom with his mouth pulled back to his ears and the cart and Miss Judith Dannaher yawing and gybing behind him like a boat in a following sea. Whoa, whoa, ye whore, I'll knock shite out of yez was the battle-cry of this ill-assorted equipage as it shaved corners, the village bus, slow children and old Mr. Fintan Maloney on his crutches, and joyous dogs pursued its course with hopes of receiving a flight of sausages from one of its better rebounds.

Upon unharnessing the now demure and extinguished Jimmy, Miss Judith Dannaher would apply her arm, voice, and boots to him, and a fury of dust would erupt as she beat and whacked his hide like a carpet.

Miss Judith Dannaher lived on one side of the Maiden's Tower, and the brothers Johnny and Jimmy O'Neill lived on the other. Between their cabins ran a stream, and over the stream a plank bridge, and behind them a tangled patchwork of small fields and miniature forests of scrubby oaks, thorns and ash. In front lay the Burrows, mile upon mile of sand dunes, and in front of these a swish down on to the white miles of strand and the moody sea.

Miss Judith Dannaher's fields contained, as well as the occasional Jimmy, three old cows and three young heifers, her hens, some geese and a few ducks, and a tethered community of nanny goats, all spinsters like Miss Judith Dannaher and with therefore not a drop of milk between them.

The fields of Johnny and Jimmy O'Neill contained but themselves, some blackberries and fungi at the right seasons, and the brothers O'Neill let them get on with it.

The Maiden's Tower was a long pinnacle of stone, mushroom-capped with small square inlets to keep arrows out of spying eyes and was a fair example of the old round tower of Irish history. Legend and history however ran a race with truth, and all deadheated.

The Maiden had watched her Captain sail away on the tides of spring and whiled away the time and her heart's desire by building the Tower to his memory and to his return. Which he never did. That the Maiden chose to erect a peculiarly phallic edifice did not go unnoticed among the unsophisticated of the region, and private additions and ramifications to the Maiden's tale abounded in every family.

Every morning the brothers O'Neill arose and breakfasted without one word between them, and they both stalked down to their boat and its nets on the estuary shore. With long, deliberate strides they heroned down the shingle together, each one to his own task in the boat, moving together and each other like pieces in a jig-saw.

All day they rowed and netted at the river mouth close by, slow yet deft, unhurried yet quick enough, and without one word between them.

A lorry came out from the town each day to buy whatever catch they and the other scattered fishermen of the area might bring in, but on days of wind and white water the day began as usual with their Trappist breakfast, but no fishing could be attempted, and so Johnny and Jimmy O'Neill would stare at the sea from either side of the plank bridge, and without one word between them. Then Johnny would take the track over the Burrows, and Jimmy would follow the frothy tideline beside the sea, and a few hundred yards apart they would stalk the three miles into Coneytown village and bend into Barney Hagan's within a bootfall of each other. Seated on opposite sides of the Vandyke interior, they would drink time and the sea into an opacity of oblivion without one word between them and return under the moon and the flying clouds and the spit of the rain, Johnny taking the track over the black Burrows, and Jimmy following the luminous tideline beside the sea, a few hundred yards apart and so blind, so deaf, and so dumb that they could not, had they wanted to, have uttered one word between them. At the cabin, at which they arrived within each other's shadows, they unbooted and undressed to their combinations and, turning their backs to each other, fell asleep to the thunder of the surf and of their own snores.

Their lives, in this manner, had creaked apart and together down the same rut like the hub of a loosening wheel since the year of 1916 when Johnny joined the British Navy and Jimmy remained at home at his nets. In those days Miss Judith Dannaher had been as a lily in her fields, a shy wild violet of the Burrows. She and Johnny were to marry on his return from the wars. But one day she thought of the other bereft and languishing Maiden, decided a bird in the hand was better than an absent heart, and settled in its absence for Jimmy.

There was no haste, as Miss Judith had her farm and Jimmy his fish, and the rain and the sun and the winds rolled the seasons around them. Until, suddenly, there was Johnny. And from that one day the brothers O'Neill rethreaded the hole in their lives and went on with their netting as before, but now without one word between them. Miss Judith, after a suitable period of furious lament, rethatched her cabin, made herself a new apron, shot her father's old donkey, and bought a new one, a black jack she named Johnny, and out of which, for the next twenty-three years, she knocked shite.

Over the years she lost both her beauty and her old father and gained very little else but a whetstone of a temper upon which she honed her tongue.

On the day of the Second World War, Miss Judith lost her asinine fiancé in a plot of cabbages behind Michael Murphy's shed, ballooned with the bloat and upturned like a small, black currach with his four legs as stiff at each corner as bedposts.

A few days later Miss Judith, advertising, became engaged to the equally black-hearted Jimmy, then a winsome three-year-old with a shiny coat, and they settled into their mutual years of deadlock and checkmate, with Miss Judith knocking shite out of Jimmy as she had out of the late Johnny.

Thus the ordered years passed. They rolled by the brothers O'Neill with the porpoises of summer and the westerlies of winter, their wordless days punctuated by the flap of soles and bass, mullet and pollock on the boards of the boat at their feet. Their years of snapping congers, of turbot heavy as anchors, of fatuous skate and of quicksilver sprats, and of the rainbow leap of the salmon and the strange ungodliness of the huge angler fish with its mantrap jaws and its ventral parody of hands.

The years bloomed and seeded and withered too for Miss Judith Dannaher, with the harebells and the froggy marsh flowers, the mossy gates which opened her days into one field from another, and the faded finality of the grained back door shutting out the night's black paw. The days of unborn calves and ice on buckets, of geese on the high wind of Christmas, and of a striped snail on summer's rosetted wall.

The years of thistledown and blown spindthrift, the years of mustardseed.

The years changed, and to those who say there is no change their changeling lives must suffer the strangest of them all.

Like leaves, one falls on a bright day of frost, and the other is left for the night wind. One drifts to the wet grass, and one remains to tap in the sunlight.

It is a slow pavane, and yet those that are left say how swift is the end, how unexpected, how terrible. They cannot see the unravelling of the net, the break in the web, the turning of the inexorable kaleidoscope to bring about a new pattern, the new enigma.

On a December day, Miss Judith Dannaher closed all her windows and wedged the doors, fed her stock, and made up her fire. There could be no work until the sheeting rain and savage wind eased.

162

The hens peered out of their houses at the roar, and the tucked cows shivered at the closed door of their byre.

The wind flung the sand off the beach, and the sea ran against the sullen river's push, and they fought each other into a great, toothed, lionheaded wall of grey water.

The brothers O'Neill were caught up as their boat scraped ashore, and they were rolled in their black oilskins under its sucking arch like peas down a drain. The wind caught the ghosts of two words and tore them into infinity.

O Judith, cried Johnny.

O Judith, cried Jimmy.

In the dim cabin Miss Judith Dannaher had fallen asleep by her bright fire.

In a hollow of the whistling Burrows nine grey asses and one black with a broken hobble sheltered against the driving sand, patiently enduring the stinging fury of the wind with the humble acceptance of martyrs.

On the strand the whirling paper shell of a sea-urchin blew against a white branch of driftwood and disintegrated in a puff of fragments.

Her head settling further down on to her chest, Miss Judith Dannaher exhaled a strangled snore, and the light ashes of her dead fire stirred and fluttered on the cold hearth.

Park-going Days

Evelyn Conlon

They took their chairs and children, of whom they were terribly proud today, to the park on the first day of summer, relieved that the darkness was over and repeating again and again great day so that maybe such sunworship would bring them a summer. You would never have believed that in those few houses there could be so many children—you could easily have forgotten Kathleen's fifth or that Bridie during the winter had had another because naturally you never saw it, Bridie's new one, due to the freezing conditions. If you did Bridie was a bad mother and there were no good or bad mothers around here, (even the ones whose sons were inside)—just mothers. It was a Thursday after dinner—the one man who had a job nearby had been fed—no one would have gone to the park before that happened, not in deference to Jack eating but because Jack's wife wouldn't be free until then and there was nothing to make a woman feel housebound like all the other women trooping up to the park before her and there was nothing worse than feeling housebound on a sunny day.

The park-going days of sunshine were truly numbered in this country—fifteen last year, two the year before, ten the year before that and forty on the year that god was otherwise occupied and forgot to switch off the heat or else decided to tease us and make us mournful for the next five years. No woman in this country had any doubt but that god was a man—*is* a man. There's no was about that fellow unfortunately. Some had the view that the man himself was intrinsically all right and that it was the ones who took over after him who mucked the whole thing up. Could be true—he may have been all right. Perhaps. But it's a hard thing to believe in a country that only once had forty days of sunshine. It's amazing the amount of preparations women used to working can put into a trip to the park. One folded up light deck chair, suntan oil, facecloth, sandwiches which will avoid having to make a children's tea at six, rug to put sandwiches and children on, sunglasses, small lightish jumpers in case it turns cold suddenly, drinks, the antibiotics that the child is on, some toys for the baby—for the ones who were pregnant last summer—the baby's bottle, one nappy and ALL that baby stuff, *and* ice cream money.

At ten past two all the doors opened and out they poured nearly invisible behind all the paraphernalia, calling around them the children who had been dreamy and inside and the ones who had already been outside getting burned and thirsty and cranky. And dirty.

"Look at the face of her. Come here to me until I give you a wipe. Disgracing me." She dug the facecloth into the child's face disgracing her in front of friends who hadn't noticed at all.

They went and Rita went after them not to the park but past the park on the way to the shops, half hoping that if there was a summer next year, or if this one lasted beyond the day, that they would ask her to join them, knowing that it would be better if they didn't because if they ran out of steam—which they would when they realised the sort of her and why—there could be no more casual comments passed between them as strangers. They and she could whistle pleasantries back and forth at the moment, they prepared to waste their sweet words on her because of curiosity—(a new resident)—she to make them less curious, and failing.

The more she said nice day the more they wanted to know. The more she felt their sniffing the more frightened she got. That sneaky-faced woman in the nylon housecoat, too old to walk to the park, polishing her brasses again. Who did she think she was fooling? Of course she was lonelier than if she was dead but Rita couldn't set her sympathy juices working.

Rita walked after them aggravated at the bits and pieces of garages built at the ends of gardens as if thrown together in shapeless anger. In winter she could escape them by looking down at her feet, which she did, but today the sun threw their shadow across the street under her eyes. A bulldozer was needed badly. Knock the whole lot of them. She had no soft spots for old farm barns, mudwall byres or extended hen houses so she couldn't see anything for them but the bulldozer. Her husband would not have agreed. But then he came from places where fields lay companionably beside other fields that ran casually into more and more fields, flat and hilly, offering place grudgingly to the occasional house that was then forced to use rickety outhouses as protection against the ever-approaching grass. She was from a geometrician's dream where back gardens were only concessions to the superior needs of houses. She passed the park and saw them.

They belonged to a time before the time of one earring. Two ears, two earrings. Fingers were the only single part of them that divided into ones. They put rings on them, most importantly they put one ring on one finger sometimes along with another varying in degrees of vulgarity and awfulness. The rings marked stages in their self denial and destruction. Rita saw the rings glistening in the sun picking out unreachable baubles in the sky. They saw her and thought different things none of them actually about her, more about her type.

"You couldn't satisfy *him*. If it's not the smog, it's the dirt or the accents. Jayzus would yeh listen to whose talkin' about an accent."

"How *does* she put up with him? An' it's made her odd."

"There's somethin' else odd about her but I can't put me finger on it."

"Ah well."

In the end they knew in their hearts that the only thing funny about her was that they didn't know her and that she was married to a culchie. Not much of a gap to be got over.

They settled in their chairs and watched their collective new generation comparing it favourably with the other groups in the park, conscious that they were all part of even more park groups, between them accounting for hundreds of miles of discarded umbilical cords.

They uttered unconnected sentences at random. Conversation was organised only when there was tragedy or scandal to be related. But the silence was never silent, it was just a space of time between words of explanation and more words of inadequate explanation.

Bridie watched hers out of the corner of her eye, Sean always dirty. As a baby he sucked the ends of his babygro and got a red wrist in his fat little cracks from wet aggravation. Now he sucked his jumper and pulled at his waist all the time ending up each evening with handmarks branded in frustration on his clothes. His pores seemed to suck in every bit of street dirt going. His cuts usually went septic. Anne. Wise. Precocious and clean. Wise as the wound. She would have children too—it didn't bear thinking about. She played with her older brothers in a superior bossy way as if she knew.

"She'll be coming out of school at half two when she makes her communion, please god."

That would be another step passed in the sending off of her to the Lord.

"It took me all day to get out of town yesterday. Pickets outside the Dáil. They should put that buildin' down the country somewhere and not be stoppin' people tryin' to get home. They wouldn't be so quick to picket it if it was down there."

They shifted their fat bodies around on the deck chairs. They had suffered from the usual emotional disappointments being married to their husbands. Kathleen's man had been mortified one day when she was nearly due and she'd sat down on the steps of the bank in town, not fit to move another inch. It was a Saturday and the bank was closed, what *could* he have been going on about? In her early marriage before having any, Molly used to call on her husband at work. She thought it was a nice thing to do and she was lonely on her own—she'd been getting eleven pounds before the wedding, now with tax it was only five, so there wasn't much point in her going to work for the short while, the bus fare was two pounds. One day he said that she'd have to stop calling and get used to their new house for both their sakes. The men at work would start talking.

"But I don't know anyone."

"You'll get to know some mothers later."

He smiled. She smiled. It was a small subtle exclusion, preparation for the major ones—the tapping on the shoulder as women walked absentmindedly, not deliberately, not provokingly, into supermarkets pushing prams. She never called again. Bridie's man, when he was young, had kept running from one country to the other filling himself up with experience, pouring himself all over the continent and still he hadn't one word to say for himself. He'd only said once I love you. He was a consumer of cultures—he had a few words of French which gave him an edge on the other men on the street but that was no help to Bridie. Susan's man—the drinker—did his bit for his children. He talked about them occasionally in pubs in the serious way that drunk men do, once getting first day issue covers for them from a man who worked in the P & T who happened, just happened, to be drinking beside him. Now that was more than a woman could do. Kathleen had broken her mother's heart—Ma I wasn't going to tell you this but seeing we're out for the day and that it's on my mind and I have been keeping it to myself and all that and it's no good for me or anything and all that and no good for you either and I'm pregnant. Kathleen sighed. Bridie put her varicose veins on the wheel of the pram. These— the fat, the veins, the sighs—were the shapes of the backbone of the country. You'd never think it to see the corkscrew frown-free pictures that poured from the admen's anorexic fantasies.

"Great day."

"A doctor said to my mother once that there are two terrible bad things for a woman, ironing and not dropping everything to run outside when she sees the first blink of sun."

"Yeah, it's a great day."

"I'd like a cigarette. Funny the way you feel like it sometimes and not at others."

"I didn't know you smoked Molly."

Molly raised her voice to panic pitch.

"Smoke. Smoke is it? I was a chain smoker. What! I had meself burnt. Me lips, me skirts, me bras, me slips. One match would do me the whole day. Lit one off the other."

"What did you smoke?"

It was neither a question nor a statement after Molly's emotion.

"Albany."

"Were they a special cigarette, I don't remember them. I used to smoke Woodbine. No one ever died that smoked Woodbine."

"It's near tea-time."

That was a grand day. No one had got cut or desperately badly hurt. There had been the odd row but not enough to deserve a beating. One woman, not belonging to their group, had set her child up for a bat- tering. She hit her because she wanted to go on the swings too often. The child kicked her back. The women nodded a sort of ungrudging serve you right nod. The mother hit her more. The incident might have spiralled into murder but the floating disapproval, the soul sym- pathy, and the take-it-easy-it'll-get-better thoughts made the mother acknowledge defeat. Yes, a great day.

They were gathering up their stuff when Rita walked past on her way home. They delayed, to let her go on. They were sick of her kind, really, never any children, coming to live in that rented house, teasing their curiosity and staying aloof.

"You wouldn't mind so much marrying a culchie but getting *used* to him."

They laughed. They could have remarked that she was unhappy but they denied her that status in the mean way that city people can, surrounded as they are by so many, some of whom, precisely because of the number, are dispensable. They turned their noses up and pulled their curtains down an inch from their faces like country wans could never do. (Perhaps you might need her in twenty years when all the rest would be gone, to America, or Dublin.) As they struggled nearer their doors, exhausted from heat, children whinging, when *they* saw the prospect of home looming closer, that they hadn't stayed long enough in the park, only three hours Mammy; they each withdrew themselves from collective experience and concentrated on their individual problems. Parks were all right—open-air sum totals of lives that were normally lived in box rooms with thick enough doors and walls to shut out obscenities—but all the same you wouldn't want to live in a park all your life and you wouldn't want to behave in your own house as if you were in a park. After a while people get on your nerves, even on sunny days—that was why the tenants in the rented house were always handy. Everyone on the street could take their collective spite against each other out on them and so avoid major street fights.

Rita knew what they were thinking. Sometimes at four in the morning—she often woke at four—she would look out and see reflections of their lights and she would feel like forgiving them because who couldn't forgive a woman anything when they saw her struggling at that unearthly hour to silence a crying, hungry baby. Rita *had* had a child of her own. The child had died and she wasn't allowed to think about it. What had happened was anyone's guess—it just died. But Rita was fine now. Fine. The street would have gushed with sympathy if it had known. One thing Rita regretted not having was park days with mothers. She'd noticed the way mothers made up to the children on park days. Made up to them for all sorts of troubles, things like concentrated compressed family violences that emptied onto children's backsides when men and women decided at the same moment that they would have to put manners on the offspring who was at that second holding their nerves to ransom. They could do that because they knew that mothers would make it up sometime soon—certainly in a park if it was a sunny day. Rita would have liked the making up bits.

It was Bridie in the end who asked Rita if she wanted to sit down with them in the park just for a few minutes, for a little rest. She stretched her legs out in front of her and said to herself now I'll have to leave. They talked busily as they watched the replay of yesterday and yesterday, Rita not thinking all the time of her own because she wasn't allowed to, each of the other women remarking to herself how nice she was really. The next day it rained. Clouds stalked over the bit of sunshine they'd had and Rita started packing. She said goodbye before herself and her culchie husband left, knocked on the single doors and got away before they learned anything about her. A week later if you could have cut bits out of the walls you would have seen them bending over the baby in the way that causes bad backs, cleaning noses, swiping at bare legs, sneaking off for a rest and drying clothes, again, again, as the tenants moved in and the rain poured on them all.

Trio

Jennifer Johnston

In spite of the brilliant, sliding sun the evening was cold. Frank pushed his hands deep down into his pockets and stamped his feet uselessly.

"What a wind."

Dust and an empty cigarette-box skeltered past their feet, down the hill past the waiting gateways and the neat hedges.

"West. It's from the west. That means rain. More rain. God, I'll be glad when this winter's over."

Murphy pulled on his cigarette and let the smoke trickle slowly out through his nose. He was wearing a knitted hat pulled well down over his ears.

Frank shuffled his feet on the pavement again.

"I get chilblains," he complained. "Every bloody winter. There's nothing you can do about it. There was one year I didn't, that was the time I was working in London. It's the damp. So they say. Drive you crazy sometimes, so they would. Just that one year I didn't get them."

Murphy sighed. Talkers. He was always lumbered with a talker. Voices always nagging away, nudging their way into his head, never letting him be at peace with his own thoughts. Silence was good. Golden, his mother used to say. He turned and squinted his eyes towards the setting sun. Golden, but you couldn't see with it dazzling in your eyes, even when you turned your head away again you couldn't focus for a moment or two. He walked back up the street towards the main road. With a bit of luck the sun would be behind the hill in about ten minutes.

"Did you ever suffer with chilblains?" asked Frank behind him.

"No."

"You wouldn't know then what it's like at all."

"No."

They stood at the corner for a few moments, watching the cars go by. Behind them, below where they had been standing, a man sat, reading a book, in a parked car. Murphy dropped the butt of his cigarette on the pavement and then put his foot on it.

"What's the time?"

Murphy looked at his watch.

"Ten to."

"He's late."

They stared across the valley at the distant hills, the glitter.

"It'd be a great evening if it wasn't so cold. Maybe he'll not come."

They turned and strolled back down the road again.

"He'll come all right."

Patrick opened the door of his car and threw his briefcase over onto the back seat. Late. He got into the car and slammed the door. Meticulously he placed his thin white hands on the steering-wheel and stared at them. What does it matter anyway? Late or early. Nobody else worries. No one gets agitated. We all have our own obsessions. I like to treat time with care. He started the engine and sat listening to the comfortable sound of it. Like a cat by the fire. What precisely do I consider myself to be late for? The small preoccupations of domestic life. The kiss on the cheek. The careful arrangement of glasses on a tray. Clink, clink across the hall, taking care not to slip on the Persian carpet. Last shafts of sun and then pull the curtains, keep our privacy to ourselves. No dreams. No time for dreams. The stir and tumult of defeated dreams . . . who could have said that? From those years when I read books and nervously brooded on the meanings of things. I must tidy things up and have a break. I'm tired. He laughed and moved the car slowly forward across the yard. A break indeed. What happens I wonder when you, for a moment, realize the emptiness of the future, oh and God the past. The dreamlessness even of the past. Forget it. Impeccable safety.

"Good evening, sir."

George, the security man, opened the gate into the street.

Patrick smiled and nodded.

"You're late tonight, sir. It's ten to."

"Telephones should never have been invented."

"Good-night."

"Good-night George. See you in the morning."

"Of course he'll come."

"But if he doesn't? What do we do?"

"We come back tomorrow."

Murphy's voice was exasperated.

The wind was banging at their backs, pushing them firmly down the hill.

"I suppose we would." Frank sighed. "My sister's just been took into the hospital. Just, there a few minutes before I came out. Her first. Ay. I know she'll be expecting me up to see her tomorrow."

The way of the world, thought Murphy, one goes, another comes. Apart from his own somewhat amazed arrival into the world, he had no close, touching experiences of either birth or death. It didn't do to look at the whole thing in a broad, emotional way. Achievement was what mattered.

"That is, if he comes . . ."

Murphy's cap had worked its way up on to the top of his head. He pulled it firmly, warmly down over his ears again.

The gate closed behind him. The traffic was edging slowly along between the high warehouses. Time, as usual, being wasted, maltreated. Then suppose, just suppose that I treated time as if it belonged to me. I am no longer time's servant. What then? It becomes at once a precious commodity. The only one worth having. Will I turn on the radio and listen to the news? Drown the sound of my own thoughts? I hate this street, the unpainted windows and the dirty walls. Hate is a word I haven't used since I was a child, and now, having used it, I feel myself filling with it, feel it burning inside me. It feels good. I must be having a little madness of some sort. I don't want to hold things together any longer. Not even at home. In the words of the immortal Greta Garbo, I want to be alone. Free. Me and my servant Time. Unobtainable, before it is too late. Christ. To have to watch yet again the great triumphal renewal of the earth as we ourselves decay. Break. I must break. My life in shreds.

"It's her first."

"So you said."

"Mam went with her in the ambulance. Just to give her a bit of . . . well you know . . . moral support like. Sean's in England. That's her husband. She thought she'd like to have it here. At home. I suppose you're nervous with the first one. Mam went with her. I'd say she'd be all right, wouldn't you?"

"You're to cover me. That's all you're to do."

"I'll try and get to see her tomorrow. That is . . ."

"Did you hear me?"

A small girl with a dog on a lead walked past them down the hill. She walked past the gate and the parked car and then crossed the road and went into a garden on the other side. Inside the gate she stooped and let the dog free. Huge clouds were beginning to pile up in the sky. The sun was almost gone. The hedge beside them smelt sweet.

"Whose child is that?"

"How the hell would I know whose child it is."

They turned and walked slowly up towards the corner again. The man in the car put down his book and switched on the engine. Down the road a door banged. Frank groped in his pocket.

"Would you like a fag?"

"No. Did you hear what I said? You are to cover me. Nothing more. Just keep your eyes skinned."

"I wonder will it be a boy or a girl."

Only a golden line of sun. Rain was blowing from the west. It was going to be a stormy night.

So many wrong decisions I have made all the way down the line. I never searched for courage, never realized the possible need for it. Can I summon that neglected asset now, before it is too late? If . . . It's just nerves Mary would say. The situation is getting you down. You should take a break . . . pull yourself together. That's what I'll do. I'll go home and have a large drink and pull myself together. Face whatever it is she has arranged for me to face. It is unkind and totally unrealistic to throw the blame on her. Face my own music. Or else I could do the other thing.

He slowed down the car and pulled in to the side of the road.

I could. There is nothing to stop me. I could fill the car with petrol, I could . . . Commitments, aged commitments. Lack of courage. Worse, of hope. They would bring me back. I would blow it. He moved back into the mainstream of traffic.

"I wouldn't mind what it was really. She'd like a wee boy. You want it to be all right. That's what really matters. You know, all right. One of my aunties had one that was . . . well . . . not quite right. That'd be always in your mind. He's grown up now. He's not too bad, just a bit soft, you know . . . but nice enough."

Paining my head, all this talk. But maybe he's right, time is getting on. Maybe he's not coming.

Several large drops of rain, blown by the wind, scattered themselves on the ground.

Frank ducked his head into the collar of his coat.

"What did I tell you? Rain."

Behind the clouds the sky was stained pink now.

"Red sky at night . . ."

"Oh, for Jesus' sake . . ."

"What's up, Murphy?"

They stood for a moment and then turned their backs on the west.

"Nerves?"

Slowly they moved down the street once more. Murphy felt in his pocket for a cigarette.

"Nerves got you?"

He put the cigarette into his mouth.

"I'd say you're right. He's not coming," he said at last. His hand fumbled for the matches.

"It's late now. Too late."

The car down the street revved its engine. Murphy dropped the cigarette on the ground.

"Just cover me," he said. "Don't do another bloody thing."

Patrick slowed down and turned into the street. There was a car moving towards him and then past him as he swung the wheel to turn in the gate.

The spring will come and then the summer. I have no energy, no will. I will put on my smile. I will resume my role. I will wait.

175

He became aware of the two men walking down the path towards him. Quite casually they seemed to come, the guns raised in their hands.

How strange, how very, very strange . . .

There was no more time.

The echoing frightened some birds, who flew uneasily into the air. Far away a dog barked. The car accelerated and was gone. It was almost dark.

All Fall Down

Helen Lucy Burke

There was not an ounce of innate prejudice against me in the heart of Miss O'Leary. Every now and then she took us on "Nature Walks" to point us out interesting weeds and mushrooms that would clarify the botanical bits in our reader. In the same way she used me and my family to illustrate her thesis on alcohol.

By disposition she was very strong against the drink. The Parish Priest urged her to still greater extremities of zeal—our parish was a horror for alcohol. Who could blame her for her enthusiasm when daily, opposite her very window, she was presented with a text-book example?

Who but me?

Each day at half-past two came my moment of torture: for that was the time when my father, chased out of the pub for the regulation hour, went staggering home past the windows of the school.

"See, children," Miss O'Leary would cry, all professional interest, "how alcohol depresses the brain, causing loss of muscular control."

My father was a long, thin man. His legs wobbled about as awkwardly as the legs of a newly-dropped colt. There was a bit of a rise in the boreen outside the school, and there he always fell. It used to take him a long time to get up. He would throw one leg out in front of him, stiff as the fork of a compass: but then the other leg pivoted away, and there he was again, sprawling in the mud. His face was very calm and serious all the time. None of us ever attempted to help him. Miss O'Leary instructed us that drunks had terrible tempers and that we were not to trust ourselves near them, any more than we would go beside a ram or a bull.

Of course the other kids had fathers who got drunk—there was not an abstainer in the whole parish—but they did it in a jollier way altogether, at fairs and card-parties: and afterwards they went home and beat the tar out of their wives and children, which was thought nicer and more natural.

Basically, the great local failing was not alcohol but excess. The women never touched a drop of fermented liquor, but instead got their release in exaggerated fervour of church-going. They practised bowings before the altar, daily Communion, weekly Confession at which they accused themselves of interesting faults like over-zealousness and scruples, and all sorts of other religious *bonne-bouches* in the style of Sodalities and Leagues against Swearing. At night while their husbands were out drinking and gambling, they cautioned their huge families against marriage and did their best to turn their minds in the direction of monasteries and nunneries.

Among this crew my father was an oddity. He did not beat my mother or me. He drank alone. He showed no loud enjoyment of his drink—poor man, what was wine to them was blood to him. Worst of all he was a sort of gentleman, and the wrong sort, the quiet standoffish kind. If he had turned out for the first meet of the season and galloped his half-mile with the hounds there would have been no animosity. Even attendance now and then at a point-to-point would have been better than nothing.

Quite simply, I hated him. At night, lying with the blankets drawn over my head and tucked in the far side of the pillow, I used to scheme how I would kill him before I was eighteen. A push down the stairs from the top landing—now that would be a fine thing!

Most of the time I think he did not know I was there. If by chance he noticed me, I embarrassed him so much that he gave me all his loose change.

One night, coming home from the village, my father was knocked down by a straying cow who rolled him into the ditch. There he lay, all the freezing night. When he was found next morning his condition was grave. My mother had him conveyed to the hospital forty miles away. So that she might be free to sit at his bedside—his death was expected—she sent me by train to Dublin as a boarder in a convent school. I believe she was quite fond of him.

I was ten years old.

For the next two days I cried steadily, more because it was expected of me than from grief. After this purge I settled down into the bliss of a life that I could build to my own specifications.

There are strange paradises in this world. Mine was compounded of long dark corridors smelling of paraffin polish and disinfectant, a playground paved with cinders, staircases hollowed out of the mouldering walls, a corner of the nuns' garden where we dug plots for seeds.

Oh, the strangeness of the customs! The nuns bowed as they passed each other in the corridors. If they were alone they swept down the middle of the passages, majestic in their white starched bonnets as ships in full sail; and we pupils crowded in against the walls and bowed humbly with hands folded. Impassive, they never returned our reverences but floated rapidly on, their faces adorned with little mysterious smiles.

They filled me with awe. Nature must have moulded them from a different clay. Surely they were not of the same make as the harried red and brown women of Kilanore. I remember my horror when one day, peeping from a forbidden window, I saw the nuns' knickers hanging like great white spinnakers from the clothes-line. I told my infamy later in Confession.

We went to bed at nine o'clock and we rose at six. Once a month we had a bath. Hair-washing was not permitted for the whole length of the term. Some abandoned girls secretly used to wash their hair after the lights were out, and dried it on their pillows; but we were told that God had His eyes on them and sooner or later He would punish them by striking them deaf.

A number of the girls had lice. When this was spotted—we were watched pretty sharply for undue scratching—they were combed over an enamel basin with a fine comb dipped in paraffin. For weeks these victims went round smelling of paraffin and howling for grief that their shame had been exposed.

All this was paradise because my father was not near. In fact I spread it around that I had no father. Died while I was small, I said, and basked in the caressing sympathy of the older girls.

I never heard from him, of course, and when my mother wrote it was just dry little notes saying that things were going well, or things could be better, or things were not so well. The nuns opened the letters and read them before we got them, but that did not disturb me. I did not even wonder what would happen if they got to hear of my fictions. Life was taking place on two planes, and the plane of the imagination was the more real. Religion helped. Sin was all around us, we were told, lurking like a worm at the heart of an apple, invisible until you got to the ruined core. Opportunities for virtue were offered as plentifully. At lunch in the refectory one day Frances Boylan got a decayed human tooth in her stew. She wept and complained, but the refectarian pointed out the great opportunity she had missed for gaining grace by "offering it up" and saying nothing. Next day they read to us from the "Lives of the Saints" about a French lady who developed her sanctity by eating spits off the ground.

Heaven lay about us, and so did Hell, and the school was an infinite wonder, a battleground of forces contending for possession of us; and yet pure, unsensual, unworldly, a place where everything including sin could take place in the mind.

Kilanore and its grossness became a memory.

Easter came, making a dent in the routine. Christ died. Prayerbooks banged with sinister noise in the darkened chapel at Tenebrae. He rose again from the dead. We were allowed to attend three Masses on Easter Sunday. Afterwards there were boiled eggs for breakfast, and in the afternoon there was a film about the Missions. A number of girls, including myself, did not go home for the Easter holidays. We all cried a little each night, and the other girls petted me and stroked me because my father was dead and I was so brave. Frances Boylan, who was two months older than me, said she would be my best friend. The sun shone and my whole body seemed to blossom and send out green shoots. I knew at last that God lived and loved me.

I prepared with fervour for my Confirmation.

Not long after term started again my mother wrote to say that himself was out of hospital. The two of them planned to attend my Confirmation.

It was my sentence of death.

Closing my eyes tightly to shut out the pictures that presented themselves I could see them all the more clearly. My father lurching over the parquet floor . . . the fall and the sprawl and the dreadful efforts to get up . . . the girls turning kindly away so as not to see and not to know that I had lied.

I wrote to him for the first time in my life, told him what I had done, and demanded that he stay his distance. A few days later I got a letter from my mother saying that she and my uncle would be arriving for the Confirmation.

I had no uncle.

We walked—no, proceeded, slowly up the aisle, heads bent in reverence. Our white dresses creaked over layers of petticoats. The weather had turned cold, but none of us wore a coat that might hide the glory of our rows of picot-edged frills. Frances Boylan beside me had only four rows of frills: I had six, and this was a triumph that made me love her even more. When the Bishop tapped us on the cheek with a withered hand that rustled like paper she grabbed my arm and held it tightly, not daring to look up, while I stared boldly into the beaky face, lemon-coloured under the mitre, and the Bishop stared back at me the way an angry cock does.

Later, we promised to abide by the truths of our religion and to refrain from alcohol under the age of twenty-one. We chorused this in unison, and no voice was stronger than mine.

Parents and children met afterwards in the Middle Parlour. Awkwardly, on the chill expanse of waxed parquet, the family groups talked in low embarrassed voices. Even Frances Boylan's father, who was a stout red-faced bookmaker, planed the rough race-course edges off his voice and fluted out his conversation in a genteel treble.

My father seemed at ease. He did not come forward to meet me but stood quietly waiting, as if he were ready to be disowned without making a fuss.

My mother and he kissed me. I noticed at once that he did not smell of drink. There was a carnation in the buttonhole of his suit. It was a new suit, dark-brown fine tweed with a little hair in it that scratched my cheek when he pressed me against him.

"Your uncle came out of hospital a fortnight ago," said my mother.

I nodded my head politely up and down. "I hope you're better," I said.

"Not too bad." He spoke in a sort of ghost voice, that seemed to come with great effort from a great distance. His face had got smaller and was a funny clear colour, a bit like the tracing paper we used for making maps, but grayer. His moustache was gone, so that it was easier to see his mouth, and to see that his lips trembled slightly but continually. Each time he caught my eye he tried to smile, but could not quite make it. I left them and went to the table where tea and sandwiches and seedcake were set out.

Frances Boylan and Una Sheedy asked me was that my uncle.

"It is," I said. "He's just after coming out of hospital."

"He's lovely looking," said Frances. Flabbergasted, I realised that she meant it; and that she was comparing his emaciated elegance with her stout common father. And I realised that she too was ashamed of her father. Did all children hate their parents, I wondered? It seemed a new strong bond. I led them over to be introduced.

"This is my mother and my Uncle Matthew," I said.

He stood up at once and shook hands. Then he asked their permission to smoke. Reverent in their awe for his politeness they assured him that they did not mind. My mother stood in the background with a shut-off expression on her face. Presently she said that they must go. My father gave me a five-pound note, and bowed to Una and Frances.

We left the parlour all five of us together, like a family, or like a herd of does with the stag. No, that was not it either, for he deferred to us so lightly and gently that it was more like a king with a group of young queens, his equals in rank, but younger.

Worshipping, Frances and Una drifted forward beside him, while my mother and I as proprietors hung back a little and let them have their fill. He told them to call him uncle, and they did so. He took the carnation from his buttonhole and presented it to them jointly, regretting that roses were not in season. We came to the head of the marble stairs. Frances and Una drew back, I moved forward to escort my visitors down to the door.

The saints smiled at us from the walls. He turned back to wave to my friends and his footing went. His stick tumbled before him down to the foot of the stairs. Behind it he rolled, threshing with his arms for a hold to save himself. There was a dull sound from each stair as he struck, then silence when he reached the bottom. We stared down at him, an insect on its back, waving its legs. There was no power in them, like tentacles they moved. His head came up several times and turned vaguely about.

"He's killed," screamed Frances and Una. They started down the stairs. I ran past them and picked up his stick.

It took the combined strength of my mother and two nuns to get me away from him. As I struck, his eyes looked up at me for each blow and winced away as the stick fell. He said nothing, although his mouth writhed. He did not cry out.

They sent me to the sickroom with hot milk and aspirin. Later the priest came. He sat at the end of my bed for a long time. All I would say in answer to his questioning was: "He fell down again."

A few weeks afterwards I got word that my father had died. It was alcohol poisoning, I learned later.

A Day in the Dark

Elizabeth Bowen

Coming into Moher over the bridge, you may see a terrace of houses by the river. They are to the left of the bridge, below it. Their narrow height and faded air of importance make them seem to mark the approach to some larger town. The six dwellings unite into one frontage, colour-washed apricot years ago. They face north. Their lower sash windows, front steps and fanlit front doors are screened by lime trees, making for privacy. There are area railings. Between them and the water runs a road with a parapet, which comes to its end opposite the last house.

On the other side of the bridge picturesquely rises a ruined castle—more likely to catch the tourist's eye. Woods, from which the river emerges, go back deeply behind the ruin: on clear days there is a backdrop of Irish-blue mountains. Otherwise Moher has little to show. The little place prospers—a market town with a square, on a main road. The hotel is ample, cheerful, and does business. Moreover Moher is, and has been for ages, a milling town. Obsolete stone buildings follow you some way along the river valley as, having passed through Moher, you pursue your road. The flour-white modern mills, else-where, hum.

Round the square, shops and pubs are of many colours—in the main Moher looks like a chalk drawing. Not so the valley with its elusive lights.

You *could*, I can see, overlook my terrace of houses—because of the castle, indifference or haste. I only do not because I am looking out for them. For in No. 4 lived Miss Banderry.

She was the last of a former milling family—last, that is, but for

183

the widowed niece, her pensioner. She owned the terrace, drew rents also from property in another part of the town, and had acquired, some miles out of Moher, a profitable farm which she'd put to management. Had control of the family mills been hers, they would not have been parted with—as it was, she had had to contend with a hopeless brother: he it was who had ended by selling out. Her demand for her share of the money left him unable to meet personal debts: he was found hanged from one of the old mill crossbeams. Miss Banderry lived in retirement, the more thought of for being seldom seen—now and then she would summon a Ford hackney and drive to her farm in it, without warning. My uncle, whose land adjoined on hers, had dealings with her, in the main friendly—which was how they first fell into talk. She, a formidable reader, took to sending him serious magazines, reviews, pamphlets and so on, with marked passages on which she would be dying to hear his views. This was her way of harrying him. For my uncle, a winning, versatile and when necessary inventive talker, fundamentally hated to tax his brain. He took to evading meetings with her as far as possible.

So much I knew when I rang her doorbell.

It was July, a sunless warm afternoon, dead still. The terrace was heavy with limes in flower. Above, through the branches, appeared the bridge with idlers who leaned on the balustrade spying down upon me, or so I thought. I felt marked by visiting this place—I was fifteen, and my every sensation was acute in a way I recall, yet cannot recall. All six houses were locked in childless silence. From under the parapet came languidly the mesmeric sound of the weir, and, from a window over my head, the wiry hopping of a bird in a cage. From the shabby other doors of the terrace, No. 4's stood out, handsomely though sombrely painted red. It opened.

I came to return a copy of *Blackwoods*. Also I carried a bunch of ungainly roses from my uncle's garden, and a request that he might borrow the thistle cutter from Miss Banderry's farm for use on his land. One rose moulted petals on to her doorstep, then on to the linoleum in the hall. "Goodness!" complained the niece, who had let me in. "Those didn't travel well. Overblown, aren't they!" (I thought that applied to her.) "And I'll bet," she said, "*he* never sent those!" She was not in her aunt's confidence, being treated more or less like a slave. Timed (they said) when she went errands into the town—she dare not stay talking, dare not so much as look into the hotel bar while the fun was on. For a woman said to be forty, this sounded mortifying.

Widowed Nan, ready to be handsome, wore a cheated ravenous look. It was understood she would come into the money when the aunt died: she must contain herself till then. As for me—how dared she speak of my uncle with her bad breath?

Naturally he *had* never thought of the roses. He had commissioned me to be gallant for him any way I chose, and I would not do too badly with these, I'd thought, as I unstrangled them from the convolvulus in the flowerbed. They would need not only to flatter but to propitiate, for this copy of *Blackwoods* I brought back had buttery thumbmarks on its margins and on its cover a blistered circle where my uncle must have stood down his glass. "She'll be mad," he prophesied. "Better say it was you." So I sacrificed a hair ribbon to tie the roses. It rejoiced me to stand between him and trouble.

"Auntie's resting," the niece warned me, and put me to wait. The narrow parlour looked out through thick lace on to the terrace, which was reflected in a looking-glass at the far end. Ugly though I could see honourable furniture, mahogany, had been crowded in. In the middle, a circular table wore a chenille cloth. This room felt respected though seldom entered—however, it was peopled in one way: generations of oil-painted portraits hung round the walls, photographs overflowed from bracket and ledge even on to the centre table. I was faced, wherever I turned, by one or another member of the family which could only be the vanished Banderrys. There was a marble clock, but it had stopped.

Footsteps halted heavily over the ceiling, but that was all for I don't know how long. I began to wonder what those Banderrys saw—lodging the magazine and roses on the table, I went to inspect myself in the glass. A tall girl in a sketchy cotton dress. Arms thin, no sign yet of a figure. Hair forward over the shoulders in two plaits, like, said my uncle, a Red Indian maiden's. Barbie was my name.

In memory, the moment before often outlives the awaited moment. I recollect waiting for Miss Banderry—then, nothing till she was with me in the room. I got over our handshake without feeling. On to the massiveness of her bust was pinned a diamond-studded enamelled watch, depending from an enamelled bow: there was a tiny glitter as she drew breath.—"So he sent *you*, did he?" She sat down, the better to look at me. Her apart knees stretched the skirt of her dress. Her choleric colouring and eyeballs made her appear angry, as against which she favoured me with a racy indulgent smile, to counteract the impression she knew she gave.

185

"I hear wonders of you," said she, dealing the lie to me like a card.

She sat in reach of the table. "My bouquet, eh?" She grasped the bundle of roses, thorns and all, and took a long voluptuous sniff at them, as though deceiving herself as to their origin—showing me she knew how to play the game, if I didn't—then shoved back the roses among the photographs and turned her eyes on the magazine, sharply. "I'm sorry, I—" I began. In vain. All she gave was a rumbling chuckle— she held up to me the copy of *Blackwoods* open at the page with the most thumbmarks. "I'd know *those* anywhere!" She scrutinized the print for a line or two. "Did he make head or tail of it?"

"He told me to tell you, he enjoyed it." (I saw my uncle dallying, stuffing himself with buttered toast.) "With his best thanks."

"You're a little echo," she said, not discontentedly.

I stared her out.

"Never mind," she said. "He's a handsome fellow."

I shifted my feet. She gave me a look.

She observed: "It's a pity to read at table."

"He hasn't much other time, Miss Banderry."

"Still, it's a poor compliment to you!"

She stung me into remarking: "He doesn't often."

"Oh, I'm sure you're a great companion for him!"

It was as though she saw me casting myself down by my uncle's chair when he'd left the room, or watching the lassitude of his hand hanging caressing a dog's ear. With him I felt the tender bond of sex. Seven, eight weeks with him under his roof, among the copper beeches from spring to summer turning from pink to purple, and I was in love with him. Such things happen, I suppose. He was my mother's brother, but I had not known him when I was a child. Of his manhood I had had no warning. Naturally growing into love I was, like the grass growing into hay on his uncut lawns. There was not a danger till she spoke.

"He's glad of company now and then," I said as stupidly as I could.

She plucked a petal from her black serge skirt.

"Well," she said, "thank him for the thanks. And you for the nice little pleasure of this visit.—Then, there's nothing else?"

"My uncle wants—" I began.

"You don't surprise me," said Miss Banderry. "Well, come on out with it. What this time?"

"If he could once more borrow the thistle cutter . . . ?"

" 'Once more'! And what will he be looking to do next year? Get his own mended? I suppose he'd hardly go to that length."

His own, I knew, had been sold for scrap. He was sometimes looking for ready money. I said nothing.

"Looking to me to keep him out of jail?" (Law forbids one to suffer the growth of thistles.) "Time after time, it's the same story. It so happens, I haven't mine cut yet!"

"He'd be glad to lend you his jennet back, he says, to draw the cutter for you."

"*That* brute! There'd be nothing for me to cut if it wasn't for what blows in off his dirty land." With the flat of her fingers she pressed one eyeball, then the other, back into her head. She confessed, all at once almost plaintively: "I don't care to have machinery leave my farm."

"Very well," I said haughtily, "I'll tell him."

She leaned back, rubbed her palms on her thighs. "No, wait—this you may tell my lord. Tell him I'm not sure, but I'll think it over. There might be a favourable answer, there might not. If my lord would like to know which, let him come himself.—That's a sweet little dress of yours," she went on, examining me inside it, "but it's skimpy. He should do better than hide behind *those* skirts!"

"I don't know what you mean, Miss Banderry."

"He'd know."

"Today, my uncle *was* busy."

"I'm sure he was. Busy day after day. In my life, I've known only one other man anything like so busy as your uncle. And shall I tell you who that was? My poor brother."

After all these years, that terrace focuses dread. I mislike any terrace facing a river. I suppose I would rather look upon it itself (as I must, whenever I cross that bridge) than be reminded of it by harmless others. True, only one house in it was Miss Banderry's, but the rest belong to her by complicity. An indelible stain is on that monotony—the extinct pink frontage, the road leading to nothing but those six doors which the lime trees, flower as they may, exist for nothing but to shelter. The monotony of the weir and the hopping bird. Within that terrace I was in one room only, and only once.

My conversation with Miss Banderry did not end where I leave off recording it. But at that point memory is torn across, as might be an

intolerable page. The other half is missing. For that reason my portrait
of her would be incomplete if it *were* a portrait. She could be novelist's
material, I daresay—indeed novels, particularly the French and Irish
(for Ireland in some ways resembles France) are full of prototypes of
her: oversized women insulated in little provincial towns. Literature,
once one knows it, drains away some of the shockingness out of life.
But when I met her I was unread, my susceptibilities were virgin. I
refuse to fill in her outline retrospectively: I show you only what I saw
at the time. Not what she was, but what she did to me.

Her amorous hostility to my uncle—or was it hostility making use
of a farce?—unsheathed itself when she likened him to the brother she
drove to death.

When I speak of dread I mean dread, not guilt. That afternoon, I
went to Miss Banderry's for my uncle's sake, in his place. It could be
said, my gathering of foreboding had to do with my relation with him—
yet in that there was no guilt anywhere, I could swear! I swear we did
each other no harm. I think he was held that summer, as I was, by
the sense that this was a summer like no other and which could never
again be. Soon I must grow up, he must grow old. Meanwhile we
played house together on the margin of a passion which was impossible.
My longing was for him, not for an embrace—as for him, he was glad
of companionship, as I'd truly told her. He was a man tired by a lonely
house till I joined him—a schoolgirl between schools. All thought well
of his hospitality to me. Convention was our safeguard: could one have
stronger?

I left No. 4 with ceremony. I was offered raspberry cordial. Nan bore
in the tray with the thimble glasses—educated by going visiting with
my uncle, I knew refusal would mark a breach. When the glasses were
emptied, Nan conducted me out of the presence, to the hall door—
she and I stopped aimlessly on the steps. Across the river throve the
vast new mills, unabashed, and cars swished across the tree-hidden
bridge. The niece showed a reluctance to go in again—I think the bird
above must have been hers. She glanced behind her, then, conspira-
torially at me. "So now you'll be going to the hotel?"

"No. Why?"

" 'Why?' " she jibed. "Isn't he waiting for you? Anyway, that's where
he is: in there. The car's outside."

I said: "But I'm taking the bus home."

"Now, why ever?"

"I said I would take the bus. I came in that way."

"You're mad. What, with his car in the square?"

All I could say was: "When?"

"I slipped out just now," said the niece, "since you want to know. To a shop, only. While you were chatting with Auntie." She laughed, perhaps at her life, and impatiently gave me a push away. "Get on— wherever you're going to! Anybody would think you'd had bad news!"

Not till I was almost on the bridge did I hear No. 4's door shut.

I leaned on the balustrade, at the castle side. The river, coming towards me out of the distances of woods, washed the bastions and carried a paper boat—this, travelling at uncertain speed on the current, listed as it vanished under the bridge. I had not the heart to wonder how it would fare. Weeks ago, when first I came to my uncle's, here we had lingered, elbow to elbow, looking up-river through the green-hazed spring hush at the far off swan's nest, now deserted. Next I raised my eyes to the splendid battlements, kissed by the sky where they were broken.

From the bridge to the town rises a slow hill—shops and places of business come down to meet you, converting the road into a street. There are lamp posts, signboards, yard gates pasted with layers of bills, and you tread pavement. That day the approach to Moher, even the crimson valerian on stone walls, was filmed by imponderable white dust as though the flourbags had been shaken. To me, this was the pallor of suspense. An all but empty theatre was the square, which, when I entered it at a corner, paused between afternoon and evening. In the middle were parked cars, looking forgotten—my uncle's was nearest the hotel.

The hotel, glossy with green creeper, accounted for one end of the square. A cream porch, figuring the name in gold, framed the door-way—though I kept my back to that I expected at any moment to hear a shout as I searched for the independence of my bus. But where *that* should have waited, I found nothing. Nothing, at this bus end of the square, but a drip of grease on dust and a torn ticket. "She's gone out, if that's what you're looking for," said a bystander. So there it went, carrying passengers I was not among to the scenes of safety, and away from me every hope of solitude. Out of reach was the savingness of a house empty. Out of reach, the windows down to the ground open upon the purple beeches and lazy hay, the dear weather of those rooms in and out of which flew butterflies, my cushions on the floor, my blue striped tea mug. Out of reach, the whole of the lenient meaning of my uncle's house, which most filled it when he was not there . . . I did not want to be bothered with him, I think.

"She went out on time today, more's the pity."

Down hung my hair in two weighted ropes as I turned away.

Moher square is oblong. Down its length, on the two sides, people started to come to the shop doors in order to look at me in amazement. They knew who I was and where he was: what should *I* be wanting to catch the bus for? They speculated. As though a sandal chafed me I bent down, spent some time loosening the strap. Then, as though I had never had any other thought, I started in the direction of the hotel.

At the same time, my uncle appeared in the porch. He tossed a cigarette away, put the hand in a pocket and stood there under the gold lettering. He was not a lord, only a landowner. Facing Moher, he was all carriage and colouring: he wore his life like he wore his coat—though, now he was finished with the hotel, a light hint of melancholy settled down on him. He was not looking for me until he saw me.

We met at his car. He asked: "How was she, the old terror?"

"I don't know."

"She didn't eat you?"

"No," I said, shaking my head.

"Or send me another magazine?"

"No. Not this time."

"Thank God."

He opened the car door and touched my elbow, reminding me to get in.

The Foundress

Emma Cooke

Ellie was so tired that she could have cried, but if she told Dot what time she had got home Dot would probably say that she was mad. Maybe she was, or regressed into a state of perpetual adolescence. Four twenty a.m. she had arrived in and look at her this morning, treadling the old sewing machine over dark green brocade while Dot stood staring out of the window at the sun and the snow and predicting fearfully that anyone who set foot on the drive would break a leg.

In fact, Dot, while giving lip-service to the elements, was lost in calculations which did not deal directly with Ellie, or the empire-line dance dress she was so crudely piecing together in the hopes that it would bestow an illusion of flatness on her five months pregnant belly. Not that she wasn't sympathetic. She would have cut off her right arm for Ellie if she had thought it necessary; but all she seemed called on to do at the moment was stand here shivering in her slacks and two jumpers; keeping her fingers crossed so that the tanker would arrive with the central heating oil before dinner time.

Val had vanished again to God knows where. "I am his favourite, his only wife," Ellie told Dot. "The important thing is that you should multiply," Dot said, tucking Ellie's arm into hers as they travelled the long slippery road to the grocer's shop. The emerald empire dress had been finished and worn. The oil had come. The snow still lay on the ground.

They both remembered Grandmother's slogan—especially Dot. Increase and multiply. And Grandmother, buried now behind the French Church; her house, a Huguenot house, stripped of all she had ever owned. Nothing left but the crumbling roof beams, silt in the powder room, cobwebs hanging in the linen press, arches falling. Grandmother's house where, before Grandmother was born, the Duke of Wellington scratched his name on a windowpane. Which made them all famous! So Grandmother said, lighting a fresh cigarette from her old one, which she threw out of the half-moon window into the street. Increase and multiply and inherit the earth. She pulled a face at Dot and Dot pulled one back.

Time passed. The child in Ellie's womb continued to grow. Ellie continued to turn night into day, dancing—dancing while Val was away, with sundry escorts and gate-crashers, protected wherever she went by the soft mountain beneath her matron's skirts.

Content as she was to stay at home wearing her pants and writing her treatise, Dot understood. When Ellie fluttered in in the small hours with her moth-pale face Dot made tea and brought it to where Ellie had flopped on the yellow sofa. "You should dress yourself up and come too," Ellie said. "I'm too busy," Dot said.

She was as busy as a bee. Grandmother's voice buzzed in her ears. When Ellie dropped the tongs in the fireplace the crash brought back Grandmother on a Christmas Eve, standing in her tiled kitchen with her beret on the back of her head, banging saucepans together and crying "Laugh, girls, laugh" while Dot laughed and Ellie whimpered. "She is on the sherry again," Mumsie said when Ellie told her.

"And I don't mind staying with the boys," Dot said. For Ellie had four sons already. Four heralds and a child on the way. Dot was afraid to think of a daughter as she put up her notes on celibate motherhood.

Val returned to check up on his encumbrances. Dot hoped that his stay would be for hours rather than days. Ellie took him to the kitchen to be introduced to the new cleaning woman, Nancy Spratt—then to the drawing room to see the new hearthrug, then up to the bed she had been keeping warm.

Ellie looked young enough to be the oldest boy's girlfriend, Val said next morning to Dot, his goat's eyes shining. He and Dot were alone in the kitchen. Nancy Spratt did not come in until eleven o'clock. The boys were gone about their business. Dot, chewing her toast over Simone de Beauvoir, answered him with silence. He entertained the thought of ordering her to go. Up in the bedroom Ellie lay in a pool of bliss. She had forgotten, had truly forgotten. But he had to leave again straight away. Seamus was dead. He had to see him down. He recited a translation of one of Seamus's poems to make Ellie bold. She laughed as she mopped her tears. "And tell your reverend sister to get herself raped," he said. She laughed again.

Late Spring. Ellie killed time by patching old chair covers, buying teatowels and cushions, playing bridge. At intervals Val came back, but he was busy. Nancy Spratt scrubbed the tintawn matting all along the length of the landing and half-way down the stairs before she upped and left. Crows cawed in the trees. On the tarmacadam snow was replaced by moss. Clouds lay heavy as concrete.

Dot made lists of things she wanted to remember. Grandmother had been a clergyman's widow. Sometimes she borrowed the key from his successor and brought Dot and Ellie down to the church to look at the Huguenot silver. "It must be worth a fortune," Ellie whispered, chin-high to the lowest shelf of the cabinet containing the flagon and chalice, the alms dish, the paten, the present from the Princess of Wales. They passed from there out into the deserted church, sat down in Grand-mother's pew, shut its wooden door and hooked the latch. Grand-mother's pew was like all the other pews but the kneelers were shiny and tasselled and nicer than anyone else's. Dot loved it all, the hush, the tablets, the cross of red poppies, the brass eagle, the brown and creamy marble and Grandmother with her rakish beret, plucked eye-brows and smoker's cough. Nowadays Dot smoked herself.

A few months previously, when their mother died and Dot came to stay with her, Ellie dug out a photograph and put it on the piano. It was the only one she could find. Mumsie planked forlornly in a grassy field somewhere in the nineteen forties. She reminded Ellie of herself, all bosom and belly as she sat here in a pink maternity dress—although, of course, Mumsie was not pregnant. A man's hat, presumably the photographer's, lay on the grass beside her. It was not father's, although he had been alive at the time. He never went in for outings. Mumsie held something in her hands that, on close scrutiny, looked like the end of a sash. Mumsie had gone in a lot for sashes and strings of beads, bracelets, head bands, fancy bows, angora jumpers and crochet work. She and Grandmother had been opposites—poles apart.

Perhaps if Dot could have got a job . . . However, she had not worked for twenty years. Being well-read made very little difference. She had thought that she might become an organizer, an entity in the outside world while Ellie found bargain jumpers for the boys at sales of work, or walked the pavements of the city from Mass to market to gynaecologist.

She approached several men, chasing them into their offices with her *curriculum vitae* in her hand. It seemed that nothing she had to offer would mean tuppence to the farmer in the snipe grass or the members of the Irish Countrywomen's Association. She could not seem to explain in a way that the men understood why she had not worked for twenty years. She went back to Ellie's house and took Mumsie's picture off the piano. She climbed to her bedroom with the photograph in her hand and dropped Mumsie—grassy field, friend's hat, hem of skirt tugged fussily down to her ankles, and all—into the wastepaper basket.

When Ellie came home from the doctor all she noticed was that someone had dusted the piano and that the pin-cushion crinoline doll was back in its place. She had forgotten why she moved it. She knocked at Dot's door and Dot came out, red-eyed, with a book of stories by Doris Lessing in her hand. "Promise me you'll stay with us anyway," Ellie said. "For ever if you like. I need you Dot. I really do." They pressed cheeks and clasped each other's shoulders. It was a pact.

She did need Dot, now in the seventh month of pregnancy. It was early April. The scope of Ellie's activities became sadly limited. Her breasts bulged uncomfortably over the top of the empire-line dress she had worn so successfully in January. She felt like a bird trapped in an oil spill. Val hardly ever slept at home. The boys had impetigo.

One of the boys had a birthday. Val turned up with a gift for his son and a silver dish he had bought for Ellie. He watched her set the birthday table, "her breasts beneath her smock like the paps of Kerry, her beautiful breasts!" The description was Val's. Dot excused herself and retired to the sitting room where she sat raking the ashes of last night's fire into barrow mounds.

Ellie was getting increasingly tired. She spent a great deal of her time in bed, a great deal more in her dressing gown. Three cleaning women since Nancy Spratt had come and gone. "Was your Grandmother very odd?" one of the boys asked Dot as she acted surrogate mother in a shoe shop.

Dot remembered trembling with sorrow as Grandmother raked in her and Ellie's pocket money and dealt another hand of cards; Grandmother rubbing a raw onion on her chilblained feet; Grandmother reading her horoscope and spending the day in bed because any new venture would be unlucky; pencil and paper games Grandmother knew that discovered who you loved, liked, hated or adored.

"Your great-grandmother was a famous woman," Dot said. "The first woman in Co. Leix to drive a motor car. The Duke of Wellington carved his name on her windowpane."

"Was that before the Second World War?" the youngest boy asked. He was only five.

"An old Morris. It belonged to our grandfather and she drove it, once, before even we were born, up to her friends the Dells. She killed a hen driving out the gate," Ellie said at the tea table.

Ellie had never felt so unattractive. She was glad that Val had to be away so much—this time he was in Germany. She loved him, she said into the crackling holes of the telephone receiver. She understood the absence. The floors of the house had a cover crop of toy cars, torn books, meccano, action men and dirty clothes. Dot spent most of her time in her room practising transcendental meditation and trying to levitate. Ellie looked in the hall mirror at herself, huge in her printed smock and white woolly, clumsy in her navy stockings and clogs. Increase and multiply. No hope of levitation, she could hardly lift her feet to walk. She felt as if she would never have the child but continue to stretch and waddle for ever.

Val had arranged to be at home for the birth of his child. He turned up just as Ellie and Dot had settled into a pattern of television, bed, coffee, forays with the boys and periods when Dot ministered to Ellie's aches and pains that seemed about to become permanent.

Things changed. Dot was no longer consulted about the daily menu. Ellie made Baked Alaska and served it to Val and the boys, who applauded as she lumbered towards the table with the platter of flaming meringue. The boys ran wild in new lederhosen. Ellie powdered her nose and put the new powder compact away in the new leather bag.

Dot dressed herself in her woollen suit and disappeared into town to poke around the shops while Val took Ellie up to the bedroom to rub her back.

Ellie bore children easily. This time her first pains were nothing more than a small bird pecking away at her innards. She was still lying on her own bed, Val beside her, when the membranes broke.

"Why was I not called?" Dot challenged Val when he returned from the nursing home, shaken by the headlong dash and the sight of nurses hauling Ellie away from him and lifting her, overcoat and all, onto a stretcher. Dot and the boys had slept through their departure. "I should have been with her when you brought her in," she reiterated. They eyed each other across the boys' heads and the scattered cornflakes. At breaking point the telephone rang. Val and Ellie had another son.

"It was a panic," Ellie laughed. She did not seem the least bit disturbed. "The waters broke and there was poor Val." She lay in her high nursing home bed and looked at Dot and her visitors. Her stomach felt as if it had been flattened by a steam-roller. Val could come in later when Dot went home to hold the fort. "How long is your sister staying?" asked a woman whom Dot had never met. A woman with ruined red hair who was going to be the baby's godmother. "Years I hope," Ellie said, pointing to the table in the corner for Dot to pour out some drinks. "My only sister," she told the woman with the withered chrysanthemum hair. "She came down to us after Mumsie died." "Which one of the boys is your godson?" the woman asked and was surprised when it turned out that Dot was a Protestant. She would never have guessed from Ellie. Never in a million years. The other visitors clucked and coughed. "Church of Ireland, if that means any-thing to you, May," Ellie said. "Calvinist. Huguenot in fact. They came over for the Battle of the Boyne," Dot said. "I think you're pulling my leg," the woman said, finishing her gin and tonic in a mildly insulted fashion.

"I'm taking you away for the weekend as soon as you get out of this kip," Val said when he came in. He hated the nursing home, the antiseptic, the smells of floor polish and cabbage, the dusty window that looked out on a pub, the chrome trolley that pinioned Ellie on the high bed, the kidney shaped receptacles for God knew what. Hated it even more than his house full of yelling children and Dot, who sat this evening like a queen bee in his back garden, under a sun parasol he had bought for Ellie. "I wish I could creep in there beside you," he said, knowing that he was going to go off somewhere and get drunk.

The baby was down in the nursery, wrapped and labelled. Neither Val nor Dot went to look at it.

"You were very unhappy when you were sixteen," said the man with the cards. "Isn't everyone!" Dot said.

Val had brought the man home from the pub to fill the night-time silence. He wore jeans and mountaineering boots, a denim shirt and a woollen waistcoat that Mumsie could have crocheted. He had spectacles and thick white hair.

"Both my parents were alive when I was sixteen," Dot said. The man shrugged.

(And Mr. Henderson who took Mumsie out driving and down to Millar's Wood where Dot sat pretending that she was Anne of Green Gables.

Mumsie's lips twitched as she stepped past Dot in her laced two-tone shoes. She had surprisingly big feet. Mr. Henderson let go of Mumsie's hand and they both walked on a little way before Dot summoned the strength to scream. "Your blouse is open, Mumsie!" Mumsie looked back over her shoulder. Mr. Henderson had bits of grass stuck to the back of his coat. "I'm sorry, Dot," Mumsie said, nodding her head like a frightened horse.)

"Of course my Grandmother had just died," Dot said to the man but he had lost interest. Val was pouring him out a drink.

Ellie came home, glad of her own bed again and the boys and Val and an end to draw-sheets and thermometers. She behaved in a casual way towards Dot, ignoring her ups and downs. They were sisters. She was giving Dot houseroom. She held her new son to her breast and sighed. If only Dot had married . . . Val was on the telephone making a reservation. His packed suitcase rested on a stool.

Nancy Spratt resurfaced. A rape victim, found in the Shannon at low tide, her hands lashed behind her back. Dot and Ellie, for want of something more constructive, cracked a bottle of gin over the disaster. Perhaps, thought Ellie, if I had acted with more prescience, asked Dot to scrub the tintawn, given Nancy Spratt the gold sovereign of mine she admired . . .

When Ellie had gone to bed Dot walked along the river bank. Now and then her heart skipped a beat as a twig snapped or something seemed to appear and disappear on the surface of the water. She vomited up her gin. Nothing else happened. She came back by the main road, passing people were turned to waxwork by the fluorescent street lights. They were all strangers.

It was July. The Guards had searched for a month for Nancy Spratt's attacker. Now it seemed that they had given up hope. Banks were being robbed, houses ransacked; old women cooked their cupboards bare at knife point for vagrants. She was a loser anyway, Ellie thought, as Nancy Spratt's florid face and corkscrew curls, her fat thighs and broken shoes blurred in her memory.

Dot would have preferred a more stylish martyr for her pantheon. However, it was Nancy Spratt who appeared in her bedroom, over near the fireplace. She was concerned in case Grandmother would object. It seemed to be O.K. Sometimes she felt confused and seemed to see Mumsie's face peeping from under the garish hair-do, and Mumsie's brown and cream walkers hovering over the purple flames that rose mysteriously from a wicker chair seat. Mumsie who had gone to join Mr. Henderson in Hell.

Mumsie had known her destination at the end, sitting in her bedroom, her latest craze of costume dolls dangling from the picture rail for company. Her face had turned as white as the white bedroom furniture with the dabs of gilt. Her waywardness was contained at last in an arthritic prison. "I have been cursed," she whispered to Dot. Dot nodded as she combed the sparse white hairs out of Mumsie's bristle brush.

Something had to give. They said that it had been coming on slowly for some time. With drugs now, and so much sleeping, it was best to keep Dot where she was as a safeguard to herself. She hardly suffered. They could guarantee that.

She had suffered horribly, a pain that exploded in a series of anguished yelps, the day she hobbled into the kitchen while Ellie was making apple pie. She had stopped, clinging onto the door, and made sounds as if she was going to throw a fit. Ellie thought of all she had ever heard about epilepsy or brain tumours as she ran across to where Dot had sunk onto the kitchen step and held out a foot which bled because nails had been upended through the hole of her sandal like an Indian fakir. Grandmother told Nancy Spratt to tell her, Dot said. Ellie recollected from years ago a trip to the National Museum with Grandmother and a sandal with spikes which Grandmother said was a sign of holiness on the part of its owner. Grandmother had said it was the only way. "For you, Ellie," Dot said while Ellie tried to disentangle herself and get to the phone.

Not until after her next child was born—a girl at last—did Ellie even begin to think she could understand. She was lying again in the nursing home, the baby beside her in its steel cot, her nipples making milky patches on her nightgown. She was drowsy and Mumsie's friend, Mr. Henderson, flitted into her mind. A harmless poor man. Not Antichrist. It was Dot who said that he was Antichrist. That Grandmother had told her so on the night that she pushed back from the supper table and made a sound like a pigeon's coo before keeling over, dead. Ellie had not been there so she was in no position to contradict. However, she had always thought Mr. Henderson a comic person, because everyone knew that he wore a hairpiece. What Dot said could only be a fiddle-de-dee. And then she thought of Dot in the time that she lived with herself and Val. It must have been Mr. Henderson who inspired Dot in those last weeks in her room. Weeks when she was writing— writing terrible things about Val and Nancy Spratt and Mumsie and Antichrist and the Duke of Wellington and the prophets whose names were those of Ellie's sons.

In between her writing she knelt or sat with her eyes closed. "Listening to the whispering wives," she said when Ellie asked her what she was trying to do. "Beautifying the place," she said, when she came home from Woolworth's with an armload of artificial flowers and stuck them between the wallflowers in the beds under the windows. "My thesis," she called the bundle of papers, mostly scraps, that she clutched to her jumper while the doctor spoke gently, prising it from her grasp. (It had been such a blessing, such an ease for Ellie to hand Dot over to the whitecoat brigade). "God help you, my dear," a nursing sister said, squeezing Ellie's arm as if she was the one in trouble.

She felt a queer sympathy now for all those notebooks of Dot's that Val had burned in the bonfire; along with Dot's penitential sandal which the bonfire swallowed and regurgitated as a pathetic clutch of bent nails. "She couldn't even hammer straight," Val said.

When Val came in looking like a hobo in an old anorak and a tartan cap she asked him if he thought that they should let Dot know about the baby. He couldn't be bothered thinking about it, Val said. Surely Ellie knew the hell he had had finding a baby-sitter. By Christ! They were going on a holiday as soon as Ellie got herself out of this place.

"Did I ever tell you about Mr. Henderson, my mother's friend?" Ellie said. "He used to wear a toupee."

"Another bloody West Briton, I'll bet," Val said.

"We weren't. We were Huguenots," Ellie said.

"Don't start giving me that guff," Val said. "I had a bellyful of it from your crazy sister."

"Tell your reverend sister to get herself raped," Ellie said in a clipped tone, very like Dot's.

"Ha! She never did. That was her trouble," Val said.

Ellie lay back on her pillows and closed her eyes. Her head felt full of squiggles and whirling colours. She remembered a cry from Dot's room in the middle of the night. She remembered muffled footsteps walking along the corridor. She saw new meaning in Dot's pleas when she visited her. "Ellie, take care of yourself." "Ellie, don't let it all go." "Ellie, don't leave me here." She thought of Grandmother warning the two of them never to let a man get his hand under their skirts and the way Dot sat clutching her hem as if she was trying to make her dress stretch to her ankles whenever Ellie introduced Val's name. She remembered Grandmother's other slogan, "Men are only after one thing." A counterpart to "Increase and multiply." She remembered the picture of Mumsie that she had once placed on the piano and knew what had happened to it. She felt as if she was looking into Dot's head. She felt that she would rather be Nancy Spratt.

"I think it's time for you to go, Val," Ellie said.

When she opened her eyes it did not bother her that he had already gone. She lifted her daughter out of her cot. Val would be back. In the meantime, she thought, I'll see what I can remember. I'll try to figure something out.

Shepherd's Bush

Maeve Binchy

People looked very weary, May thought, and shabbier than she had remembered Londoners to be. They reminded her a little of those news-reel pictures of crowds during the war or just after it, old raincoats, brave smiles, endless patience. But then this wasn't Regent Street, where she had wandered up and down looking at shops on other visits to London, it wasn't the West End, with lights all glittering and people getting out of taxis full of excitement and wafts of perfume. This was Shepherd's Bush, where people lived. They had probably set out from here early this morning and fought similar crowds on the way to work. The women must have done their shopping in their lunch hour because most of them were carrying plastic bags of food. It was a London different to the one you see as a tourist.

And she was here for a different reason, although she had once read a cynical article in a magazine which said that girls coming to London for abortions provided a significant part of the city's tourist revenue. It wasn't something you could classify under any terms as a holiday. When she filled in the card at the airport she had written "Business" in the section where it said "Purpose of journey."

The pub where she was to meet Celia was near the tube station. She found it easily and settled herself in. A lot of the accents were Irish, workmen having a pint before they went home to their English wives and their television programmes. Not drunk tonight, it was only Monday, but obviously regulars. Maybe not so welcome as regulars on Friday or Saturday nights, when they would remember they were Irish and sing anti-British songs.

Celia wouldn't agree with her about that. Celia had rose-tinted views about the Irish in London, she thought they were all here from choice, not because there was no work for them at home. She hated stories about the restless Irish, or Irishmen on the lump in the building trade. She said people shouldn't make such a big thing about it all. People who came from much farther away settled in London, it was big enough to absorb everyone. Oh well, she wouldn't bring up the subject, there were enough things to disagree with Celia about . . . without searching for more.

Oh why of all people, of all the bloody people in the world, did she have to come to Celia? Why was there nobody else whom she could ask for advice? Celia would give it, she would give a lecture with every piece of information she imparted. She would deliver a speech with every cup of tea, she would be cool, practical, and exactly the right person, if she weren't so much the wrong person. It was handing Celia a whole box of ammunition about Andy. From now on Celia could say that Andy was a rat, and May could no longer say she had no facts to go on.

Celia arrived. She was thinner, and looked a little tired. She smiled. Obviously the lectures weren't going to come in the pub. Celia always knew the right place for things. Pubs were for meaningless chats and bright, nonintense conversation. Home was for lectures.

"You're looking marvellous," Celia said.

It couldn't be true. May looked at her reflection in a glass panel. You couldn't see the dark lines under her eyes there, but you could see the droop of her shoulders, she wasn't a person that could be described as looking marvellous. No, not even in a pub.

"I'm okay," she said. "But you've got very slim, how did you do it?"

"No bread, no cakes, no potatoes, no sweets," said Celia in a businesslike way. "It's the old rule but it's the only rule. You deny yourself everything you want and you lose weight."

"I know," said May, absently rubbing her waistline.

"Oh I didn't mean *that*," cried Celia, horrified. "I didn't mean that at all."

May felt weary, she hadn't meant that either, she was patting her stomach because she had been putting on weight. The child that she was going to get rid of was still only a speck, it would cause no bulge. She had put on weight because she cooked for Andy three or four times a week in his flat. He was long and lean. He could eat forever and he wouldn't put on weight. He didn't like eating alone so she ate with him. She reassured Celia that there was no offence and when Celia had gone, twittering with rage at herself, to the counter, May wondered whether she had explored every avenue before coming to Celia and Shepherd's Bush for help.

She had. There were no legal abortions in Dublin, and she did not know of anyone who had ever had an illegal one there. England and the ease of the system were less than an hour away by plane. She didn't want to try and get it on the National Health, she had the money, all she wanted was someone who would introduce her to a doctor, so that she could get it all over with quickly. She needed somebody who knew her, somebody who wouldn't abandon her if things went wrong, somebody who would lie for her, because a few lies would have to be told. May didn't have any other friends in London. There was a girl she had once met on a skiing holiday, but you couldn't impose on a holiday friendship in that way. She knew a man, a very nice, kind man who had stayed in the hotel where she worked and had often begged her to come and stay with him and his wife. But she couldn't go to stay with them for the first time in this predicament, it would be ridiculous. It had to be Celia.

It might be easier if Celia had loved somebody so much that everything else was unimportant. But stop, that wasn't fair. Celia loved that dreary, boring, selfish Martin. She loved him so much that she believed one day he was going to get things organized and make a home for them. Everyone else knew that Martin was the worst possible bet for any punter, a Mamma's boy who had everything he wanted now, including a visit every two months from Celia, home from London, smartly dressed, undemanding, saving away for a day that would never come. So Celia did understand something about the nature of love. She never talked about it. People as brisk as Celia don't talk about things like unbrisk attitudes in men, or hurt feelings or broken hearts. Not when it refers to themselves, but they are very good at pointing out the foolish attitudes of others.

Celia was back with the drinks.

"We'll finish them up quickly," she said.

Why could she never, never take her ease over anything? Things always had to be finished up quickly. It was warm and anonymous in the pub. They could go back to Celia's flat, which May felt sure wouldn't have even a comfortable chair in it, and talk in a businesslike way about the rights and wrongs of abortion, the procedure, the money, and how it shouldn't be spent on something so hopeless and destructive. And about Andy. Why wouldn't May tell him? He had a right to know. The child was half his, and even if he didn't want it he should pay for the abortion. He had plenty of money, he was a hotel manager. May had hardly any, she was a hotel receptionist. May could see it all coming, she dreaded it. She wanted to stay in this warm place until closing time, and to fall asleep, and wake up there two days later.

Celia made walking-along-the-road conversation on the way to her flat. This road used to be very quiet and full of retired people, now it was all flats and bed-sitters. That road was nice, but noisy, too much through traffic. The houses in the road over there were going for thirty-five thousand, which was ridiculous, but then you had to remember it was fairly central and they did have little gardens. Finally they were there. A big Victorian house, a clean, polished hall, and three flights of stairs. The flat was much bigger than May expected, and it had a sort of divan on which she sat down immediately and put up her legs while Celia fussed about a bit, opening a bottle of wine and putting a dish of four small lamb chops into the oven. May braced herself for the lecture.

It wasn't a lecture, it was an information sheet. She was so relieved that she could feel herself relaxing, and filled up her wineglass again.

"I've arranged with Dr. Harris that you can call to see him tomorrow morning at eleven. I told him no lies, just a little less than the truth. I said you were staying with me. If he thinks that means you are staying permanently, that's his mistake not mine. I mentioned that your problem was . . . what it is. I asked him when he thought it would be . . . em . . . done. He said Wednesday or Thursday, but it would all depend. He didn't seem shocked or anything; it's like tonsillitis to him, I suppose. Anyway he was very calm about it. I think you'll find he's a kind person and it won't be upsetting . . . that part of it."

May was dumbfounded. Where were the accusations, the I-told-you-so sighs, the hope that now, finally, she would finish with Andy? Where was the slight moralistic bit, the heavy wondering whether or not it might be murder? For the first time in the eleven days since she had confirmed she was pregnant, May began to hope that there would be some normality in the world again.

"Will it embarrass you, all this?" she asked. "I mean, do you feel it will change your relationship with him?"

"In London a doctor isn't an old family friend like at home, May. He's someone you go to, or I've gone to anyway, when I've had to have my ears syringed, needed antibiotics for flu last year, and a medical certificate for the time I sprained my ankle and couldn't go to work. He hardly knows me except as a name on his register. He's nice though, and he doesn't rush you in and out. He's Jewish and small and worried-looking."

Celia moved around the flat, changing into comfortable sitting-about clothes, looking up what was on television, explaining to May that she must sleep in her room and that she, Celia, would use the divan.

No, honestly, it would be easier that way, she wasn't being nice, it would be much easier. A girl friend rang and they arranged to play squash together at the week-end. A wrong number rang; a West Indian from the flat downstairs knocked on the door to say he would be having a party on Saturday night and to apologize in advance for any noise. If they liked to bring a bottle of something, they could call in themselves. Celia served dinner. They looked at television for an hour, then went to bed.

May thought what a strange empty life Celia led here far from home, miles from Martin, no real friends, no life at all. Then she thought that Celia might possibly regard her life too as sad, working in a second-rate hotel for five years, having an affair with its manager for three years. A hopeless affair because the manager's wife and four children were a bigger stumbling block than Martin's mother could ever be. She felt tired and comfortable, and in Celia's funny, characterless bedroom she drifted off and dreamed that Andy had discovered where she was and what she was about to do, and had flown over during the night to tell her that they would get married next morning, and live in England and forget the hotel, the family, and what anyone would say.

Tuesday morning. Celia was gone. Dr. Harris's address was neatly written on the pad by the phone with instructions how to get there. Also Celia's phone number at work, and a message that May never believed she would hear from Celia. "Good luck."

He was small, and Jewish, and worried, and kind. His examination was painless and unembarrassing. He confirmed what she knew already. He wrote down dates, and asked general questions about her health. May wondered whether he had a family, there were no pictures of wife or children in the surgery. But then there were none in Andy's office, either. Perhaps his wife was called Rebecca and she, too, worried because her husband worked so hard, they might have two children, a boy who was a gifted musician, and a girl who wanted to get married to a Christian. Maybe they all walked along these leafy roads on Saturdays to synagogue and Rebecca cooked all those things like gefilte fish and bagels.

With a start, May told herself to stop dreaming about him. It was a habit she had gotten into recently, fancying lives for everyone she met, however briefly. She usually gave them happy lives with a bit of problem-to-be-solved thrown in. She wondered what a psychiatrist would make of that. As she was coming back to real life, Dr. Harris was saying that if he was going to refer her for a termination he must know why she could not have the baby. He pointed out that she was healthy, and strong, and young. She should have no difficulty with pregnancy or birth. Were there emotional reasons? Yes, it would kill her parents, she wouldn't be able to look after the baby, she didn't want to look after one on her own either, it wouldn't be fair on her or the baby.

"And the father?" Dr. Harris asked.

"Is my boss, is heavily married, already has four babies of his own. It would break up his marriage, which he doesn't want to do . . . yet. No, the father wouldn't want me to have it either."

"Has he said that?" asked Dr. Harris as if he already knew the answer.

"I haven't told him, I can't tell him, I won't tell him," said May.

Dr. Harris sighed. He asked a few more questions; he made a telephone call; he wrote out an address. It was a posh address near Harley Street.

"This is Mr. White. A well-known surgeon. These are his consulting rooms, I have made an appointment for you at two-thirty this afternoon. I understand from your friend Miss . . . " He searched his mind and his desk for Celia's name and then gave up. "I understand anyway that you are not living here, and don't want to try and pretend that you are, so that you want the termination done privately. That's just as well, because it would be difficult to get it done on the National Health. There are many cases that would have to come before you."

"Oh I have the money," said May, patting her handbag. She felt nervous but relieved at the same time. Almost exhilarated. It was working, the whole thing was actually moving. God bless Celia.

"It will be around £180 to £200, and in cash, you know that?"

"Yes, it's all here, but why should a well-known surgeon have to be paid in cash, Dr. Harris? You know it makes it look a bit illegal and sort of underhand, doesn't it?"

Dr. Harris smiled a tired smile. "You ask me why he has to be paid in cash. Because he says so. Why he says so, I don't know. Maybe it's because some of his clients don't feel too like paying him after the event. It's not like plastic surgery or a broken leg, where they can see the results. In a termination you see no results. Maybe people don't pay so easily then. Maybe also Mr. White doesn't have a warm relationship with his income tax people. I don't know."

"Do I owe you anything?" May asked, putting on her coat.

"No, my dear, nothing." He smiled and showed her to the door.

"It feels wrong. I'm used to paying a doctor at home or they send bills," she said.

"Send me a picture postcard of your nice country sometime," he said. "When my wife was alive she and I spent several happy holidays there before all this business started." He waved a hand to take in the course of Anglo-Irish politics and difficulties over the last ten years.

May blinked a bit hard and thanked him. She took a taxi which was passing his door and went to Oxford Street. She wanted to see what was in the shops because she was going to pretend that she had spent £200 on clothes and then they had all been lost or stolen. She hadn't yet worked out the details of this deception, which seemed unimportant compared to all the rest that had to be gone through. But she would need to know what was in the shops so that she could say what she was meant to have bought.

Imagining that she had this kind of money to spend, she examined jackets, skirts, sweaters, and the loveliest boots she had ever seen. If only she didn't have to throw this money away, she could have these things. It was her savings over ten months, she put by £30 a month with difficulty. Would Andy have liked her in the boots? She didn't know. He never said much about the way she looked. He saw her mostly in uniform when she could steal time to go to the flat he had for himself in the hotel. On the evenings when he was meant to be working late, and she was in fact cooking for him, she usually wore a dressing gown, a long velvet one. Perhaps she might have bought a dressing gown. She examined some, beautiful Indian silks, and a Japanese satin one in pink covered with little black butterflies. Yes, she would tell him she had bought that, he would like the sound of it, and be sorry it had been stolen.

She had a cup of coffee in one of the big shops and watched the other shoppers resting between bouts of buying. She wondered, did any of them look at her, and if so, would they know in a million years that her shopping money would remain in her purse until it was handed over to a Mr. White so that he could abort Andy's baby? Why did she use words like that, why did she say things to hurt herself, she must have a very deep-seated sense of guilt. Perhaps, she thought to herself with a bit of humour, she should save another couple of hundred pounds and come over for a few sessions with a Harley Street shrink. That should set her right.

It wasn't a long walk to Mr. White's rooms, it wasn't a pleasant welcome. A kind of girl that May had before only seen in the pages of fashion magazines, bored, disdainful, elegant, reluctantly admitted her.

"Oh yes, Dr. Harris's patient," she said, as if May should have come in some tradesman's entrance. She felt furious, and inferior, and sat with her hands in small tight balls, and her eyes unseeing in the waiting room.

Mr. White looked like a caricature of a diplomat. He had elegant grey hair, elegant manicured hands. He moved very gracefully, he talked in practised, concerned clichés, he knew how to put people at their ease, and despite herself, and while still disliking him, May felt safe.

Another examination, another confirmation, more checking of dates. Good, good, she had come in plenty of time, sensible girl. No reasons she would like to discuss about whether this was the right course of action? No? Oh well, grown-up lady, must make up her own mind. Absolutely certain then? Fine, fine. A look at a big leather-bound book on his desk, a look at a small notebook. Leather-bound for the tax people, small notebook for himself, thought May viciously. Splendid, splendid. Tomorrow morning then, not a problem in the world, once she was sure, then he knew this was the best, and wisest, thing. Very sad the people who dithered.

May could never imagine this man having dithered in his life. She was asked to see Vanessa on the way out. She knew that the girl would be called something like Vanessa.

Vanessa yawned and took £194 from her. She seemed to have difficulty in finding the six pounds in change. May wondered wildly whether this was meant to be a tip. If so, she would wait for a year until Vanessa found the change. With the notes came a discreet printed card advertising a nursing home on the other side of London.

"Before nine, fasting, just the usual overnight things," said Vanessa helpfully.

"Tomorrow morning?" checked May.

"Well yes, naturally. You'll be out at eight the following morning. They'll arrange everything like taxis. They have super food," she added as an afterthought.

"They'd need to have for this money," said May spiritedly.

"You're not just paying for the food," said Vanessa wisely.

It was still raining. She rang Celia from a public phone box. Everything was organized, she told her. Would Celia like to come and have a meal somewhere, and maybe they could go on to a theatre?

Celia was sorry, she had to work late, and she had already bought liver and bacon for supper. Could she meet May at home around nine? There was a great quiz show on telly, it would be a shame to miss it.

May went to a hairdresser and spent four times what she would have spent at home on a hairdo.

She went to a cinema and saw a film which looked as if it were going to be about a lot of sophisticated witty French people on a yacht and turned out to be about a sophisticated witty French girl who fell in love with the deckhand on the yacht and when she purposely got pregnant, in order that he would marry her, he laughed at her and the witty sophisticated girl threw herself overboard. Great choice that, May said glumly, as she dived into the underground to go back to the smell of liver frying.

Celia asked little about the arrangements for the morning, only practical things like the address so that she could work out how long it would take to get there.

"Would you like me to come and see you?" she asked. "I expect when it's all over, all finished you know, they'd let you have visitors. I could come after work."

She emphasized the word "could" very slightly. May immediately felt mutinous. She would love Celia to come, but not if it was going to be a duty, something she felt she had to do, against her principles, her inclinations.

"No, don't do that," she said in a falsely bright voice. "They have telly in the rooms apparently, and anyway, it's not as if I were going to be there for more than twenty-four hours."

Celia looked relieved. She worked out taxi times and locations and turned on the quiz show.

In the half-light May looked at her. She was unbending, Celia was. She would survive everything, even the fact that Martin would never marry her. Christ, the whole thing was a mess. Why did people start life with such hopes, and as early as their mid-twenties become beaten and accepting of things. Was the rest of life going to be like this?

She didn't sleep so well, and it was a relief when Celia shouted that it was seven o'clock.

Wednesday. An ordinary Wednesday for the taxi driver, who shouted some kind of amiable conversation at her. She missed most of it, because of the noise of the engine, and didn't bother to answer him half the time except with a grunt.

The place had creeper on the walls. It was a big house, with a small garden, and an attractive brass handle on the door. The nurse who opened it was Irish. She checked May's name on a list. Thank God it was O'Connor, there were a million O'Connors. Suppose she had had an unusual name, she'd have been found out immediately.

The bedroom was big and bright. Two beds, flowery covers, nice furniture. A magazine rack, a bookshelf. A television, a bathroom.

The Irish nurse offered her a hanger from the wardrobe for her coat as if this were a pleasant family hotel of great class and comfort. May felt frightened for the first time. She longed to sit down on one of the beds and cry, and for the nurse to put her arm around her and give her a cigarette and say that it would be all right. She hated being so alone.

The nurse was distant.

"The other lady will be in shortly. Her name is Miss Adams. She just went downstairs to say good-bye to her friend. If there's anything you'd like, please ring."

She was gone, and May paced the room like a captured animal. Was she to undress? It was ridiculous to go to bed. You only went to bed in the daytime if you were ill. She was well, perfectly well.

Miss Adams burst in the door. She was a chubby, pretty girl about twenty-three. She was Australian, and her name was Hell, short for Helen.

"Come on, bedtime," she said, and they both put on their night-dresses and got into beds facing each other. May had never felt so silly in her whole life.

"Are you sure we're meant to do this?" she asked.

"Positive," Helen announced. "I was here last year. They'll be in with the screens for modesty, the examination, and the premed. They go mad if you're not in bed. Of course that stupid Paddy of a nurse didn't tell you, they expect you to be inspired."

Hell was right. In five minutes, the nurse and Mr. White came in. A younger nurse carried a screen. Hell was examined first, then May, for blood pressure and temperature, and that kind of thing. Mr. White was charming. He called her Miss O'Connor, as if he had known her all his life.

He patted her shoulder and told her she didn't have anything to worry about. The Irish nurse gave her an unsmiling injection which was going to make her drowsy. It didn't immediately.

Hell was doing her nails.

"You were really here last year?" asked May in disbelief.

"Yeah, there's nothing to it. I'll be back at work tomorrow."

"Why didn't you take the Pill?" May asked.

"Why didn't you?" countered Hell.

"Well, I did for a bit, but I thought it was making me fat, and then anyway, you know, I thought I'd escaped for so long before I started the Pill that it would be all right. I was wrong."

"I know." Hell was sympathetic. "I can't take it. I've got varicose veins already and I don't really understand all those things they give you in the family planning clinics, jellies, and rubber things, and diaphragms. It's worse than working out income tax. Anyway, you never have time to set up a scene like that before going to bed with someone, do you? It's like preparing for a battle."

May laughed.

"It's going to be fine, love," said Hell. "Look, I know, I've been here before. Some of my friends have had it done four or five times. I promise you, it's only the people who don't know who worry. This afternoon you'll wonder what you were thinking about to look so white. Now if it had been terrible, would I be here again?"

"But your varicose veins?" said May, feeling a little sleepy.

"Go to sleep, kid," said Hell. "We'll have a chat when it's all over."

Then she was getting onto a trolley, half asleep, and going down corridors with lovely prints on the walls to a room with a lot of light, and transferring onto another table. She felt as if she could sleep forever and she hadn't even had the anaesthetic yet. Mr. White stood there in a coat brighter than his name. Someone was dressing him up the way they do in films.

She thought about Andy. "I love you," she said suddenly.

"Of course you do," said Mr. White, coming over and patting her kindly without a trace of embarrassment.

Then she was being moved again, she thought they hadn't got her right on the operating table, but it wasn't that, it was back into her own bed and more sleep.

There was a tinkle of china. Hell called over from the window.

"Come on, they've brought us some nice soup. Broth they call it."

May blinked.

"Come on, May. I was done after you and I'm wide awake. Now didn't I tell you there was nothing to it?"

May sat up. No pain, no tearing feeling in her insides. No sickness.

"Are you sure they did me?" she asked.

They both laughed.

They had what the nursing-home called a light lunch. Then they got a menu so that they could choose dinner.

"There are some things that England does really well, and this is one of them," Hell said approvingly, trying to decide between the delights that were offered. "They even give us a small carafe of wine. If you want more you have to pay for it. But they kind of disapprove of us getting pissed."

Hell's friend Charlie was coming in at six when he finished work. Would May be having a friend, too, she wondered? No. Celia wouldn't come.

"I don't mean Celia," said Hell. "I mean the bloke."

"He doesn't know, he's in Dublin, and he's married," said May.

"Well, Charlie's married, but he bloody knows, and he'd know if he were on the moon."

"It's different."

"No, it's not different. It's the same for everyone, there are rules, you're a fool to break them. Didn't he pay for it either, this guy?"

"No. I told you he doesn't know."

"Aren't you noble," said Hell scornfully. "Aren't you a real Lady

Galahad. Just visiting London for a day or two, darling, just going to see a few friends, see you soon. Love you, darling. Is that it?"

"We don't go in for so many darlings as that in Dublin," said May.

"You don't go in for much common sense either. What will you gain, what will he gain, what will anyone gain? You come home penniless, a bit lonely. He doesn't know what the hell you've been doing, he isn't extrasensitive and loving and grateful because he doesn't have anything to be grateful about as far as he's concerned."

"I couldn't tell him. I couldn't. I couldn't ask him for £200 and say what it was for. That wasn't in the bargain, that was never part of the deal."

May was almost tearful, mainly from jealousy she thought. She couldn't bear Hell's Charlie to come in, while her Andy was going home to his wife because there would be nobody to cook him something exciting and go to bed with him in his little manager's flat.

"When you go back, tell him. That's my advice," said Hell. "Tell him you didn't want to worry him, you did it all on your own because the responsibility was yours since you didn't take the Pill. That's unless you think he'd have wanted it?"

"No, he wouldn't have wanted it."

"Well then, that's what you do. Don't ask him for the money straight out, just let him know you're broke. He'll react some way then. It's silly not to tell them at all. My sister did that with her bloke back in Melbourne. She never told him at all, and she got upset because he didn't know the sacrifice she had made, and every time she bought a drink or paid for a cinema ticket she got resentful of him. All for no reason, because he didn't bloody know."

"I might," said May, but she knew she wouldn't.

Charlie came in. He was great fun, very fond of Hell, wanting to be sure she was okay, and no problems. He brought a bottle of wine which they shared, and he told them funny stories about what had happened at the office. He was in advertising. He arranged to meet Hell for lunch next day and joked his way out of the room.

"He's a lovely man," said May.

"Old Charlie's smashing," agreed Hell. He had gone back home to entertain his wife and six dinner guests. His wife was a marvellous hostess apparently. They were always having dinner parties.

"Do you think he'll ever leave her?" asked May.

"He'd be out of his brains if he did," said Hell cheerfully.

May was thoughtful. Maybe everyone would be out of their brains if they left good, comfortable, happy home setups for whatever the other woman imagined she could offer. She wished she could be as happy as Hell.

"Tell me about your fellow," Hell said kindly.

May did, the whole long tale. It was great to have somebody to listen, somebody who didn't say she was on a collision course, somebody who didn't purse up lips like Celia, someone who said, "Go on, what did you do then?"

"He sounds like a great guy," said Hell, and May smiled happily.

They exchanged addresses, and Hell promised that if ever she came to Ireland she wouldn't ring up the hotel and say, "Can I talk to May, the girl I had the abortion with last winter?" and they finished Charlie's wine, and went to sleep.

The beds were stripped early next morning when the final examination had been done, and both were pronounced perfect and ready to leave. May wondered fancifully how many strange life stories the room must have seen.

"Do people come here for other reasons apart from . . . er, terminations?" she asked the disapproving Irish nurse.

"Oh certainly they do, you couldn't work here otherwise," said the nurse. "It would be like a death factory, wouldn't it?"

That puts me in my place, thought May, wondering why she hadn't the courage to say that she was only visiting the home, she didn't earn her living from it.

She let herself into Celia's gloomy flat. It had become gloomy again, like the way she had imagined it before she saw it. The warmth of her first night there was gone. She looked around and wondered why Celia had no pictures, no books, no souvenirs.

There was a note on the telephone pad.

"I didn't ring or anything, because I forgot to ask if you had given your real name, and I wouldn't know who to ask for. Hope you feel well again. I'll be getting some chicken pieces so we can have supper together around 8. Ring me if you need me. C."

May thought for a bit. She went out and bought Celia a casserole dish, a nice one made of cast iron. It would be useful for all those little high-protein, low-calorie dinners Celia cooked. She also bought a bunch of flowers, but could find no vase when she came back and had to use a big glass instead. She left a note thanking her for the hospitality, warm enough to sound properly grateful, and a genuinely warm remark about how glad she was that she had been able to do it all through nice Dr. Harris. She said nothing about the time in the nursing-home. Celia would prefer not to know. May just said that she was fine, and thought she would go back to Dublin tonight. She rang the airline and booked a plane.

Should she ring Celia and tell her to get only one chicken piece? No, damn Celia, she wasn't going to ring her. She had a fridge, hadn't she?

The plane didn't leave until the early afternoon. For a wild moment she thought of joining Hell and Charlie in the pub where they were meeting, but dismissed the idea. She must now make a list of what clothes she was meant to have bought and work out a story about how they had disappeared. Nothing that would make Andy get in touch with police or airlines to find them for her. It was going to be quite hard, but she'd have to give Andy some explanation of what she'd been doing, wouldn't she? And he would want to know why she had spent all that money. Or would he? Did he know she had all that money? She couldn't remember telling him. He wasn't very interested in her little savings, they talked more about his investments. And she must remember that if he was busy or cross tonight or tomorrow she wasn't to take it out on him. Like Hell had said, there wasn't any point in her expecting a bit of cossetting when he didn't even know she needed it.

How sad and lonely it would be to live like Celia, to be so suspicious of men, to think so ill of Andy. Celia always said he was selfish and just took what he could get. That was typical of Celia, she understood nothing. Hell had understood more, in a couple of hours, than Celia had in three years. Hell knew what it was like to love someone.

But May didn't think Hell had got it right about telling Andy all about the abortion. Andy might be against that kind of thing. He was very moral in his own way, was Andy.

Failing Years

Mary Beckett

Nora sat tense in the upright chair she used nowadays until her daughter banged the door behind her without saying goodbye. Then she went to the front window and watched as Una eased herself into her car. She wished she had not snapped at her. But Una so seldom left the house for any length of time that when she said she'd be away until tea-time, and then fussed, upstairs and down, giving directions about the fire and the lunch, Nora could bear the delay no longer and said, "Una, I can manage without you. I am not a fool. And it *is* my house."

She felt no kinship with this sedate, solid, middle-aged woman. She tried to remember the slim, lively girl who had been such a delight to Alec and herself. She was the eldest of the family and Alec and Nora had congratulated each other while she was growing up that no matter what bother they had with the four boys who came after her, they never had to trouble about Una. They had been completely taken aback by her unsuitable marriage. Why should she have married before she was twenty a man so old for her? His stiff, polite manner to her parents seemed a continual reproach. When he died eventually, Nora wondered what sympathy she should feel for her daughter. "It was not," she said to Alec, "as if it was a real marriage, like ours." Alec had looked doubtful and had worried about Una alone, growing fat, but Nora had never felt welcome in that big, pompous house with the heavy blinds at the windows, so she expected no support from Una when Alec himself died suddenly.

He had been retired for some years, the family was gone and Nora and he were very happy together in the routine they made for themselves. Then the night after he had got injections for varicose veins he

216

had been restless, and she worried about him. The next morning was a First Friday and they decided to walk to Mass, since the doctor had told him to use his legs instead of his car. Just inside the church he fell full length on his back. "Pole-axed"—the word sat in her mind. The priest rushed to give him the last rites. They sent for an ambulance. Some woman whispered, "Such a fine figure of a man." Nora knew he was dead. She stood looking at his high colour fade and his white shining hair seemed to lose its vitality while she watched. She had often said to him that it would be nice if his car would go out of control and smash into a wall and kill the both of them and not leave one lonely. Now he was gone and she was left waiting. Of course he had gone off and left her waiting many a time on his trips abroad, but then she knew he'd be back with a present for her and a suitcase full of dirty clothes. She'd often thought, as the smell of exotic cigarettes and strange rooms rose out of the washing-machine, that that was her share of the foreign travel. She had never been out of Ireland. He promised that they would go when he retired but she had been afraid of the effort it would have meant for both of them. They used to do shopping some-times in Dun Laoire on sunny, summer Fridays and watching the big white ferry and the sharp blue sea and the painted terraces, she used to say, "Isn't this as good as the south of France any day?" Now he was gone for good. At first she couldn't sleep and when she mentioned that, they gave her sleeping tablets. So she slept sound and wakened in the morning feeling the empty half of the bed, wondering, "How could he be up without my noticing," and then, remembering, felt such a heaviness in her chest that she decided sleeplessness was preferable any time.

She began to feel old. For years before Alec died she had noticed casually the signs of age. When she looked in the mirror with her glasses on she was disgusted, so she took off her glasses and smiled at the improvement. She had always made the effort to keep her shoulders straight, and when she was able to buy expensive clothes her long, thin figure looked elegant, but most of her life she could only afford cheaper ones. Her sisters in Belfast sometimes presented her with things to wear. Alec always told her she looked well. She thought it didn't mean a thing to her because he did not discriminate. But with him gone there was no one to praise her, no one to laugh at her, no one to touch her.

Fending for herself, her main trouble was the new range in the kitchen. All her married life she had lamented the lack of her mother's black, burnished range in the three-storey terrace house where she had been reared in Belfast. The bread baked in it was so much better than anything she could produce in her electric cooker. It had heated the water so well that on winter evenings the whole house rumbled and shook with the vibrations of the boiler. So when Alec retired and he had time to listen to her, he had a modern range installed. He took great satisfaction in stoking it, praising its warmth and everything Nora cooked on it. Nora didn't feel it was as good as the fires of her childhood where the glow behind the bars was a dangerous delight, but she joined in Alec's praises with gratitude. Now she had difficulty with it. She had not the strength in her hands to riddle it properly so that ash prevented it burning as brightly as it should. The ash pan was so heavy she needed two hands to lift it and so had nothing to lean on to help herself off her knees. She didn't complain, even to herself, because she had a fear that if she did, it would postpone Alec's happiness in the next world. Summers were easier. She cooked and cleaned and shopped and visited the two sons who were married in Dublin and wrote letters to the two who were away. She chatted with the neighbours and because she had lived there so long the familiar faces were a strength to her—until she too fell in the church.

It was Sunday and the church was crowded so she was waiting to kneel at the altar rail when the whole sanctuary turned copper colour and then purple so that she staggered and sat back on the seat behind her. She could hear the voice of the priest: "Body of Christ, Body of Christ," but she couldn't see, and she thought she was going to die and felt terror. Somebody helped her out of the church and after Mass drove her home. A neighbour telephoned for Una, who insisted she'd had a stroke and that it would be necessary for her to move into the house. Nora said such nonsense, it was only chapel sickness, other people suffered it frequently but of course Una could come and stay if she wished to. And before she had really collected herself Una's house was sold, the money in the bank and Una was in charge. When the neighbours called to welcome Una back it was Una who had their sympathy. When they asked Nora how she felt she was cross, "I am perfectly well," but sometimes she worried. She had difficulty with words. She noticed it first when some of her grandchildren came in the summer and she cut up a block of ice-cream and asked them to pass her the rashers instead of the wafers. She had to laugh with them at how stupid Granny was. A few days later she asked in a shop for coconut twist instead of buttonhole twist. Sometimes she couldn't think of the words she wanted at all and her tongue felt heavy in her mouth.

Anxiety kept her lying awake at night. Before Una moved in she hadn't really minded waking up in the night. She switched on her lamp and read a book, or went downstairs and sat drinking tea while she read. Now she had to lie still or Una was up enquiring what was wrong, was she all right, when would she go back to bed, when would she put out her light, would she have a sleeping tablet. It was easier to stay quiet. She remembered the advice she had always given to children wakening from nightmares—"Think of something pleasant." So she thought of the security of that warm house in Belfast with her own energetic mother who never completely reconciled herself to town life. During school holidays she often gathered up her children and took them down to the farm near the shores of Lough Neagh where she had been reared. There they tore through the fields, slid down haystacks, rode on the ruck shifter and ran in and out of the draughty stone-flagged kitchen to take turns at the clackety wheel of the fan-bellows blazing the fire up the wide chimney so that her grandmother feared for the thatch. Coming back there was the excitement of the pony and trap tilting downhill and up so that Nora was afraid she'd fall out over the pony's head, or back against her stout grandfather of whom they were all nervous. The road ran between orchards with the trunks white-washed so that they stood in the evening like neat, well-ordered ghosts. Nora was glad of the safety of trains and trams, and even her mother when she entered her own cluttered, red-papered hall used to say "Well, we had a great day but it's not bad to be home."

"Well, now I've the house to myself," Nora said aloud after Una's car had disappeared. She moved from room to room taking possession, enjoying the freedom. She came back into the kitchen heated by the range well lit and smiled with pleasure in the warmth of the November sun on her legs.

She could not relax with Una in the house whether she was in the same room with her or not. Una's ways filled her with impatience. She tried to contain it but often she heard herself speaking irritably, criticising what Una was doing. Una then went about for long hours in an awkward silence. She put the transistor on the table between them at mealtimes. Nora tried to make conversation in spite of it. She tried to talk about what she thought might interest Una. Una looked at her blankly, as if what she was saying did not make sense. Maybe it didn't. Una had bought brown plates for everyday use to save her mother's good china. On the brown were black, skeletal birds top and bottom, intertwined, with big bills meeting and eyes staring. There was no expression in those eyes but they menaced Nora. She thought Alec would have managed Una far better. At the time of his death she had consoled herself that it was better for him to go first than be left helpless, but now with Una in the house he would not have been unhappy at all. Alec and Una might have enjoyed life without her quite well.

She took the meat for her lunch from the fridge and looked at it with distaste. "We'll have a tea-dinner," her mother used to announce long ago whenever there were no men or boys to cater for, and they would be treated to an omelette or pancakes or potato bread with caraway seeds and then one of the hot, sugary things her mother made with apples. They grew apples in the long garden behind the house. Nora used to climb one of the trees and sit contentedly in it eating the small green apples that the others scorned. Once she fell down on a wooden box with a nail which tore the top of her leg. She went in sore and frightened and was told to put iodine on it. As she sat on the sofa in the kitchen dabbing at it, she found a pea-sized lump of her flesh separate and she lifted it out, pink and solid. She held it up, asking what she would do with it and her mother gasped, "Oh Nora, put it in the fire," but her brother shouted, "No, no, we must have a funeral," and they put it in a little match-box and dug a hole in the garden and buried it. Then they stood around, feeling something else was necessary, but they had never been at a funeral. "We'll sing 'Nearer by God to Thee.' " Nora had suggested. Their father had said that somebody he knew called Johnnie Donnelly had told him that on the Titanic before it went down they all sang "Nearer by God to Thee" and her parents had laughed and then said, "It's not right to be laughing." The children couldn't understand the joke as they had never heard the hymn. They didn't know the tune either so they just shouted the words over and over into the golden September garden and Nora came in feeling much better. Her mother, dressing it daily, marvelled that the ugly scar was exactly the shape of Lough Neagh.

Nora's own apple trees were neglected, the branches green and strappling. Alec had planted them for her when she came to live in Dublin. He had pruned them and sprayed them. At Hallow Eve he had picked off the Bramleys, apple by apple, and sorted them according to size in three or four boxes to keep Nora supplied until Easter. The

autumn after his death two of her sons came with their children and
Nora's heart had warmed watching them do as Alec had done, and
listening to them laughing. Then it appeared that they were dividing
them evenly between themselves with one small box for her. Of course
she would have given them the apples but she would have liked to
have the giving of them. They would never have treated Alec like that.
She was annoyed because she felt such resentment. Very early in her
marriage she had made up her mind never to resent anything and had
disciplined herself to keep to that. Now she felt resentment again as
she looked for something interesting to have with her "tea-dinner."
There were no scones, no cake, no tart, no home-baked bread even,
because Una was slimming and believed that if there was no food to
tempt her she would lose weight. But Nora had seen her many times
eating bars of chocolate after a meagre lunch. All her life Nora had
taken great satisfaction in well-stocked cupboards. Now the presses were
empty.

The house in Belfast was empty too. The last time Nora had visited
her sisters she had gone to see the old house and found it bricked-up,
inaccessible. An army car drove past slowly with two bored soldiers in
the back, their guns pointing down the road. The pub at the corner
was burnt out, its pitted brick blackened and the pavement shattered.
Nora had been in that pub only once. She had been seventeen and
running home from a friend's house at curfew time when shots rattled
in the next street. A man pulled her into the pub and shut the door
behind her. He was young and a stranger. The only other person there
was the middle-aged barman whom she knew by sight. He looked
annoyed. "Aren't you a young Magee from up the road? What in the
name of God are you doing out after the curfew?" She couldn't make
herself answer. She was shivering. She was completely out of place.
Then the young man in the raincoat smiled at her and she felt deep
inside her the beginning of something almost like laughter. When they
checked that the road was clear she slipped home and while her harassed
parents scolded her she was looking at herself smiling in the oval, oak-
framed mirror in the red hall. For years that smiling face occupied her
day-dreams. Even after she was married to Alec it was not entirely
obliterated. Sometimes at night while he was asleep and she lay worrying if Una was warm enough in bed or if Andy's cough would ever
clear up she would close her eyes and the disembodied smile would
taunt her.

Now looking out at the pale sun shining through the cypresses at the end of the garden she suddenly decided she would go to Belfast and she began to tremble with excitement. There was a train at half past five—there was always the Enterprise at half past five. She had plenty of time to catch it. She rang a taxi—she was still good at remembering numbers—and went upstairs to get ready. She was going only for a visit to her sisters, she told herself. It didn't matter that the house was gone. She'd meet all her old friends and have great evenings by the fire, talking. She'd listen to all the gossip even if she couldn't remember the people, and relish the old jokes and the occasional spurt of venom. She had to look well, going up. She put on her good winter coat and her fur hat. There had been a row with Una over buying that hat. It cost twenty-seven pounds and Una had held up her hands in horror but Nora bought it. "Your father always liked me to have a fur hat to keep my head warm." And when Una insisted that the price was exorbitant, she retorted, "You say yourself money has no value any more." Her bag and gloves were years old but still good, she thought, as she settled back happily into the corner of the taxi.

"You'll love Dublin," Alec had told her when they got married. "We'll have great times there." But she had not loved Dublin. She had been lonely and homesick, totally dependent on Alec for comfort. It had been many years before she became accustomed to the strange streets and difficult distances. In the crowds downtown she never met by chance a familiar face. And the arrival of one child after the other finished any possibility of "great times." Then one St. Patrick's night a neighbour insisted on baby-sitting for them. It was too late to book for a play and when they went into town the restaurants and cinemas were all full so they strolled round arm-in-arm looking at shop-windows. It was a mild night and hundreds of other people were doing the same. Nora became aware of a light, bubbling sound rising from the streets and she realised it was people laughing all over the town. So she began to have an affection for Dublin as one can grow fond of someone else's child.

She paid the taxi-man outside the station. "My case?" she said.

"You hadn't got any case," he said and then looked concerned. "Did you forget it? We'd never make it back again in time." She was confused but assured him she was quite all right without it. At the ticket office she was told: "This train only travels to Dundalk."

"But I want to buy a second-class return for Belfast," she repeated.

"Bus connections to Portadown," the man said impatiently and she drew her money back out again, murmuring she'd better think about it. She stopped a uniformed railway man who was limping in a hurry over to the Enterprise gate and asked him to explain.

"You get the train to Dundalk, ma'm, buses to Portadown and train again to Belfast. It's a long old journey. Tiresome."

"But what can be the reason?" she asked.

"Bombs along the line, ma'm. That's it. Bombs along the line."

"But I thought they'd stopped all that," she said.

"Sure, didn't we all. But they've started again. There y'are." He went off but came back in a moment to find her still standing there. He assured her, "If you have to get home to Belfast, ma'm, we'll get you there all right. Only it'll be a bit longsome."

"Oh no," she said, "my home is in Dublin."

"Ah well then you're all right. I'd get back there then and ring up your friends in Belfast and tell them you're not coming. They'll know what it's like."

"How will I get home?" she asked helplessly.

"You'll get a bus at the foot of the steps there," he pointed. "Can you manage the steps?"

"Of course I can," she said indignantly and started off urgently, hoping to get home before Una. But no bus came until she was frozen and despairing. She looked round for support and saw another woman waiting in the shelter of the wall. She was perhaps not as old as Nora but she was poor and bent, in a shapeless coat and thin headscarf.

"Oh isn't the buses brutal?" she sighed and Nora agreed.

"The trains too."

"I didn't know there was anything wrong with the trains," the woman said. "But then it's years and years since I was on a train. Not since I used to bring the children to the seaside." She laughed. "They were great days. I used to pack all the picnic and bathing things in the bottom of the pram—do you remember the big deep prams there were then— and wheel them down to the station here with the smallest two in the pram and the others holding on at the sides. But sure they're only lent to you. Isn't that true?"

"Do you live with any of your children?" Nora asked.

"I do not," she said. "Since *he* died I've the pension myself. I have my independence. It's a great thing to have."

Eventually arriving home to find lights on all over the house she determined she would say nothing of where she had been. Her cold fingers had difficulty turning the key in the lock and before she could manage, Una flung open the door, her face anxious, her voice sharp, harassing her mother with questions. Nora said, "If you don't mind, Una, I'm going straight up to bed. I am very, very tired." She leaned against the wall to rest her legs and in the bright hall the unframed mirror reflected a wrinkled, powdery face with a wisp of grey hair untidy on the forehead. She looked down to the hall table where the big blue and white jug Dermot had brought her home years ago from some student trip held white chrysanthemums slightly browned at the under edges. She didn't like white chrysanthemums. They reminded her too much of funerals—real, unhappy funerals. She remembered, fleetingly, daffodils covering banks at the side of the road and the corner of a field, escaped probably from some big house.

"The flowers are withered, Una," she said. "We must buy different ones tomorrow."

"But where did you go?" Una repeated. "What did you think I'd feel coming home to find the house in darkness and the fire out and you not here?"

"I'm sorry it was uncomfortable for you, Una," Nora apologised sarcastically. "You haven't managed to warm up the house much yet."

"How could I?" Una demanded. "I've been on the phone to everybody I knew to find out where you were. You went off in a taxi?"

"I did," Nora answered. "Thank God I have a little money left to save me from hardship."

"Oh, Mother," Una said, "why do you say such things?"

"Why indeed?" Nora wondered to herself as she went slowly upstairs. Una followed her into her bedroom and stood looking at her uncertainly while she struggled to open her hot water bottle. She could not unscrew the cap. Una said she would go down and ring her brothers to tell them their mother was safely home. "I'd like you to fill my bottle first," Nora had to ask. "You need be in no hurry ringing Andy or Donal. They don't care what happens to me."

"Mother, are you out of your mind?" Una exclaimed. Nora sat down on the stool at her dressing-table, huddled in her good coat and fur hat until the electric heater had taken the chill off the room. "Will you have a hot bath?" Una asked, coming back.

"I don't think I could," her mother answered.

"Will I get the doctor for you then?"

"Indeed you will not. What good would the doctor do? I'm beginning to warm now, but I'm hungry."

"Hungry?" Una echoed.

"I haven't had a thing to eat since morning," Nora began and then shut her lips tight. When Una was gone she undressed in a hurry, leaving her clothes untidily on the stool but taking her handbag within reach on the bedside table. There were warm spots in the bed but most of it was so cold it felt damp.

She would never let them know where she'd gone, she repeated to herself. It was something of her own to hold on to. Then she realised that if she were very careful and kept Una at bay, Belfast would still be there for her. She would try again some time in the spring, when the weather was warmer or the Troubles were over. She was afraid though it would all come out somehow, some way or another, during the dark enclosed days.

*

A Curse

Brenda Murphy

She awoke in stages, aware of the humming sound that filled the space she was in. The fan, they had said. But that was not what had tugged her out of sleep. Cramping pains gripped her lower belly, holding her, then tightening their grip by spasms. A deep ache in the small of her back. She lay huddled, knees drawn up, face to the wall, eyes closed to block out the constantly burning light.

She sat up and looked about her. The yellow dimpled walls covered in graffiti stared back. She coughed and felt the ooze between her legs, the familiar ooze, the heat, the wetness. Her mother called it "the curse." A curse it was for her right then.

How long had she been asleep? What time was it? She could smell her own sweat, sniffed under her arm as if to confirm it. She felt a desperate need to wash herself, to be clean again. She took off her shoe, went over to the cell door and banged hard. After a while she heard footsteps, the jangle of keys. The door unlocked, a policeman stood before her.

"What do you want?"

"Can I speak to a policewoman?"

"No." After a pause, "There's none here at the minute. Now what is it?" He eyed her impatiently.

"I've taken my period," she said simply. "I need some sanitary towels and a wash. I've not been allowed to wash since I was arrested, days ago."

He looked at her with disgust. "Have you no shame? I've been married twenty years and my wife wouldn't mention things like that."

What is the colour of shame? All she could see was red as it trickled down her leg.

"Look, mister, I asked for a policewoman. I'm filthy, I'm bleeding, I need a wash and a change of clothes. Ask them to ring my mother. She'll bring them down for me. I don't think even your wife would stand here and bleed in silence."

"Don't you foul-mouth my wife, you wee hussy!" His face contorted with rage as he slammed the cell door.

She sat down again on the raised wooden boards and watched the blocked-out window in the ceiling. An hour, maybe two passed. She couldn't tell. Then footsteps again and the cell door opened. The policeman and a policewoman stared in at her.

"Right you, up!" said the woman officer, handing the prisoner a sanitary towel. Her voice was high-pitched and squeaky. "Follow me and hurry up about it. You have to go to the interview room again."

They walked along a corridor and a door was opened to reveal a toilet, wash basin and urinal. The stench was overwhelming. The girl went in. The toilet was blocked. She tried to flush it but it didn't work. She put on the sanitary towel then went to the basin. No soap, no towel, no hot water. She splashed her face with water, drying it on the bottom of her sweater.

"Hurry up," piped the policewoman from the doorway, reluctant to go in any further.

"Look, could you see if I can have a change of clothes and a proper wash? You know what it's like when you have your period."

The woman officer appeared not to hear, looking away as she repeated, "Hurry up. You're wanted for interview."

She stepped past the policewoman, who walked her upstairs to the interview room. It was exactly as she remembered it. Bright, electric, windowless.

Village without Men

Margaret Barrington

Weary and distraught the women listened to the storm as it raged around the houses. The wind screamed and howled. It drove suddenly against the doors with heavy lurchings. It tore at the straw ropes which anchored the thatched roofs to the ground. It rattled and shook the small windows. It sent the rain in narrow streams under the door, through the piled-up sacks, to form large puddles on the hard stamped earthen floors.

At times when the wind dropped for a moment to a low whistling whisper and nothing could be heard but the hammering of the sea against the face of Cahir Roe, the sudden release would be intolerable. Then one or another would raise her head and break into a prayer, stumbling words of supplication without continuity or meaning. Just for a moment a voice would be heard. Then the screaming wind would rise again in fury, roaring in the chimney and straining the roof-ropes, the voice would sink to a murmur and then to nothing as the women crouched again over the smouldering sods, never believing for a moment in the miracle they prayed for.

Dawn broke and the wind dropped for a while. The women wrapped their shawls tightly round them, knotted the ends behind them and tightened their headcloths. They slipped out through cautiously opened doors. The wind whipped their wide skirts so tightly to their bodies it was hard to move. They muttered to themselves as they clambered over the rocks or waded through the pools down to the foaming sea.

To the right Cahir Roe sloped upward, smothered in storm clouds, protecting the village from the outer sea. The ears of the women rang with the thunder of the ocean against its giant face. Salt foam flecked their faces, their clothes as they struggled along in knots of three or four, their heads turned from the wind as they searched the shore and looked out over the rolling water. But in all that grey-green expanse of churning sea, nothing. Not even an oar. All day long they wandered.

It was not until the turn of the tide on the second day that the bodies began to roll in, one now, another again, over and over in the water like dark, heavy logs. Now a face showed, now an outstretched hand rose clear of the water. John Boyle's face had been smashed on the rocks, yet his wife knew him as an incoming wave lifted his tall lean body to hurl it to shore.

For two days the women wandered until the ocean, now grown oily but still sullen with anger, gave up no more. Niel Boylan, Charley Friel and Dan Gallagher were never found.

The women rowed across the bay to the little town of Clonmullen for the priest. After the heavy rain the road across the bog was dangerous, and the village was cut off by land. The young curate, Father Twomey, came across. When he looked at the grey haggard faces of these women, all words of comfort deserted the young priest. His throat went dry and his eyes stung as if the salt sea had caught them. What comfort could words bring to women in their plight? He could with greater ease pray for the souls of the drowned than encourage the living to bear their sorrow in patience.

The women had opened the shallow graves in the sandy graveyard. They lowered the bodies and shovelled back the sand. Then for head-stones, to mark the place where each man was laid before the restless sand should blot out every sign, they drove an oar which he had handled into each man's grave and dropped a stone there for every prayer they said. The wind blew the sand into the priest's vestments, into his shoes, into his well-oiled hair and into his book. It whirled the sand around the little heaps of stones.

As the women rowed him home across the bay, the priest looked back at the village. The oars in the graves stood out against the stormy winter sky like the masts of ships in harbour.

The midwife was the first to leave the village.

As they brought each dead man up from the sea, she stripped him and washed his body. For most of them she had done this first service. From early youth, first with her mother, then alone, she had plied her trade on this desolate spit of land. These same bodies which once warm, soft, tender and full of life, had struggled between her strong hands, now lay cold and rigid beneath them. She washed the cold sea-water from these limbs from which she had once washed the birth-slime. Silently she accomplished her task and retired to her cottage. Of what use was a midwife in a village without men?

She wrote to her married daughter in Letterkenny who replied that there was work in plenty for her there. Then two weeks later when the hard frosts held the bog road, she loaded her goods on a cart and set out for Clonmullen from where she could get the train to Letterkenny. She took with her young Laurence Boyle, John Boyle's fourteen-year-old son, to bring back the donkey and cart.

The women watched her go. A few called God-speed but the others, thin-lipped, uttered no word. Silently they went back to their houses and their daily tasks. From now on their bodies would be barren as fields in winter.

All winter the village lay dumb and still. The stores of potatoes and salt fish were eaten sparingly. The fish might run in the bay now, followed by the screaming seagulls, but there were no men to put out the boats or draw in the gleaming nets. The children gathered mussels to feed the hens.

Then in the early spring days, the women rose from their hearths, and tightly knotted their headcloths and shawls. They took down the wicker creels from the lofts, the men's knives from the mantleshelves and went down to the rocks below Cahir Roe to cut the seawrack for the fields. The children spread it on the earth. Then with fork and spade the women turned the light sandy soil, planted their potatoes, oats and barley. The work was heavy and backbreaking but it had to be done. If they did not work now with all their strength, their children would be crying for food in the coming winter.

Driven, bone-tired, sick at heart, they rose early and worked all day, stopping at midday as their husbands had stopped, to rest in the shelter of a stone wall, to drink some milk or cold tea and to eat some oatbread the children brought to them in the fields. At night they dragged their bodies to bed. There was no joy, no relief to be got there now. Nothing but sleep, easing of weary muscles.

Their work in the house was neglected. The hearths went untended, their clothes unwashed. They no longer white-washed the walls of the cottages or tended the geraniums they grew in pots. They did not notice when the flowers died.

The next to leave the village was Sally Boyle. She was to have married young Dan Gallagher after the next Lent. There at the end of the straggling village was the half-built ruin of the house he had been getting ready with the help of the other men in the village. All winter she moped over the fire, only rousing herself when her mother's voice rose sharp and angry. Now in the spring she began to wander about restlessly. She would leave her work and climb the great headland of Cahir Roe, there to look out to where Tory rose like a fortress from the sea—out there across the sea in which Dan Gallagher had been drowned, the sea which had refused to surrender what should have been hers. At night in bed she could not control the wildness of her body. She pitched from side to side, moaning and muttering. Her whole mind was darkened by the memory of soft kisses on warm autumn nights, of strong hands fondling her. She felt bereft, denied.

She slipped away one day and joined the lads and lasses in Clonmullen who were off to the hiring fair at Strabane. Later her mother got a letter and a postal order for five shillings. Sally was now hired girl on a farm down in the Lagan.

Then in ones and twos the young girls began to leave. With the coming of spring their eyes brightened, their steps grew lighter. They would stop and look over their shoulders hurriedly as if someone were behind. They would rush violently to work and then leave their tasks unfinished to stand and look out over the landscape, or out to sea from under a sheltering hand. They became irritable, quarrelsome and penitent by turns. Somewhere out there across the bog, across the sea, lay a world where men waited; men who could marry them, love them perhaps, give them homes and children.

The women objected to their going and pleaded with them. Every hand was needed now. The turf must be cut in the bog, turned and stacked for the coming winter. Surely they could go when the crops were gathered in. But tears and pleading were in vain. Nature fought against kindness in their young bodies. Here no men were left to promise these girls life, even the hazardous life of this country. They gathered their few garments together and departed, promising to send back what money they could. But their mothers knew that it was not to get money they left. It was the blood in their veins which drove them forth. And though the women lamented, they understood.

No use now to give a dance for the departing girls. There were no men with whom they could dance. No use to gather the neighbours into the house to sing. The voices of women are thin and shrill without men's voices to balance them.

Larry Boyle found himself the only lad in the village. The other boys were many years younger and those who were older had been lost with their fathers in the storm. The winter gloom, the silence of the women and his loneliness drove him to daydreaming, to the creation of a fantasy world. He saw himself, in coming years, stronger and taller than any man, towering over humanity as Cahir Roe towered over the sea, impregnable, aloof. Boats, fields, cattle, houses, everything in the village would belong to him. For as yet the outside world meant nothing to him and women had no power over his dreams. They existed but to serve him.

At first the women paid no more attention to him than they did to the other children. He ate what food was set before him. Some potatoes, a piece of dried salt fish, a bowl of buttermilk. He performed such tasks as were set him, helping with the few cows, carrying the seawrack, heeling the turf. Indeed he was despised rather than otherwise, for the girls of his age were more nimble and less absent-minded than he. But slowly, as if in answer to his dreams, his position changed. In every house he entered he was welcomed and given the seat by the fire. He was never allowed to depart without food and drink. The older women baked and cooked for him, kept the best for him, gave him small presents from their hoard; a husband's knife; a son's trousers. They began to compliment him at every turn on his strength and growth. No one asked him to work.

Now he allowed his hair to grow like a man's. The stubby quiff vanished and a crop of thick, fair curls crowned his forehead, giving him the obstinate look of a fierce young ram. He became particular about the cleanliness of his shirt, refused to wear old patched trousers and coats. Gradually he dominated the whole village. Even the dogs owned him sole master, and snarled savagely at one another when he called them to heel. The younger boys were his slaves, to fetch and carry for him. He scarcely noticed the girls of his own age, never called them by name, never spoke directly to them. Unlike them, he had no wish to leave the village.

A day came when Larry Boyle went from house to house and collected the fishing lines, hooks and spinners which had belonged to the drowned men. They were granted him as if by right. He took them to the rock behind the village where formerly the fish had been dried and where the men had then met in the summer evenings to talk, away from their womenfolk. It was a day of shifting sun and shadow and the wind from the west broken by the headland.

He sang as he carefully tested, cut and spliced each line. He rubbed the hooks and spinners clean of rust with wet sand from the stream. He made a long line, tested each length and wound it in a coil between hand and elbow. He fastened the hooks and the lead weight. Then, satisfied, he went down to the shore to dig bait.

He swung his can of bait over his shoulder, picked up his line and made for Cahir Roe. He was going to fish for rockfish.

A deep shelf ran round part of the headland and from this the men had fished in the drowsy heat of summer days when they could spare time from the fields. He clambered along the shelf and stood on the edge. The sea heaved and foamed beneath him. Far out, Tory rose, a castle against the white line of the horizon.

He fixed his bait carefully and placed the loose end of the line beneath his heel. Then, clear of the beetling rock behind, he swung the coil of line above his head and threw it far out. His body, balanced over the edge, seemed to follow it as his eye watched the untwisting of the cord, the drop of the lead towards the sea. He bent down and gathered up the end.

He could feel the movement as the length of line ran through the sea and the weight sank slowly through the heavy water. His hand knew what was happening down there beneath the surface of the water. He felt the lead strike the bottom. His fingers, born to a new delicacy, held the line firmly so that the bait should float free. He could feel the gentle nibbling of the fish at the bait, nibbling cautiously, daintily, as sheep nibble grass. Twice he drew in his line to rebait the hook. Then one struck.

Excited, breathing heavily, his eyes distended, he drew in the line slowly, letting it fall in careful coils at his feet. Then the fish left the water and the full weight hung on the line. It plunged about madly in the air, twisting and flapping. The cord rubbed against the edge of the shelf as it passed from hand to hand, dislodging small stones and dirt from the crumbling surface. He had to lean out to jerk the fish over the edge, at that moment unaware of everything but the twisting, flapping fish. He threw it well behind him so that it could not leap back into the water. It lay there, twisting and turning, its brilliant orange and green colouring coming and going, its belly heaving, its panting gills shining red. Then it lay still and from its open mouth the brick-red blood flowed over the stones. Another leap, another twitch. It was dead.

Larry passed the back of his hand across his forehead to wipe away the sweat. Before he stooped to disengage the hook from the jaws of the fish, he looked around him, at Tory on the far horizon, at the towering cliff above, the heaving sea beneath. For a moment his head reeled as he felt the turning of the world.

The women liked the new schoolmistress. They liked her modesty and reserve. Though young she knew how to keep the children in order, teach them their lessons and their manners. They looked after her with approval when they saw her walk precisely from the school to the cottage where she lived, her hands stiffly by her sides, her eyes lowered. They admired her round, rosy face, her light hair, her neat figure. She appeared so young and lovely to these women whose bodies were lean and tired from hard work and poor food.

She never stopped at the half-door for a chat, nor delayed for a moment to pass the time of day with a neighbour on the road. She never played with the younger children. She walked around encased in herself.

Every Saturday while the road held, she would mount her clean, well-oiled bicycle and cycle to Clonmullen. On the way she did not speak to anyone nor answer a greeting. With gaze fixed on the road before her, she pedalled furiously. In Clonmullen she would make one or two purchases, post her letters and cycle back home. All attempts at conversation were firmly repulsed. She did not even stop to have tea at the hotel.

She lived alone in a small cottage built on the rise of ground just beyond the village. For an hour at a time she would kneel in the shelter of the fuchsia hedge and gaze hungrily at the houses she did not wish to enter, at the women to whom she did not care to speak. She knew all their comings and goings, all the details of their daily life. She watched them at their work, in their conversation. She watched the children at play. She watched Larry Boyle as he wandered along the shore towards Cahir Roe to fish, or passed her cottage on his way to set rabbit snares in the burrows.

The July heat beat down on the earth and the blue-grey sea moved

sleepily under a mist. He was returning home when he saw her, standing in the shelter of the bushes that grew over the gateway. She was
looking at him with fierce intentness. He stood still and gazed back,
his eyes wide and startled. The fear of unknown lands, of uncharted
seas took hold of him. His mouth dropped open, his skin twitched.
His throat hurt and there was a hammering in his ears like the heavy
pounding of the surf on Cahir Roe. He could not move hand nor foot.
With a sudden movement her hand darted out and caught his wrist.
She drew him towards her, in the shelter of the thick fuchsia hedge.
Frightened by her intent stare, her pale face, her quick uneven breathing, when she put out her other hand to fondle him, he pulled away
and burst through the bushes. Quietly, with lowered eyes, she listened
as his boots clattered over the rocky road. She sighed and turned back
into her house.

But he came back. Furtively. He would steal into her kitchen when
she was at school and leave some offering; a freshly caught fish, a
rabbit, some rock pigeon's eggs. He had so little to give. She did not
seem to notice. She did not stop him to thank him when they met.
She passed without even a greeting, once again encased in her rigid
calm. Then one evening, as darkness fell, he lifted the latch of her
door. She was seated on her hearthrug, gazing at the glowing turf fire.
He approached in silent desperation and with the same wild desperation
she answered.

Such happenings do not long remain hidden in a small world.
Without a word spoken, the women came to know. Primitive anger
seized hold on them. They said nothing to Larry. Their belief in man's
place in life and the fact that they had denied him nothing shut their
mouths. All their rage turned against the young teacher whom they
had thought so modest and gentle. They became as fierce as hawks at
the theft of their darling.

They ceased work. They came together in groups, muttering. They
buzzed like angry bees. Their lips spoke words to which their ears were
long unaccustomed as they worked themselves into an ancient battle
fury. They smoothed their hair back from their foreheads with damp
and trembling hands. They drew their small shawls tightly round their
shoulders.

From behind the fuchsia hedge the girl saw them coming like a
flock of angry crows. Their wide dark skirts, caught by the light summer
breeze, bellowed out behind them. Their long, thin arms waved over

235

their heads like sticks in the air. Their voices raised in some primitive battle cry, they surged up the road towards her.

Terrified of this living tidal wave, she rushed out. The uneven road caught her feet. It seemed to her that she made no headway as she ran, that the surging mass of women came ever nearer. Stones rattled at her heels. She ran on in blind panic, unaware of where she was going. Her chest began to ache, her throat to burn. A stone caught her shoulder but she scarcely felt the blow. Then another hit her on the back and she stumbled. Still she ran on, not daring to look back. A stone struck her head. She reeled and fell. Over the edge of the narrow bog road, down the bank towards the deep watery ditch. Briars caught her clothes. Her hands grasped wildly at the tufts of rough grass. There she lay, half in, half out of the water, too frightened to move or struggle.

When they saw her fall, the women stopped and stood there in the road, muttering. Then they turned back. They burst into her neat little cottage. They threw the furniture about, broke the delft, hurled the pots out of doors, tore the pretty clothes to ribbons. Then they left, still muttering threats, like the sea after storm.

Later, shivering, aching, sick, the girl dragged herself back onto the road. There was no one there now. The flock of crows had gone. She stood alone on the empty road. There was no sound but the lonely call of a moor bird overhead.

The next day Larry, too, left the village.

The war when it came meant little to these women. The explosions of mines on the rocks could not harm them now that there were no men to risk their lives on the water. The aeroplanes which from time to time circled over the coast seemed to them no more than strange birds, at first matter for wonder and then taken for granted. Sometimes the sea washed up an empty ship's boat, some timbers or empty wooden cases. One morning scores of oranges came dancing in on the waves. The children screamed with delight and, not knowing what they were, played ball with them. But since the oranges did not bounce they soon tired of them and left them along the shore to rot. The women only realized that the war could touch them when the supplies of Indian meal ran out.

All that winter storms lashed the coast. Snow whirled around the houses, blotting out the sight of the fierce sea which growled savagely against the headland of Cahir Roe day and night. Not once during the bitter months did the snow melt on the mountains beyond Clonmullen. The wind tore at the ropes which tethered the thatched roofs, rotting and grass-grown from neglect. The north-east wind drove under the doors, roared in the chimneys; it hardened the earth until it was like a stone.

Yet now it seemed that the silence was broken, that terrible silence they had kept in mourning for their dead. Now in the evenings they gathered round one another's firesides. They told stories, old Rabelaisian tales heard when they were children from the old men of the village. Such tales as lie deep in the minds of people and are its true history. Tales of old wars, of great slaughter of men, of the survival of the women and children, of tricks to preserve the race. They told of the Danes and their love of the dark-haired Irishwomen. They laughed quietly and spoke in whispers of the great power of the Norsemen's bodies, of the fertility of their loins.

Over and over again they told the story of the women of Monastir, who, when widowed and alone, lured with false lights a ship to their shore. What matter that their victims were dark-skinned Turks. Their need was great.

The eyes of the women grew large and full of light as they repeated these tales over the dying embers of their fires. A new ferocity appeared in their faces. Their bodies took on a new grace, grew lithe and supple. As the body of the wild goat becomes sleek and lovely in the autumn.

Spring came suddenly. After the weeks of fierce winds and wild seas, followed days of mild breezes and scampering sunshine. The women threw open their doors and stepped out with light hearts. As they cut the seawrack for their fields, they called to one another and sang snatches of old songs. Sometimes one or another would stop in her work and look out over the water at the sea-swallows dipping and skimming over the surface of the water, at the black shags as they swam and dived, at old Leatherwing standing in his corner in wait. The older children laughed and shouted as they helped to spread out the wrack on the fields. The younger ones screamed as they ran along the shore and searched under the rocks for crabs. They called and clapped their hands at the sea-pies as they bobbed up and down on the waves.

On and on the children ran, their toes pink in the seawater. They chattered together like pies over each fresh discovery. They travelled along the shore until they found themselves out on the point of land beside Cahir Roe, facing the open sea. There they stood and looked out to sea from under sheltering hands.

For some minutes they stood and stared. Then in a body they turned and ran towards the women, shouting all together that out there, coming in closer every minute, was a strange boat.

The women straightened their backs and listened. Even before they understood what the children were shouting, they let down their petticoats and started for the point. There they stood in a group and stared, amazed that a boat should put in on that inhospitable shore. Close in now, with flapping sail, the boat came.

They could make out only one man and their eyes, used to long searching over water, could see that he was lying across the tiller. Was he alive or dead? Could he not see where he was going? If he did not change his course now he would fetch up on the reef below Cahir Roe. They rushed forward to the water's edge and shouted. The man bent over the tiller did not move. They continued to shout. They waded into the sea until the water surged against their bodies and threatened to overbalance them. Their dark skirts swirled round them in the heavy sea as they shouted and waved their arms.

Then the man at the tiller slowly raised his head. He looked around him, at the sea, at the screaming women, at the great red granite face of Cahir Roe. With great effort he pulled his body upright and swung the tiller over. Then he fell forward again. Even before the keel had grounded on the gravel, the women had seized the boat and dragged it up onto the beach.

Six men lay huddled in the bottom of the boat. Great, strong men, now helpless. The women turned to the helmsman. He looked at them with dull, sunken eyes. He moved. He tried to speak. His grey face was stiff, his lips cracked.

"Scotland?" he asked and his voice was hoarse.

The women shook their heads. Then the man slowly lifted one hand, pointed to the men at his feet and then to himself.

"Danes. Torpedoed. Ten days."

The women cried aloud as they lifted the heavy bodies of the men. Their voices sang out in wild exultation.

The Danes. The Danes were come again.

Checkpoint

Ann McKay

He was a gangster, Damian, a gangster of hearts. Like Humphrey Bogart, Glennie Barr, and Heathcliff merged in shades of grey, all rolled into one hell of a desperate man. Of all those heroes of my wet dreams, he was the one. His image haunts me, like some glamorous good angel, or a battered photograph which leaves more and more to the imagination as time goes on.

But you can still see the hardman's skullface, the mouth childish and expectant as a woman's, and the well-armed eyes. "Keeps himself to himself, MacCauley does, he's dead witty, though." He was a legend at school for the drink and the fags and the poker and not much else, least of all rugger. I don't know why, but even the thought of him makes me ache and damp and smile, the way he used to get so husky tender and fumbling.

My God, but those were some enchanted evenings down by the riverside, on Derry's chilly wooden docks, where the winos dine on chips and peas, and the bad girls roam on tottered heels, and the seagulls peer like voyeurs from their squalid lonely posts. Not that there was much to see, as far as we were concerned. The fact is, our poignant love was full of tragic bliss, for we could neither of us fathom the mysterious potential of our mutual presence. We knew passion all right, but in mind, from A level texts and Sunday colour magazines. Somehow we couldn't connect that vestige of privilege and well-being with the incomprehensible stirrings that were furtive as our glances and uneasy as the talk.

We would meet after school, uniformed and blushing, walking down town the long way, rather than pass bus queues of merciless innocents and precocious fellow sixth-formers already in the know. So we braved instead the Taigs perched like injuns on the concrete steps of the Tech and the cocky Brits lounging behind sandbags. Until we sat camouflaged in the busmen's café, where across the sloppy veneer table I gazed at your warm neck when you had undone your school tie, you stared at my grey woollen breasts, and we gladly guzzled tea and chips, the only sensuality our rigourously inbred protestant morality would admit. And then the goodbye, dreaded by both, and always deferred by the promise of a phonecall after tea. "Bye, then." "Yes, bye." And both our faces beamed with smiling, so relieved we might almost have dived into a kiss, but never did, running away after different buses.

"You say it."

"Only if you will."

"Awright. Ready?"

"Mmm . . ."

A warm and tender pause.

"Damian?"

"Yes."

"You still there?"

"Yes. Are you?"

"Yes."

A warm and tender pause. While in my secret head I'm screaming, howling with laughter, lowly sobbing, "Damian Damian Damian love I love you love you love you." And in the breathy silence of the telephone we shift and sigh, wishing and wondering and wanting.

You have to laugh. Even then we had to laugh. At me and you and us and what the hell this is one love will last forever, unrealized. "Better go then, do this damned physics."

I loved it when he swore. Grinning, "Yes, me too."

"So I'll see you tomorrow."

"Yes."

"If you want."

"I do, Damian, really. Same time?"

"Yeah. Bye, honey."

"Bye, honey."

A warm and tender pause. Then we both held our respective receivers at arm's length, and with trembling fingers disconnected.

Needless to say, the parents couldn't understand it, even apart from the pennies accumulating on the phone bills. "Why don't you say whatever it is you want to say during the day, for it's not as if you never see him, not to be wasting time and money on the phone." So I said, all right then, I'll use the call box up the road, but they didn't like that either. Didn't like the secrecy, not knowing what was going on.

As it was now fully apparent to me and to him that we were actually going together, we felt obliged to make it official and go out on a date. Meeting at eight at the bus depot, where rival obscenities were scored and crossed like equations on the wooden shelters. Too excited to be embarrassed, I would alight, nervy and awkward in my ordinary clothes, to see Damian skulking in the doorway of the sweetshop, dragging gulps of smoke from his cigarette. We faced each other in the dusk. Where now? In the end we headed for Free Derry, where we would be sure of seeing nobody we knew, so there would be no scenes of wretched embarrassment, and no disasters, no catharsis.

You had to go through an army checkpoint. Which involved a spontaneous moral decision, whether to be civil and politely submissive, or whether to stand by instinctive integrity and challenge the imposition of constraint. No time for heroics, girls showed their handbags with a minimum of fuss or thrill, but men were frisked, leaning against the wall. I didn't watch, only heard the rasping slap of hard hands on clothes. After the soldiers there were tinker kids from Donegal, runny-nosed and looselipped, who scrambled at my coat for spare pennies. "Ah go on miss, please, please." We paid them to go away. And winos on the corner of William Street, and dogs and streams of piss on the footpath. Shouting and smoke from the flats behind. Waterloo Street was full of men—wordpassing in doorways, locking or unlocking cars, lugging crates and barrels. Every stranger was watched who came in.

Alert to every move, we were horrified and fascinated by the world beyond the barriers. We sat in the corner of the pub, out of the light and near the door, talking about it, the terrible squalid energy of the place. Inhibitions suspended, we talked like friends, Damian drinking whiskey and water, I with my glass of Guinness, our legs beneath the table close and warm.

The barman in slow motion wiped a glass, watching up at the TV where Paisley flickered and gaped. We cringed guiltily, glad of the dim lights. But what the hell, aren't we all in this together, so Fuck the Queen and Up the Pope and God save Ulster in the green in the green, every laugh a conspiracy, we clinked glasses. Men at the bar, slanging one bastard and praising another. There was a thump outside, another bomb. Nobody flinched but me. My hand jumped for the table, grabbed your leg, shocking warm like a dog's back, and we both flinched. Hard on the oul nerves this, enough to make you lose the head altogether, and if my heart could speak knowing that I want you in me however hard I can't imagine sore I'm sure but this is like a forest as one wolf to another. "Sorry," I said. We left the pub and walked. Apart from a few cross-clinched, quickmarching couples, the street was empty, wide and high with tension as a mountain pass. Damian in front, his coat undone and I holding back, using my painful good shoes as an excuse. A car came from behind, spotlighting the back before me. I felt the now familiar dreadthrill of sudden bullets in the night. The car slowed to a stop, jerked into reverse and eased towards the pavement. I recognized my mother in the passenger seat before I recognized the family car.

"On your way hame?" says the mother.

"Hop in and we'll give you a lift," says the father in a gay magnanimous tone; so we did, our moments together in the wide dark suspended.

"Did you hear that explosion just now? Another good business up in smoke, I suppose. But you know what they said about the country, if they couldn't have it, they would destroy it. . . . " An impressive silence, nobody rising to the bait. "Well now," says the mother straining round, all smiles and diplomacy, "you must be the famous Damian."

"That's right," he mutters, scrambling at a cigarette packet, offers one all round.

"No thanks," the father laughs at the naïvety of the gesture. "We don't smoke." Damian's match hisses, flares, and he breathes a car full of smoke. My mother winds down the window.

He refused to come in for a cup of tea, no thanks, he had to be getting back, and the offer of a lift home, no thanks, I'd rather walk, goodnight now.

At the gate, under a heavy sagging sycamore tree, in a dark that was dank with slight rain and midges, we confronted each other again, drawing back embarrassed as a snogging couple lurched up the road, on the near side the breadman's notorious wife and mother of five. She always looked harrowed, her matching lips and nails livid as bruises. Unmistakable, even in the dark, she was five foot eleven.

"She's a big woman." His voice was low and harsh. I chewed a thumbnail, tasting skin. The midges were biting, striking softly with invisible fangs, not really deterred by cigarette smoke. Damian threw his butt across the road. It fell, a tiny spark among nettles.

"It's a bloody hangover from childhood, this damned ignorance, bloody innocents the pair of us, rotting on the branch like unpicked apples."

"That's a fine literary allusion."

"Oh fuck off."

And hearing in his voice all the wrapped-up misery I knew in his eyes, I would gladly have fucked off and come back a new woman, bird-bodied, a painted lady with wings to enfold. Not this ingenuous fledgling who coyly coveted her swelling breasts and welcomed in secret the sordid monthly rituals with towels and talc. Sweet consolation for the tenderness and pain.

And if either of us had moved, and we couldn't with that dark space of wilful impotence between, what monstrous dream crouched waiting, hand on the hole, finger on the trigger, the taloned pointing fingers of yours disgusted, the righteous god of wrath. A hellfire cartoon of riflesticks and bottle throats assaulting the angels to tears. Or his arm around my neck, my fingers in his hair stroking to touch and feel. Coaxing with my mouth, craving the sweat of another skin, green like new grass, and then at last the breath-held pain of new-broken earth.

Will I bleed? Will you come? Will we cry or laugh or turn away from our eyes with the shame and the disappointment. And should we wait for a bed with champagne and candles or do it as the fancy takes us on the road. Behind a tree unclothed and lie in the wet among midges and twigs. It was darker and spitting rain.

"It's raining," I said. "So I'm going in."

"As you wish."

"Night then." But before I could move, his shape shifted heavily in the night, breathing fierce and sore and not for love, and he hared off down the road, pursued and overtaken by a swishing car and his own huge shadow.

The Dove of Peace

Leland Bardwell

There's a hole in my memory. I've had other holes—unimportant ones—but this one nags, some days almost to torture level. It could be three days or more or it could be weeks. Lately I have felt an urgency to recapture that dark patch. I fear the failing memory of the old, the undignified lapses, the difficulty in distinguishing one decade from another.

Yes, I'm old, arthritic. Some mornings I can barely lift the kettle. All my strength has to be tailored to my boxes. All over the world you'll find them. I have made boxes of every size and shape, every colour and hue. I have made boxes of ash and cedar wood, ebony and elder. I have made boxes inlaid with garnets and coloured glass set in garlands of flowers resembling the wild herbaceous borders of the big house where she and I used to play.

I have fought this dark patch like you'd fight to get out of a nightmare, stitching and restitching till my head swims and the events before and after become even more unyielding. I have gone back to my work saying, What does it matter now? The past is the past. Let sleeping dogs lie.

This morning again I sorted through the old trunk and reread the famous letter. The envelope was addressed to me, Miss Jessica O'Brien, c/o The Ballyronan County Asylum. Inside, dated 12th July 1946, it stated that my father Joseph O'Brien was dead.

Every time I read this letter I relive the exhilaration of those next few days. I was no longer a non-being. It was like a news flash of world importance that you get nowadays on television.

244

You see this short period I speak of is not my first experience of memory failure. For four long years I had lived in that place with no recollection of what had happened before I went there. All I could recall was the deaf man driving the old Ford and myself in the back—a bundle of clothes with nothing inside it. And the gates of the Asylum. I always remembered the gates—each individual strut pointed like a spear and the whole welded together with hefty iron cross-bars. The outside of the building, also, haunted me—the opacity, the height and the great oak door cut into the wall which was opened with a mortice key some eight inches long. And how the smells had hit me that first day—the mixture of urine and sweet powder.

Nor could I forget my first impression of the nurse who strode ahead of me like a man and had a stone-coloured featureless face that threw loops of sentences at me that made no sense but seemed to settle in my brain in strings. At first I was put in a cell with a high-up window the size of a tray through which filtered a shaft of light that barely lit the end of the bed. The bedding consisted of a white cotton cover, two thin blankets and no sheets. That night I discovered the blankets were as coarse as turf and caused sour weals to rise on my skin.

It was about a year later that a nurse casually told me that my mother had died in the same hospital in another ward and did I want to see her body? What mother? I had no mother or father. I had nobody belonging to me. I ate with old women who dribbled and had to be fed. In the exercise hall I was paired off with a harridan who cursed me all the time. This I had come to accept. This was my reality. I was a non-being, homogeneous, as though I were not composed of parts. I called myself a changeling, a moonchild, and when I wasn't eating or sleeping I paced the ward like all the others, slowly, back and forth, like floating creatures in a massive tank.

But then came the letter. The nurse read it to me as if I were illiterate and as she read the words *Joseph O'Brien is dead* my whole body underwent a physical change. I had a feeling of freshness, "young-ness," clarity of mind. I clutched the woman, implored her to repeat the news. With that one sentence she had given me back my past. Every bit of it, that is, except that short period so nearly remembered, so hidden.

Now that I am elderly and crippled those four years are of a timeless monotony—grey as the food they gave us which we shovelled into our mouths with large tin spoons.

But how I crave to find you, Columbine, in those short hours, Oh Columbine, my Dove of Peace.

It was Jessica who noticed the mother's wandering first. The trailing abstracted movements as she switched from hall to sitting room, from sitting room to kitchen. Columbine didn't notice. Columbine was Daddy's pet. Daddy bought her dresses and brooches and scarves. "Columbine can charm the birds off the trees," Daddy said, as he took her on his knee and she settled her pointed face into the lapels of his jacket. No, Columbine didn't notice the mother's pacing, nor the strain in her mouth, nor the anger in her shoulders. She was Columbine, The Dove of Peace—Daddy had chosen the name because the war was over.

The two little girls shared a bedroom. They had a high iron bed each and Jessica used to tell Columbine a story every night. The story wove its way through Columbine's head until she fell into a gentle sleep. From then on Jessica would stare vacantly into the darkness. If she dozed off, she'd wake frequently, sounds of ghostly swishings, perhaps a human sigh or something louder like a withheld yawn would cause knots of terror to gather in her stomach. Yet somehow she knew that she must not call out or make known that she was awake.

If she questioned Columbine in the morning the latter would only curl up more tightly into her silky morning warmth and say nothing.

Columbine had soft hair, light as lint, which fell each side of her face in madonna curves, while Jessica's hair was thick and dry, held back by kirby grips. But she was light as a fox and in this way she pleased Columbine, who was all movement, all grace.

Jessica was a year younger than her sister and for this reason all her thoughts, actions and mannerisms were directed towards being as exactly as possible a replica of the elder girl. To the extent that sometimes Columbine would feel irritated by the intensity of Jessica's adoration and would try to shake herself away with an angry, "Don't copy me all the time."

But mostly their games were wild and secret, beset with the lore and superstition of the countryside, overlaid by their inventiveness and natural savagery. It was only at night time that a strange anomaly manifested itself.

Jessica never quite knew when she found out the cause of her nightly terrors. It was like a gradual growth of the faculties, the inculcation of logic into her childish brain. These nocturnal noises had, after all, a human origin. There were no ghosts, no disembodied spirits, nothing, in fact, to be afraid of. It was only Daddy, who came up to give Columbine a last goodnight kiss, to hold her soft body in his arms, reassure her of his love.

There was a shed at the end of the garden in which junk of all kinds was jettisoned. When rebuffed by Columbine, Jessica would go into this shed, at first to sulk, hoping that Columbine would follow, and then when this plan didn't work, her own inventiveness took over. One day while in a complicated fantasy of delving amongst the broken furniture and odds and ends she came upon a bag of tools. A great leather bag, matted with dust, the hasp askew but crammed with the most exciting amalgam of saws, chisels, planes, adzes and such like, keenly edged and in fine condition. At first she just played with the saws, cutting broken chair-legs and the like. Gradually her fascination grew till one day the shapes began to form neatly. She had fashioned her first perfect square. She taught herself how to make tenons and mortices, how to dovetail the wood so that she could fit the squares together. She had made her first box.

She made more and more, boxes of every size and description. She became obsessed. But it was a secret obsession. No one must know about her boxes. Especially Columbine.

If Columbine found out she would only laugh at her. She could imagine what she would say.

"Making boxes? What for? They're useless."

Meanwhile the mother's pacing grew worse although sometimes she'd stand stock still and stare. It was uncomfortable, that staring. Also she sometimes stood in an awkward place, like in a doorway or blocking the cooker.

"What is wrong with Mammy?" Jessica asked.

"She's mad. Stone mad."

"Why is she mad?"

"She's mad because she can't have what she wants."

"What does she want?"

"Something big, Daddy says."

"What does that mean?"

"Dunno."

Out in the shed, Jessica planned. Perhaps she could make her Mammy a big box. A big box so as Mammy could put everything into it. All her boxes were small because the bits of wood she found were seldom more than a few inches long. It was no good. She'd have to buy her Mammy something big. An elephant? Everyone knew that elephants were the biggest things in the world. But she couldn't get her a real elephant because they were all in circuses. She'd have to get her a toy one.

The following day Jessica emptied her savings box and bought her mother a toy elephant.

"Now Mammy, you can imagine that this is a real elephant and that's a big thing."

Her mother stopped and hit her so hard she spun twice and landed against the table leg.

"Don't ever do that again," the mother screamed. And she screamed so much others came from the neighbouring house.

Jessica looked up from where she lay, the blood spurting down her chin. There was the woman from next door bending over her muttering, "Oh dear the little one is hurt."

"I'm perfectly all right." Prim little Jessica got up and ran into the kitchen to wipe the blood from her face.

But because she was bleeding her mother wanted to hit her more. And more. She picked her up, with the two neighbours watching, and shook her and shouted and the hatred ran up and down the stairs and out the back door and into the yard till the father came in and hit the mother and the neighbours ran away.

Some days after that a van came. A white van. And Jessica stood in the hall and watched her mother carrying her suitcase and climbing into the back of the van. Father was there, too. Nobody took any notice of Jessica.

"Where's Mammy gone?"

"To a mad house."

Now the girls had to grow up fast. They had to cook and do the housework as well as attend school and do their homework. Dirt piled up in odd corners. Smells accumulated. Food rotted and was thrown away. Daddy grew more and more bad tempered. At six o'clock every evening he'd return, his face ravaged from the raw winds, banging his bike through the front door and the kitchen and out into the yard, leaving a cold draught to circle through the house. When it was Columbine's turn to cook, he took pains to praise what dreadful concoction she placed before him, but when it was Jessica's turn he'd cast his plate from him, shouting, "Do you expect me to eat this muck," and storm out to the pub.

Although the girls had long since ceased their games of fantasy they were very close. At night when the wind howled outside they'd strive to get their homework done, helping each other when possible, giggling over the teacher's stupidity and drawing cartoons in their copy-books.

But when it was time to go to bed Jessica's terrible fears intruded on their intimacy. She was never allowed to mention the father's nightly visits. Starched with sleeplessness, she'd lie motionless till he went.

One morning Columbine said she couldn't get up.

"What's the matter?"

"I've got my visitor."

Jessica looked around. She thought of the nightly shufflings, the yawn-like noises.

"You're going mad, like Mammy. There's no one in the room."

"I'm not well."

There was a new smell. A not unpleasant smell but warm and penetrating, ammoniac.

"Should I get the doctor?"

"Good heavens, no!"

Jessica went off to school in a state of bewilderment.

That night, as usual, Daddy came up. He wasn't steady and there was a foul smell on him, like man. All the men in the morning bus smelled like that. This time Jessica was wide awake and for the first time felt a heavy guilt as though she were to blame. To blame for what? Perhaps, when she was a baby she had done something wrong, which was why Daddy only loved Columbine. But no. It wasn't only that. It was sorrow. Sorrow you could touch like a coat or extra padding on your body. Please go away, oh please, she wanted to scream. Tears, cooling quickly, gathered round her eyes, ran down her ears, her neck and soaked the pillow. But this time the father didn't stay long. With a furious oath he stumbled from the room. Jessica sat up in horror. In a shaft of moonlight she could see Columbine's face like a scallop above the sheets. "Are you all right?" she managed to ask.

Columbine didn't answer.

Next morning it was the same.

"Are you still sick? Please tell me what's the matter?"

"I'm bleeding. There. Are you happy now?"

"Columbine, darling, why didn't you tell me?"

"Oh go away for God's sake."

"But you must see the doctor."

She pulled the bedclothes down. "There! Look. Blood! Get me a pad from the drawer before you go."

"These?" Jessica picked up a packet wrapped in blue paper. The torn label read: Six Sanitary Towels.

"Lucky you had these."

"Wait till it happens to you."

"Me? This won't happen to me, will it?"

"God, you're an innocent fool."

"Do you not mind?"

"It means I'm a grown up girl, Daddy says."

How could she? How could she talk about that to Daddy? Columbine, still laughing, was holding out the used towel.

"Present for you," she said.

Jessica took the towel and fired it in the wastepaper basket.

It was a year later when Jessica got her first period. She didn't know what to do so she stole the towels from Columbine.

"You can buy your own. Ask Daddy for the money."

This was out of the question. She cut up rags and washed them out afterwards. Her thighs were roughened from the coarse cloth. Little scabs formed and barely healed from month to month.

About this time a deaf man became a new neighbour. He drove an old blue Ford. Jessica learnt deaf and dumb language on her fingers hoping that if they made friends he'd take them for drives.

On these excursions the two sisters would sit in the back giggling at all the passers-by. The deaf man talked in loops because he had never heard speech so they laughed at that too. And when they got home at night Daddy was usually in the pub so they'd sit together by the kitchen stove eating toast and jam and scrawling out their homework till they'd hear the dreaded noises that warned them of their father's return. At least Jessica dreaded them, Columbine still laughed at her, saying, "Poor Daddy, he's unhappy."

"So that's why you let him?"

"Mind your own business. You're supposed to be asleep."

One morning Columbine told her they were not going on any more rides.

"Why, oh why not?"

"Daddy says we're not to. Unless he comes with us."

"But he'd be horrible. He'd spoil everything."

"Not at all. He says we can take a day off tomorrow and go to the sea. For my birthday treat." It would be Columbine's fifteenth birthday.

When they reached Hunter's Cove with its small beach laid out like a custard coloured apron, the sun was shining and even Jessica in her excitement—for she loved the sea—forgot her misgivings.

The two girls ran to get undressed and put on their togs. The deaf man built a fire with driftwood to boil the kettle, while Daddy kept pulling the corks out of the bottles of stout he had brought with him. He was a different man, it seemed, not scowling, no, all smiles and little jokes. Even his crusted face looked less abandoned than usual. He had shaved tightly and put on a clean ribbed shirt and a "holiday" pullover.

The sisters bobbed up and down in the water and swam way out till they were tired, splashing each other as they trod water.

By the time they were white with cold they raced up the beach, released into gleeful cries like the gulls who circled and fought the wind overhead. Daddy began to chase them and they ran and feinted with him. Suddenly Columbine was sprawled on the sand with Daddy on top of her. He held her fast, his face gone red and powerful like he was killing a German soldier and Columbine's face was wax and her eyes searched around like they'd pop out of her head alone. Jessica ran to the deaf man, "Stop him, stop him," her fingers raced through the alphabet but he was busy and didn't or pretended not to notice. She ran back shouting at her father to get off but he just kept heaving and she could see the sand matting Columbine's hair like cake and her thin elbows red from piercing little holes by her side. There were shouts from the rocks behind them. People had arrived, picking their way carefully over the crags with their buckets and spades and baskets and towels. Daddy sprang away and faced the sea. Columbine just lay like a corpse newly dragged from the depths.

Jessica knelt beside her. "Go away. Go away. Pretend you didn't see. You didn't. Oh . . . God, I'm cold." She was twisting and turning, looking at Jessica as though she had never seen her before.

Jessica got up, exhilarated. "Now," she thought, "she'll be mine, again. She'll hate him, she'll never let him near her again." She wandered into the shelter of the rocks, barely noticing that Columbine had joined her. The sea darkened behind them when a cloud blew over the sun and the beach turned from blond to brown and the wind lifted motes of sand which raced over the surface.

As they tried to dress the towels were torn from their backs exposing their white buttocks, the sand sticking to their thighs, as they put on their knickers and their vests and fought with the openings of their dresses. Daddy remained where he was, legs apart, back hunched as though the changing pattern of the waves were his only interest.

All the way home Daddy stared out of the window, silent, and the two girls isolated in the back said nothing. Only the deaf man mouthed his deaf noises—groans, gurgles or belches—while the meadows and wheatfields sped past, interspersed by the odd useless cottage, distant sheep on a hill like lice stuck to a blanket, or the occasional wrinkle of a ploughed field.

The treat was over.

Months passed. The sisters continued to live in sly seclusion. Jessica spent much time in the shed. No one spoke of the absent mother. Every evening their father wheeled his bicycle through the kitchen and out the back door, leaving the inevitable draught behind him.

It was when Columbine was in the bath that Jessica noticed it first. Her sister was lying flat on her back, her chin hooked onto her breastbone, staring at her belly.

"My god!" Jessica said. Columbine's stomach was no longer hollow. Like an upturned saucer it seemed to palpitate beneath the water.

"What the hell are you doing in here?"

Jessica went to back out.

"Oh you needn't go. You've seen it now."

"You're . . . You're . . . " Jessica couldn't finish the sentence.

"Yes."

"Does Daddy know?"

"No. And don't tell anyone."

"Oh, Columbine, how could . . . "

"Shut up."

She rose from the bath and she'd barely stepped out when the vomit came up like a spout and splashed over the edge of the lavatory bowl. Jessica, paralysed, longed to stroke her sister's forehead, to say some words of sympathy, hold her tight, but a wave of distrust from Columbine held her back.

Some weeks later at school, Columbine was called to the headmistress's office. Jessica listened at the door. The head spoke in sepulchral tones.

"Who is the father? You must tell me. So as he can be punished too. God has punished you for your sin and will go on punishing you all the days of your life." Her sister was sobbing uncontrolledly. "Speak, child," the head kept shouting, but Columbine wouldn't or couldn't utter a word. Jessica ached to comfort her, break in and scream the truth at the woman but there wasn't time. Columbine came rushing out, her face the colour of cardboard.

Winter had scaled everything down, the land was brittle with frost. At half-past four the lights in the village were on as the bus snaked in. Their own house, dark with damp, the scuttle of mice their daily welcome. Listlessly they began their evening chores.

Suddenly Columbine crumpled in her sister's arms. "Oh god, Oh god, Oh god," she moaned.

They clung together, the dead stove, the unwashed dishes, the dirty clothes on the floor the only witnesses. The life between them jerked and cavorted.

All that night they planned. Discarded one possibility after another. Should they steal money, run away together, have the baby adopted? In the planning they grew optimistic. They put a chair against the door and huddled together in the same bed.

Some sentences emerged.

"When he touched me there first it tingled. He gave me presents to hold his thing. I didn't want to but I couldn't stop."

"I don't understand."

"You will one day."

"No. Never. Is that why Mammy went mad?"

"No, no. She was mad first, Daddy says. Always always mad."

"Poor Mammy."

"Poor Daddy."

"I hate him, Columbine. I hate him. You hate him too. Say it." But she couldn't say it.

"It's my fault, Jessica. He couldn't help it."

Jessica hugged her sister till she cried out, "Don't. You're squashing it."

Jessica was now allowed to attend to her sister, bring her water when she vomited, put compresses on her brow when her head was bad. At school they lurked around together. The headmistress ignored them.

Columbine was always in her anorak, her body at an angle to hide the swelling. Jessica felt that she was pregnant too, that she also was shielding the child from prying eyes.

She began to walk as Columbine, take on her habits, just as she had as a small child. They didn't count the months. It would soon be Columbine's sixteenth birthday. Why was that puzzling? Suddenly Jessica realised that the baby had not started that day at the seaside. There must have been times since—other secret times. Times when they both had hidden from her their fury and their pantings. Jessica felt a sickness gathering. From then on her vomit came as frequently as Columbine's. At night when she held her sister, she wondered when they had stopped, did they even still "do it"? But she knew if she asked she'd be rebuked, called an interfering fool.

It was a clear summer's night—late May or early June. They sat out before going to bed. They were as they had been that first night when they had planned. They had done nothing, time just hurtled over them. Occasionally a bird uttered or a leaf moved. The night gathered in the village, doors closed, lights went on, radios blared. To their left the cattle lowed in Long's field.

Finally they went up to bed, nothing solved, nothing changed.

When Jessica woke up it was dawn, birdsong shattering the air beyond the windows. She stretched her limbs, sat up, the other side of the bed was empty. Perhaps she's in the bathroom? She lay down again. But minutes passed, ten, fifteen. Shocked she sat up again. So this was when they "did it"? Around dawn? She felt the old paralysis of dread. "No," she screamed out loud, threw off the bedclothes and thundered into her father's room. She would kill them, kill them both and kill herself afterwards. She pulled the blankets off him, a heavy firedog in her other hand. He was alone, the body moss-green in the early light. He didn't wake even when she yelled, "Where is she, you pig? Tell me or I'll kill you."

She ran out, searched the bathroom and all the rooms. Then a new fear screwed into her throat. They had never really considered the actual birth of the baby. It was as if the baby would be born when they decided the time was ready for it. It had never occurred to them to count the months, to get clothes or nappies or a place for it to lie. Hysterical, Jessica tried to count back now over the year but how could she add or subtract when she didn't know when it had started. (The word "conception" was one she avoided as she avoided all other words that had any relation to the sexual act.)

The child must have come! They must be somewhere. She imagined Columbine perhaps struggling in a dark corner, the baby half in and half out. The shed! Perhaps she'd run there to be private. Jessica raced downstairs and out in the back garden. But no! There were all her boxes, her tools, her work bench, the little heaps of sawdust, undisturbed exactly as she'd left them. Back in through the house and out into the street she ran, banging doors behind her, her shoes clattering on the kitchen tiles. The street was dawn-empty. A distant beast, bullock or cow, gave a lamentable cry. There was the noise of the cistern in the house next door and then silence. She stood like a stopped pendulum not knowing which way to run.

It must have been my hysterics that woke the neighbours. Not the deaf man, of course, but the ones on the right hand side. She came out straggling and strealing, looking like I must look now when I'm woken early from sleep. Of course they knew why I was screaming. While we lived in our fool's paradise, imagining that only the headmistress knew, everybody in the village was exulting in my sister's pregnancy. Her pathetic anorak had hidden nothing from those sex-obsessed eyes.

I was carried or pushed into the house. I was raucous, incoherent, they—the grey faces (suddenly there were many)—were collected around me, gloating. I was shoved into bed, pills put in my mouth, a glass of water knocked against my clenched teeth. They threatened me with the doctor but it wasn't I who needed the doctor I tried to tell them. No one seemed to care. It was as if they'd caught one fish and didn't care about the other.

But, as soon as they left, thinking me asleep, I leapt up again, crept downstairs, ran out the back and across the fields. How did I know where to go? But there was purpose in my running, that I do remember. My vision was distorted—from the pills, I expect. I ran and ran, sliding over ditches, and through a bit of plough and over a further ditch beyond Long's farm. And there she was, lying in the muck, her neck twisted, her eyes closed, a small twig tangled in her hair. There was something beyond her bared feet, dark like liver, slimy. Then I noticed its shape and a little white shining through the slime like a red apple with a bite out of it. It was the child's head. It was asleep, too, it seemed.

I bent over my sister, took her in my arms.

"My dove, my Columbine, wake up. It's me, Jessica." I knelt beside her, cradled her and kissed her many times. Her body was limp. I lay down with her, opening my shirt to pour my own warmth into her. The long grass rode up around us, a thrush perched on a blackthorn. His song was sweet.

But that is all. If only I could creep back into that tunnel. The light is there somewhere, deep amongst the million cells of my brain. I can catch the sound of a twig cracking or a branch wheezing. Someone could have followed me, seen us together, carried us home. Perhaps it doesn't matter. Will I leave it there? Did I die then with her, to be reborn in a web for four years until finally released by *his* death to live alone for the next fifty years surrounded by my boxes, my pieces of wood, my delicate filigree patterns, my chisels, my complicated machines, my meaningless carvings which have made me famous, rich. Yes I will leave us there, me holding the wall of your body, you relaxed in my arms, keeping the secret of your sleep, your child's sleep. Unable to keep the two lives going you chose rather to leave me barren in the short death of days. Maybe we shared those days together. Yes I'll leave it there.

Glossary

amach leat out with you

An tUasal O Riain Mr. Ryan

ar aghaidh 's ar gcul back and forth

Aspal Mor na hEireann (Hymn to Saint Patrick) Great Apostle of Ireland

Bail o Dhia orthu (Irish greeting) God's company be on them

caint speech

camogie a girls' or women's hurling game

ceili dance

cinnte dearfa sure indeed

cinta cairbreacha centuries ago

comhra conversation

Craidhps, an dtuigeann tu bhfuil's agat Cripes! do you know what I mean

culchie derogatory term for person from the country

cursai reatha current affairs

Dail Irish Parliament

Dev nickname for Eamon de Valera

Dia duit, 'Athair. Failte romhat 'Athair (Irish greeting) God with you, Father. You are welcome, Father.

diabhal devil

Fainne ring

Garda policeman

gormless brainless

I dtigh diabhail leat to hell with you

mortler mortal sin

nadur nature

o sea sea oh, yes, yes

Sea, a chroi . . . inis dom aris . . . Beannacht De ort, a thaisce . . . agus orthsa, a Athair Yes, my love . . . tell me that again . . . The blessing of God on you, my dear . . . And on you, Father.

slans farewells

Taigs derogatory term for Catholics

taom a great wave; commonly used to describe an overwhelming wave of emotion

Notes on the Contributors

Leland Bardwell ("The Dove of Peace," p. 244) was born in India of Irish parents. She grew up in Kildare and went to school in Dublin. "The Dove of Peace" appeared in *Different Kinds of Love,* her first short story collection. She has published three novels: *Girl on a Bicycle,* described by Anthony Burgess as "a period gem," *That London Winter,* and *The House;* and two collections of poetry: *The Mad Cyclist* and *The Fly and the Bed Bug.* Bardwell has written for both Radio Television Eireann and the BBC as well as for the theater. Most recently she scripted *No Regrets,* based on the life and songs of Edith Piaf. She is the coeditor of the literary magazine *Cyphers.* Bardwell presently lives in Dublin with her three sons.

Fiona Barr ("The Wall-Reader," p. 46) was born in Derry, Northern Ireland, in 1952. She has had numerous short stories and articles published and broadcast on radio. Her short story "The Wall Reader" received first place in the Maxwell House Women Writers' Competition in 1978 and appeared with other stories from this competition in the Arlen House collection *The Wall Reader.* Her short story "Sisters," first published in the collection of the same name by Blackstaff Press, is being adapted for the BBC. A mother of four, Fiona Barr is currently television critic for the *Irish News.*

Margaret Barrington ("Village without Men," p. 228) was born in 1896 in County Donegal. She attended various private schools, including a French school in Normandy, before entering Trinity College, Dublin, in 1915. Her first marriage was to the historian Edmund Curtis in 1922. In 1926 she married the novelist Liam O'Flaherty and they traveled widely in Ireland, England, and France before separating in 1932. During the 1930s she lived in England and published a novel, *My Cousin Justine,* in

1939. Politically active, she helped refugees from Nazi Germany and organized support for the Republican forces in the Spanish Civil War. When World War II erupted, she moved to West Cork and continued to write short stories and articles until her death in 1982. Eighteen of her stories, gleaned from four decades of her work, including "Village without Men," were collected and published in *David's Daughter Tamar*.

Mary Beckett ("Failing Years," p. 216) was born in Belfast in 1926 and taught school in Ardoyne for ten years. After her marriage in 1956 she moved to Dublin where she raised five children. In the 1950s, her short stories were published in *The Bell, Irish Writing, Threshold*, and the "New Irish Writing" section of the *Irish Press*. Her stories have focused on life in Belfast and the surrounding Ulster countryside even though she has lived in Dublin for the past thirty years. Some of her stories have been broadcast by the BBC and Radio Eireann. In 1980, Poolbeg Press published a collection of stories entitled *A Belfast Woman*, reissued in the United States in 1988 by William Morrow. She has recently published her first novel, *Give Them Stones*.

Maeve Binchy ("Shepherd's Bush," p. 201) is from Dalkey, a coastal town near Dublin, and is married to the writer Gordon Snell. She took a history degree at University College in Dublin and taught in girls' schools before she joined the *Irish Times* in 1969. She has lived in London for the past ten years. Binchy is known primarily as a novelist, and her first novel, *Light a Penny Candle*, was translated into several languages and sold over one million copies. A second novel, *Echoes*, was published in 1985; a third, *Firefly Summer*, to wide acclaim, in 1988. Two of her plays, *End of Term* and *Half Promised Land*, have been staged at the Peacock Theater in Dublin. "Shepherd's Bush" appeared in *London Transports*, one of her four volumes of short stories. Her television play, *Deeply Regretted*, won the Best Script Award at the Prague Film Festival.

Elizabeth Bowen ("A Day in the Dark," p. 183), internationally acclaimed novelist, short story writer, essayist, critic, and editor, was born in Dublin in 1899. Educated in England, Bowen inherited Bowen's Court, the family estate in County Cork in 1928, although she did not live there until after her husband's death in 1952. She remained in Cork for eight years and died in London in 1973. Although her reputation rests on her nine novels, which include *The Death of the Heart, The Heat of the Day, A World of Love*, and *Eva Trout*, she is described as one of the greatest practitioners of the short story, having written over seventy in her lifetime. Although much of her work deals with the loneliness of children, reflecting her own unhappy childhood, her adult life was satisfying and included relationships with Virginia Woolf, E. M. Forster, May Sarton, Carson McCullers, Eudora Welty, and others. She is highly regarded for her strong evocation of place. Even though she was born into the Anglo-Irish gentry and lived for many years in England, she always considered herself Irish: "As long as I can remember, I've been extremely conscious of being Irish. . . . No amount of traveling between Ireland, England, and the Continent has ever robbed me of the strong feelings of my nationality."

Clare Boylan ("Housekeeper's Cut," p. 17) was born in Dublin in 1948. She is a journalist and has won the Benson & Hedges Award for "Outstanding Work in Irish Journalism." She has also written for radio and for Irish television. She established herself as a short story writer in magazines in Europe, Denmark, Australia, Sweden, South Africa, Norway, and the United States. Her stories have also appeared in anthologies, such as *Winter's Tales*. She published her first novel, *Holy Pictures*, in 1983. This was followed by a collection of short stories, *A Nail on the Head*, and another novel, *Last Resorts*. She lives in County Wicklow with her husband, who is also a journalist.

Helen Lucy Burke ("All Fall Down," p. 177) was born in Dublin and has worked in local government. She has had her short stories published in the *Irish Press* and in journals and anthologies in Ireland, Britain, and Germany. She was a contributor to two collections of short stories, *Tears of the Shamrock* and *The Seven Deadly Sins*. She published a novel, *Close Connections*, in 1979 and a collection of short stories, *A Season for Mothers*, in 1980. Her story "Trio" won the PEN International Short Story Award. She is completing a novel at present and works as a freelance journalist with a restaurant column in Ireland's *Sunday Tribune*.

Juanita Casey ("One Word," p. 158), animal trainer, artist, poet, novelist, and short story writer, was born in 1925 in England. Her teenage mother was an Irish tinker or traveler who died giving birth to her. Her father was an English Gypsy who abandoned the year-old Casey in a field belonging to the man who subsequently raised her. He brought her up in a circus background but also sent her to private boarding schools. She has lived in England and Ireland and for certain periods has traveled both with English Gypsies and Irish tinkers. She has been married three times: to an English farmer, a Swedish sculptor, and an Irish journalist who died in 1971. She has had a child from each marriage. Her first group of short stories, *Hath the Rain a Father?*, was published in 1966, and another volume, *Horse by the River*, in 1968. She has published two novels, *The Horse of Selene* in 1971, and *The Circus* in 1974. Some of her stories have been published in *The Journal of Irish Literature* and in *Juanita Casey: A Sampling*.

Evelyn Conlon ("Park-going Days," p. 164), born in rural County Monaghan in 1952, now lives with her two sons in Dublin. She has also lived in Asia and Australia, where her first poems were published. When she was nineteen she published her first short story; subsequent stories were published in the *Irish Press* and other periodicals. Her work has been influenced by the works of writers as diverse as Toni Cade Bambara, Alice Munro, Grace Paley, and Colette. She has published two collections of short stories, *My Head Is Opening* and *Crimson Houses*, and has just published her first novel, *Stars in the Daytime*. She is active in the women's rights movement in Ireland and has worked in the Rape Crisis Centre in Dublin. She is now working with the filmmaker Pat Murphy on a script tentatively entitled *Fire in a Concrete Box*.

Emma Cooke ("The Foundress," p. 191) was born in County Laois in 1934 of Huguenot ancestors. Educated in Dublin, she married John Cuddy in 1955 and has nine children. She has always been active in community affairs and has directed the short story workshop at the Writers' Week in Listowel. She has published two novels, *A Single Sensation* and *Eve's Apple*. Her short stories have been published in the *Irish Times*, the *Irish Press*, the *Irish Independent*, in popular magazines and anthologies, and have also been broadcast on Radio Eireann. She lives in County Clare on the shore of Lough Derg, where she spends most of her time writing. She is working on a new novel and a second collection of short stories.

Ita Daly ("A Family Picnic," p. 123) was born in County Leitrim in 1944. A graduate of University College, Dublin, she is a teacher in Dublin and is married to the editor and writer David Marcus. Her short stories have appeared in the "New Irish Writing" section of the *Irish Press, Threshold*, the *Irish Times, Short Story International, The Critic, Best Irish Short Stories*, and *The Penguin Book of Irish Short Stories*. Two of her stories have won Hennessy Literary Awards, and a third won the *Irish Times* short story competition. She has published one collection of short stories, *The Lady with the Red Shoes*, and a novel, *A Singular Attraction*.

Anne Devlin ("Naming the Names," p. 93) was born in Belfast in 1951 and has lived in Birmingham since 1984. Her short story, "Passages," the winner of the Hennessy Literary Award in 1982, was adapted for television as *A Woman Calling* in 1984 and won the Samuel Beckett Award for Television Drama. In 1984 a version of her radio play *The Long March* was also televised. Her first stage play, *Ourselves Alone*, was performed in 1985 and won several awards, among them the Susan Smith Blackburn Prize. She notes that she is "continually torn between writing about the 'Troubles' and wishing to ignore them; resenting the grip of history and bowing to its inevitability." Her first collection of short stories, *The Way-Paver*, contains the award-winning "Passages" and "Naming the Names," recently shown on television in the United States.

Éilís Ní Dhuibhne ("Midwife to the Fairies," p. 31) was born in Dublin in 1954. She has published short stories, poems, and scholarly articles in a variety of newspapers and journals and has written a Ph.D. dissertation on folktales. Married and the mother of two young children, she has worked as a librarian, archivist, folklore collector, and lecturer. In 1986 she participated in the National Women Writer's Workshop and her story "Fulfillment" won a place in Heinemann's *Best Short Stories 1986*. In 1987 she received a bursary in literature from the Arts Council. *Blood and Water*, which includes "Midwife to the Fairies," is her first collection of short stories and powerfully reveals aspects of modern Irish life.

Anne Le Marquand Hartigan ("Pure Invention," p. 79), poet, playwright, and painter, has lived in England and Ireland and been a farmer's wife on the banks of the river Boyne, County Louth, for fifteen years. She has two daughters and four sons. She is a prize-winning poet and her two books of poetry, *Long Tongue* (1982) and *Return Single* (1986), have been published by Beaver Row Press. Her play *Beds* was performed at the Dublin Theatre Festival in 1982. The most recent one-woman show of her paintings was in Dublin at the Temple Bar Gallery in 1985. She has given many workshops and readings. Her epic poem *Now Is a Moveable Feast* was performed on Radio Television Eireann in 1981. She now lives in Dublin.

Jennifer Johnston ("Trio," p. 171) was born in Dublin in 1930, daughter of Denis Johnston, novelist and playwright, and Shelah Richards, a noted actress and theater director. Married in 1951, she and her husband have four children and live in Northern Ireland. She has written eight critically acclaimed novels dealing with the decline of the Anglo-Irish, the events of 1918–20, and the current Ulster crisis, among them *The Captains and the Kings*, *The Gates*, *Shadows on Our Skin*, and *The Railway-Station Man*. She has received the Whitbread Prize, the Robert Putnum Award, and the Yorkshire Post Prize. Three of her novels have been made into television plays, including the BBC production of *How Many Miles to Babylon?*, dramatized by the Northern Irish poet Derek Mahon.

Maeve Kelly ("Amnesty," p. 114) was born in County Clare in 1930 and grew up and was educated in Dundalk, County Louth. She farmed for many years and now lives with her husband and two children near Limerick, where she founded a residential center for abused women and their children. A member of the Limerick Federation of Women's Organisations, she often speaks on feminist issues. For many years she wrote and published poetry. In 1971 she published her first short story in the *Irish Press* and has since become a regular contributor. One of her stories won a Hennessy Literary Award in 1972. A collection of her short stories, *A Life of Her Own*, was published in 1976 and was reissued in 1979. In 1985, she published her first novel, *Necessary Treasons*. A collection of her poetry, *Resolution*, was published in 1986. Kelly has just completed a second novel and is working on a new collection of short stories.

Rita Kelly ("The Intruders," p. 86) was born in 1953 in County Galway. She writes fiction, poetry, criticism, and drama both in Irish and in English. Her drama *Frau Luther* was produced in London. Some of her work has been translated into German, Dutch, and Italian. She has won various literary awards in Ireland, including the *Irish Times* Merriman Poetry Award, an Arlen House Maxwell House prize for the short story, and an Arts Council bursary in literature. In 1985 she coedited *Poetry-Ireland Review*. In 1980 she published a collection of poetry, *Dialann sa Díseart*; a second, *An Bealach Éadóigh*, was published in 1984. Her first collection of stories, *The Whispering Arch*, was published in 1986. She now lives in County Wexford and is at present completing a novel, a collection of poetry in English, and one in Irish.

Mary Lavin ("In the Middle of the Fields," p. 1) was born in Massachusetts in 1912, the only child of Irish immigrants who returned with her to Ireland, where she was raised in Dublin. With her first husband, she bought a farm in County Meath. She had two daughters from this marriage. Her husband's death in 1954 and her struggle to raise a family alone are reflected in her stories on widowhood. Lavin married again and had a third daughter. She has written two novels, *The House in Clewe Street* and *Mary O'Grady*, but is primarily known for her eighteen volumes of stories, which include *Tales from Bective Bridge*, *The Patriot Son*, *The Great Wave*, *In the Middle of the Fields*, *Happiness*, and *A Memory*. A member of the Irish Academy of Letters, Lavin is regarded internationally as a major literary figure, and her works are now being studied critically. Among her many awards are the Katherine Mansfield Award, the Ella Lynam Cabot Award, two Guggenheim fellowships, the James Tait Black Memorial Prize, and the literary award of the American-Irish Foundation.

Her stories deal primarily with the experiences of Irish women and contain what Benedict Kiely calls "her quiet terrifyingly intimate studies of domesticity."

Bernadette Matthews ("Granny," p. 39) lives in Galway and has had some of her work published in *Writers in the West* and *The Salmon*.

Ann McKay ("Checkpoint," p. 239) was born in County Tyrone, Northern Ireland, in 1955. She went to school in Derry and studies English literature at universities in both York and Dublin. "Checkpoint" is the first story she wrote and was published in David Marcus's *Best Short Stories 3*.

Brenda Murphy ("A Curse," p. 226) was born in Belfast in 1954 and now lives in Downpatrick. She has been writing since she was seventeen. Most recently, she has published in *No Place for Dogs* by the residents of Divis Flats. Her work has been published in *The Blackstaff Book of Short Stories* (1988). She has spent six years in Armagh Jail.

Edna O'Brien ("Sister Imelda," p. 139), the prolific novelist, dramatist, screenwriter, and short story writer, was born in County Clare in 1930 and was raised in Western Ireland. In 1959, after separating from her husband, she moved to London with her two sons. She is the author of several novels, including *The Country Girls* trilogy, *A Pagan Place*, and *Night*. Five of her novels have been banned in Ireland for their portrayal of female sexuality. O'Brien's numerous short story collections, such as *A Fanatic Heart*, *A Scandalous Woman*, and *A Rose in the Heart*, present many of the same settings and themes as her novels. O'Brien has written for television, films, and the stage. Her most recent play, *Virginia*, was a portrait of Virginia Woolf.

Harriet O'Carroll ("The Day of the Christening," p. 53) was born in Callan, County Kilkenny, in 1941. She has had short stories represented in the two Maxwell House collections of Irish writing. Her stories have been broadcast on the BBC radio, and in 1981 she won first prize in a short story competition organized by the Mental Health Association. A practicing physiotherapist, O'Carroll lives in County Limerick with her husband and three children.

Julia O'Faolain ("Melancholy Baby," p. 62), the novelist and short story writer, is the daughter of writers Sean O'Faolain and Eileen Gould. She was born in 1932 and has studied in Ireland, Paris, and Rome. She currently resides in Los Angeles with her husband Lauro Martines, a historian. O'Faolain has worked as a teacher of languages, an interpreter, translator, and editor. Under the name Julia Martines she has published several translations of nonfiction works by Italian historical figures and has edited with her husband *Not in God's Image: Women in History from the Greeks to the Victorians*. Her novel *Woman in the Wall*, reconstructed in part from original manuscripts, is an evocation of sixth-century Gaul, a time of tribal rivalries and random violence. *No Country for Young Men* addresses the issue of Irish nationalism. Many of her short stories, such as those in her first collection, *We Might See Stars* (later published as *Melancholy Baby*), treat sexual and social hypocrisies and repressions.

Eithne Strong ("The Bride of Christ," p. 41) was born in 1923 in West Limerick and since 1942 has lived in Dublin. In 1943 she married and subsequently had nine children, the youngest being mentally handicapped. A poet in English and Irish, she was among the pioneering few who presented work bilingually. Her first published poetry was in Irish and appeared in 1942. In 1943 she became a founding member of the Runa Press, which published the works of important Irish poets. She has published four collections of poetry, including *Sarah, in Passing* and the long poem *Flesh—the Greatest Sin*. In 1979 her novel *Degrees of Kindred* was published and in 1981 a collection of her short stories, *Patterns*, appeared. Many of her stories have appeared in leading periodicals and have been anthologized in volumes such as the *Penguin Book of Irish Short Stories*. For the past seventeen years she has coordinated creative writing workshops, judged literary works, and given readings in Ireland and throughout the world.

Maura Treacy ("Made in Heaven," p. 131) was born in County Kilkenny in 1946 and has published articles and short stories in many magazines and periodicals but most especially in the "New Irish Writing" page of the *Irish Press*. Her works have been broadcast on Radio Eireann and are included in *Best Irish Short Stories 1*, *Bodley Head Book of Irish Short Stories*, and *Northern Ireland: Aspects of the Conflict*. Her story "The Weight of the World" won the Writers' Week in Listowel Short Story Award and is included in her collection *Sixpence in Her Shoe*, published in 1977. Her first novel, *Scenes from a Country Wedding*, was published in 1981. Treacy was awarded a bursary by the Arts Council in 1983 and received a grant from the American-Irish Foundation in 1987.

Credits

Grateful acknowledgment is made to the following for permission to reprint the selections in this volume: Leland Bardwell, "The Dove of Peace" from *Different Kinds of Love* by Leland Bardwell, first published by Attic Press, 44 East Essex Street, Dublin 2, Ireland, © 1987, reprinted by permission of the publisher; Fiona Barr, "The Wall-Reader," first published in *The Wall-Reader*, published by Arlen House Ltd, © 1979, reprinted by permission of the author; Margaret Barrington, "Village without Men," from *David's Daughter Tamar and Other Stories* by Margaret Barrington, published by Wolfhound Press, 68 Mountjoy Square, Dublin 1, Ireland, © 1981, reprinted by permission of the publisher; Mary Beckett, "Failing Years," from *A Belfast Woman* by Mary Beckett, originally published by Poolbeg Press Ltd., Knocksdean House, Swords, Co. Dublin, Ireland, © 1980, reprinted by permission of William Morrow and Company, Inc.; Maeve Binchy, "Shepherd's Bush," from *London Transports* by Maeve Binchy, published by Century Hutchinson Publishing Group Ltd., © 1983, reprinted by permission of the publisher; Elizabeth Bowen, "A Day in the Dark," first published in *Mademoiselle* magazine, July 1957, from *The Collected Stories of Elizabeth Bowen* by Elizabeth Bowen, © 1981 by Curtis Brown, Ltd, literary executors of the Estate of Elizabeth Bowen, reprinted by permission of Alfred A. Knopf, Inc.; Clare Boylan, "Housekeeper's Cut," from *A Nail on the Head* by Clare Boylan, © 1981 by Clare Boylan, reprinted by permission of Viking Penguin Inc.; Helen Lucy Burke, "All Fall Down," from the short story collection *A Season for Mothers* by Helen Lucy Burke, published by Poolbeg Press Ltd, © 1980 by Helen Lucy Burke, reprinted by permission of the author; Moya Cannon, "Taom," first published in *The Salmon* and reprinted in *The Midland Review* 3 (Winter 1986), © 1987, reprinted by permission of *The Salmon*, Nuala Archer, and the author (the title of this volume is also used by permission of the author); Juanita Casey, "One Word," from *The Journal of Irish Literature* 1, no. 3 (September 1972), © 1972 Proscenium Press Inc., P.O. Box 361, Newark, Delaware, 19711, reprinted by permission of *The Journal of Irish Literature* and the author; Evelyn Conlon, "Park-going Days," from *My Head Is Opening*, published by Attic Press, 44 East Essex Street, Dublin 2, Ireland, © 1987 by Evelyn Conlon, reprinted by permission of the publisher; Emma Cooke, "The Foundress," from *Female Forms*, first published by Poolbeg Press Ltd, © 1980 by Emma Cooke, reprinted by permission of Enid Cuddy; Ita Daly, "A Family Picnic," from *The Lady with the Red Shoes*, published by Poolbeg Press Ltd, © 1980 by Ita Daly, reprinted by permission of the author; Anne Devlin, "Naming the Names," first published in *Good Housekeeping*, from *The Way-Paver* by Anne Devlin, published by Faber and Faber Ltd, 1986, © 1983 by Anne Devlin, reprinted by permission of the publisher; Éilís Ní Dhuibhne, "Midwife to the Fairies," from *Blood and Water* by Éilís Ní Dhuibhne, published by Attic Press, 44 East Essex Street, Dublin 2, Ireland, © 1988 by Éilís Ní Dhuibhne, reprinted by permission of the publisher; Anne Le Marquand Hartigan, "Pure Invention," © 1989 by Anne Le Marquand Hartigan, printed by permission of the author; Jennifer Johnston, "Trio," from *Best Irish Short Stories 2*, edited by David Marcus, published by Elek Books Limited, 1977, © 1977 by Jennifer Johnston, reprinted by permission of the author; Maeve Kelly, "Amnesty," from *A Life of Her Own*, published by Poolbeg Press Ltd, 1976, © 1976 by Maeve Kelly, reprinted by permission of the author; Rita Kelly, "The Intruders," from *The Whispering Arch*, published by Arlen House, Dublin, 1986, © 1986 by Rita Kelly, reprinted by permission of the author; Mary Lavin, "In the Middle of the Fields," originally published in *The New Yorker*, from *In the Middle of the Fields and Other Stories*, published by the Macmillan Company, 1961, © 1961 by Mary Lavin, reprinted by permission of the author; Bernadette Matthews, "Granny," from *Midland Review* 3 (Winter 1986), © 1987 by the Board of Regents for Oklahoma State University, reprinted by permission of Nuala Archer; Ann McKay, "Checkpoint," originally published in *The Stony Thursday Book*, Autumn 1977, reprinted in *Best Irish Short Stories 3*, edited by David Marcus, published

The Republic of Ireland and Northern Ireland
(Reprinted from A *Writer's Ireland* by William Trevor by permission of Thames and Hudson Ltd)